The Politics of
Western Water

The Politics of
Western Water,

THE CONGRESSIONAL CAREER
OF WAYNE ASPINALL

Stephen C. Sturgeon

The University of Arizona Press   Tucson

The University of Arizona Press
© 2002 The Arizona Board of Regents
First printing
All rights reserved
⊛ This book is printed on acid-free, archival-quality paper.
Manufactured in the United States of America
07   06   05   04   03   02   6   5   4   3   2   1

Library of Congress Cataloging-in-Publication Data
Sturgeon, Stephen C. (Stephen Craig), 1967–
The politics of western water : the congressional career of Wayne Aspinall /
Stephen C. Sturgeon.
p. cm.
Includes bibliographical references and index.
ISBN 0-8165-2160-3 (alk. paper)
1. Aspinall, Wayne N. 2. Legislators—United States—Biography.
3. United States. Congress. House—Biography. 4. Water rights—West
(U.S.)—History—20th century. 5. Environmental policy—West
(U.S.)—History—20th century. 6. West (U.S.)—Environmental
conditions. I. Title.
E748.A249 .S78 2002
333.91'0092—dc21   2002002786

British Library Cataloguing-in-Publication Data
A catalogue record for this book is available from the British Library.

To the memory of Jack,
the first historian in my life

Contents

Figures

Maps

Preface

The story of dams is the story of winning the West.
—U.S. Bureau of Reclamation, 1966[1]

D URING THE SUMMER OF 1981, my family made one of its regular
    automotive treks across the American West. On this particular jour-
ney we left our home in Missouri, stopped to visit the Eisenhower Presidential Library in Abilene, Kansas, and spent our first night surrounded by
the pseudo-Western atmosphere of Dodge City. Early the next morning
we continued our trip, heading west across southern Colorado on U.S.
Route 50 with the goal of reaching Durango by nightfall.

Crossing the Great Plains can, at times, inspire restlessness, and as we
approached the aptly named town of Hasty, Colorado, my father spotted
the first of the day's side trips. A sign at the side of the road told us that
we were approaching the exit leading to the John Martin Dam and Reservoir. In our various travels in the West, my family had made a practice of
"dam spotting," so my father quickly drove down the side road toward the
Arkansas River.

As we walked from the parking lot onto the dam itself, we were met
with a completely unexpected view. The reservoir contained no water.
After pondering this strange spectacle for a while, my parents and I concluded that the absence of a lake must have been a sign that the dam was
brand new, and the reservoir simply had not had time to fill. Having solved
the mystery to our satisfaction, we climbed back in our car and continued
on our way.

The image of this massive dam and empty reservoir, however, continued to linger in my mind, and later helped fuel my curiosity about the
giant reclamation projects in the American West. It would be a dozen
years before I learned the full story of this particular dam and the larger
story behind it. (The dam was not new; it had been built in the 1940s, and
the reservoir was empty because the water was routinely drained out for

irrigation purposes.) It was only later that I learned that some of the water in the Arkansas River had, in fact, been diverted from west of the Continental Divide as the result of a federal reclamation project called the Fryingpan-Arkansas. One of the key supporters of this project, and the preeminent proponent of federal reclamation in general, was a Colorado congressman named Wayne Aspinall.

First elected to Congress in 1948, Aspinall had gone to Washington with a well-defined point of view regarding natural resource development, a view shaped in large part by the economic realities of his district. Today, Colorado's Fourth Congressional District is located on the state's eastern high plains, but during Aspinall's years in the House of Representatives the district covered the state's Western Slope. Comprising approximately 150,000 people in twenty-four counties spread over an area of 43,000 square miles, the Fourth District was one of the geographically largest congressional districts in the United States; the local economy in the district depended heavily on natural resources (logging, mining, and grazing). Aspinall's success in promoting his own district's agenda resulted from the nearly unrivaled power and influence he acquired on Capitol Hill. Thanks to the seniority system, the Democratic congressman became chair of the House Interior Committee in 1959 and ruled that committee with almost dictatorial control for the next fourteen years, a position that allowed Aspinall to obtain congressional approval of much legislation that benefited his district, especially reclamation projects.[2]

Aspinall's role as chair placed him in a key position to shape the nation's natural resource legislation at a time when the growing conservation/environmental movement was calling for a sharp change in those policies. Not surprisingly, given his pro-development point of view, Aspinall frequently clashed with environmental leaders. David Brower, the executive director of the Sierra Club in the 1950s and 1960s, once commented that "We have seen dream after dream dashed on the stony continents of Wayne Aspinall." (Aspinall had expressed his own opinion of Brower a few years earlier, when he publicly confronted Brower and called him a liar.)[3]

Aspinall in many ways was an odd federal politician: he participated in, but was not part of, the national political scene. In natural resource matters Aspinall's power was unrivaled, but this clout and interest did not carry over into other legislative issues. When Congress passed major social legislation in the 1960s, Aspinall's chief interest in these issues seemed to be whether they would affect spending on reclamation. His focus on natural resource issues was so specific that Aspinall even passed on an offer to serve on the more powerful, and nationally prominent, House Ways and Means Committee.[4]

The chairman had a cordial working relationship with the ranking minority member of the Interior Committee, Rep. John Saylor (despite Saylor's active support for environmental legislation), yet Aspinall did not appear to have any close friends or allies in the House. Unlike the Arizona congressional delegation, whose members actively consulted with one another during the passage of the Central Arizona Project, Aspinall had only limited contact with the other members of Colorado's delegation. Despite having been active in Colorado politics and the state Democratic Party for twenty years prior to his election to Congress, Aspinall had little involvement with either one after becoming a representative (the state Democratic Party reciprocated this indifference). He also developed a reputation for being a weak supporter of the national Democratic Party.[5]

Aspinall's congressional peers in the field of natural resource development were Western senators, such as Henry Jackson of Washington and Clinton Anderson of New Mexico, rather than fellow representatives. The congressman, however, had little respect for the Senate, which he thought was a sloppy legislative chamber, and less respect for Senators Jackson and Anderson, who tended to be more in favor of environmental legislation. Aspinall also had a strained relationship with most of the five presidents with whom he served. He disliked Eisenhower and Nixon for both personal and political reasons. Neither did he particularly like Johnson, even though the Johnson administration actively courted his support on environmental legislation. (LBJ even went so far as to insist on appointing Aspinall's son, Owen, to the governorship of American Samoa.) The congressman did respect Truman, but as a freshman congressman he had limited contact. The president for whom Aspinall had the highest praise, and with whom he had the most contact, was Kennedy. The congressman always considered Kennedy a good friend, although it is not clear if this feeling was reciprocated.[6]

The congressman's political "loner" status may have been partly due to his personality. Throughout his life (and even afterwards), Aspinall frequently inspired strong, and often negative, comments not only from environmentalists, but also from journalists, scholars, and other politicians. Among the plethora of negative terms used to describe the congressman were "crusty," "difficult," "abrasive," "irascible," "wily," "prickly," "cantankerous," "rigid," and "autocratic." Some of the harshest comments came from Aspinall's former colleagues in government. Former Rep. Pete McCloskey described the congressman in a 1990 interview as "a waspy, hostile, bitter man." Former congressman John Rhodes privately remarked in 1967 that Aspinall was "arrogant and rude." Former Secretary of the Interior Stewart Udall in 1995 claimed that the chairman was "an obdurate hedgehog." Even a Federal Bureau of Investigation agent described Aspinall as "brusque."[7]

Perhaps the unkindest cut of all came from former Sierra Club President Edgar Wayburn, who said that Aspinall, "in many ways, including stature, was a very small man." Even so, the chairman did not automatically reject all the adjectives people used to describe him. He once told a reporter that he was crusty and cantankerous because that was what was needed to get the job done, and Aspinall did receive his share of praise from congressional colleagues for the efficient manner in which he ran his committee. They also praised him for his knowledge of technical matters affecting natural resources legislation.[8]

Just as his contemporaries had strong opinions about him, scholars and researchers have not been neutral regarding the Colorado congressman. One historian who analyzed the secondary literature on Aspinall found a consistent pattern: political scientists praise the congressman, while historians damn him. Perhaps the best example of the political science point of view comes from Richard Fenno, who in his book *Congressmen in Committees* praised the way Aspinall managed his committee and his success rate at passing legislation in the House of Representatives. In sharp contrast, Donald Worster offers a typical historical assessment, basically dismissing Aspinall as someone who used cold war ideology to justify porkbarrel budgets. The different perspectives among political scientists and historians can perhaps be explained in terms of Fenno's focus on the process, as contrasted with Worster's focus on the results.[9]

The trouble with both of these interpretations is that they fail to explain or understand the motive behind Aspinall's actions. He mastered parliamentary methods and cold war rhetoric not as political ends unto themselves, but rather as tools for a larger purpose: to secure economic prosperity for his district by protecting its share of the Colorado River through federal reclamation projects. Aspinall made this goal the centerpiece of his congressional career, and the majority of voters on the Western Slope, who shared this objective, supported him. The congressman could achieve his goal because he served as the chair of the Interior Committee in an era when committee chairs were the power brokers in Congress. Aspinall's ability to kill or bottle up any piece of legislation under consideration by his committee gave him a strong bargaining position for his own legislative efforts.

The chairman, though, typically did not have to resort to direct or implicit threats. His expertise on natural resource matters led a number of congressional colleagues to defer to his opinion on such matters. As one remarked, "If it's good enough for Wayne Aspinall, it's good enough for Ed Willis." But even as the congressman displayed nearly unrivaled political power with the passage of legislation such as the Colorado River Basin Act of 1968, his influence was beginning to erode. This erosion was due to several factors: personal arrogance, rebellious younger members on his committee, the growing cry for congressional reform, changing presidential administrations, and emerging public resistance to federal spending, as well as redistricting and changing voter demographics back home. The most significant change, however, was the emergence of the environmental movement, which directly challenged Aspinall's beliefs and eventually succeeded in turning the public against his goals. The story of Wayne Aspinall's congressional career is the story of a man achieving national power just as his power base slipped away.[10]

The chapters in this book trace the arc of Aspinall's career as a water broker, from his days as an obscure freshman congressman, to his ascendance to power, to his abrupt defeat in 1972 and the end of the so-called "golden era" of reclamation in the West. Chapter 1 examines how the political, geographic, and economic realities of the Western Slope and western water helped to shape Aspinall's political point of view. Chapter 2 discusses Aspinall's personal and political background, from his childhood in Palisade, Colorado, through his two decades in the state legislature and his early years in Congress. Chapter 3 looks at the congressman's involvement in the Colorado River Storage Project bill and his clash with conservationists over the proposed Echo Park dam. Chapter 4 recounts the fight over the Fryingpan-Arkansas Project and Aspinall's decision to support diverting water out of his own district. Chapters 5 and 6 look at the battles that occurred over the Central Arizona Project, not just between Aspinall and environmentalists, but also between the chairman and other members of Congress. Chapter 7 discusses the congressman's defeat in 1972 and his "retirement" years. The final chapter examines the legacy Aspinall left behind, including the still disputed Animas–La Plata project, and how his vision of progress shaped the history of western water development.

I do not know what my reaction would have been had I learned the larger story of western reclamation and Wayne Aspinall's role in it when I visited the John Martin Dam in the summer of 1981. Perhaps it would have inspired interest, curiosity, or (more likely for a teenager) studied indifference. Even today, I cannot be certain that I completely comprehend all the factors in this story or fully appreciate Wayne Aspinall's role in it. The journey to John Martin Dam was a matter of miles, but the journey to understanding dams has been a matter of years.

Acknowledgments

I F THE CLICHÉ THAT "it takes a village to raise a child" is true, then it seems fair to say that it takes a nation to write a book. My research for this project has literally taken me coast to coast, from national archives to local museums, and introduced me to academic topics and subfields I never even knew existed. It has also provided me with an opportunity to meet a wide variety of people with whom I otherwise never would have had contact, and to whom I owe a big debt. Typically acknowledgments can be summed up in one phrase, "thanks to those who helped, and curses to those who hindered," but this glib statement glosses over the sheer amount and variety of help I received from others (and gives the trouble-makers equal billing). So, at the risk of sounding like an Academy Award acceptance speech, I would like to thank the following people. (For a more exhaustive list of thank-yous, please see my dissertation, "Wayne Aspinall and the Politics of Western Water," University of Colorado, 1998.)

My biggest collective thank you goes to all the archivists and librarians who helped me along the way. These individuals really do represent the front line in historical research, and without their frequently underpaid and often overlooked efforts the historical endeavor would grind to a halt. I try to keep their (positive) examples in mind each day as I carry out my own work. One person in particular to whom I owe a large debt of gratitude is Bonnie Harwick, formerly of the Bancroft Library, who for many years has been an archival mentor and friend. I also owe a very big thank you to the staffs of both the Western Historical Collections at the University of Colorado and the University of Denver's Special Collections, where the bulk of the research for this project took place (and where I practically lived for several months).

Over the course of this project I have also benefited immensely from the help of other researchers and historians who were willing to share with me their expertise and the fruits of their own labors. Among them have been Richard Baker of the U.S. Senate Historical Office; Brit Storey, the senior historian for the Bureau of Reclamation; Mark Harvey of North Dakota State University; Steve Schulte of Mesa State University (who shares my passion for all things Aspinall); Chuck Coate of Eastern Oregon State College; Thomas G. Smith of Nichols College; and Byron Pearson of West Texas A & M University. I especially owe thanks to Chris Riggs of Lewis-Clark State College for his help and friendship over the years.

In addition to the help I have received from my colleagues, I have also benefited from the willingness of strangers to take time to talk with me about their past experiences. My interviews with Floyd Dominy, Sid McFarland, Tommy Neal, Howard Scott, Felix Sparks, and Stewart Udall clearly enriched this project. I owe a special thanks to Bill Cleary, who not only agreed to an interview, but also gave me the names and addresses of other possible contacts.

Perhaps the biggest challenge in the research and writing process, apart from finding an original and manageable topic, is figuring out how to pay for the whole thing. I have been extremely fortunate to have received financial support from a wide variety of sources. During my time as a graduate student at the University of Colorado at Boulder the History Department provided me with money from both the Douglas A. Bean Memorial Fellowship and the John Reinthaler Memorial Endowment Fellowship to pay part of the costs of my travels. The Graduate School awarded me a Dean's Small Grant, and the College of Arts and Sciences generously gave me a Lowe Humanities Dissertation Fellowship. I also received travel stipends from several of the institutions I visited, including the LBJ Foundation, the JFK Library Foundation, an American Heritage Center Travel Grant, and a Morris K. Udall Research Travel Grant.

In addition to providing financial support for this project, the University of Colorado also served as a wonderful intellectual incubator for my research and writing. The members of my dissertation committee, among them Phil Deloria, Gloria Main, and Charles Wilkinson, provided useful guidance and feedback. Thanks, in particular, to my second reader, Tom Zeiler, who was always supportive of my work and quick to reassure me that my efforts would eventually pay off. Finally, a very sincere thank you to my committee chair, Patty Limerick. Over the past decade she has been an adviser, mentor, and friend who gave this work a rigorous grilling that improved it immeasurably.

Almost as daunting as financing this project has been the process of finding a publisher. Many first-time authors today face the Catch-22 of not being able to get published because they have never been published. The cavalier and insulting manner in which many academic publishers now treat new authors is a sad indication of how far the publishing industry has fallen. Fortunately that is not the case with the University of Arizona Press, whose staff has been unflaggingly helpful. I owe thanks to Alan M. Schroder, Evan Young, Kathryn Conrad, and Anne Keyl for their help with various aspects of the publication process. Additionally, I owe thanks to the five anonymous outside readers, whose useful and positive comments helped me to tighten up the manuscript and reassured me that I had not been wasting my time. My deepest gratitude goes to Patti Hartmann, who expressed strong interest in and support for my manuscript from the first meeting, and who guided it through the approval process. I also owe special thanks to people not affiliated with the University of Arizona Press. Stephen Cox designed the maps in this book, Sandy Smith from Alexander Smith Design fine-tuned them, Linda Gregonis prepared the index, and Daniel Davis helped conquer the scanning challenges I faced.

Since joining the faculty at Utah State University I have benefited greatly from the support of my colleagues in Special Collections & Archives and in the History Department. I owe a special thank you to Ann Buttars, Head Curator of Special Collections, for her patience as I tried to juggle my job with the completion of this book. I am also blessed to have coworkers who are active historians in their own right. Noel Carmack, Daniel Davis, and Robert Parson have shared their own research adventures with me, and in the case of Dan and Bob, also share my passion for Western water.

Last of all I wish to thank my friends and family. Ted Bromund has been my best friend and fellow traveler in the historical profession for more than a decade. He has patiently and actively listened as I droned on about this project for years, while sharing his own historical adventures and nightmares. I can never hope to repay the debt of thanks that I owe to my wife, Stacy, for all she has done during this project. While at times it seemed like Wayne Aspinall had become a guest in our home who had long overstayed his welcome, Stacy's willingness to pitch in and type, photocopy, edit, or simply believe in me when I didn't believe in myself has made this whole effort possible. My final thanks goes to my parents, Jack and Jane Sturgeon, who proved to be an inexhaustible source of financial, editorial, emotional, and intellectual support (not necessarily in that order of importance) over the long haul, and were willing to hold my feet to the fire when necessary. One of the true regrets of my life is that my father did not live to see this book published. It is dedicated to his memory and honor.

The Politics of
Western Water

1

The Water, the Land, and the People

Here is a land where life is written in water.
—Thomas Hornsby Ferril[1]

HISTORIAN DONALD WORSTER HAS SAID, "Touch water in the West, and you touch environment, science, capital, government, ideology, and the social order," and it is true that the struggle to find, develop, and control water has done more to shape the modern West than anything else. Wayne Aspinall, a water lawyer by training, was certainly aware of the importance of water to the West and firmly believed that the key to economic progress and prosperity for the Western Slope of Colorado lay in obtaining a permanent stored supply of water. To understand the origins of this belief it is necessary to understand the land and the people where Aspinall grew up, but most of all one must understand the water.[2]

The average annual precipitation in the western half of the United States stands in sharp contrast to rainfall amounts in the east. Whereas the states east of the Mississippi River typically receive forty-eight inches a year, the Great Plains receives on average thirty inches, and the interior West receives only twelve. The quest for water in the West dates back to the earliest human settlements in the region. The pre-Pueblo civilizations of the Southwest built elaborate irrigation systems, and later settlers, such as the Spanish and the Mormons, also built small-scale irrigation projects.[3]

One of the clearest manifestations of the importance of water to the West can be seen in the area of water law. Historian Robert Dunbar explicitly states that "[c]limate has been the determining factor in the development of Western water law." The eastern legal tradition for water rights had its origins in English common law and the doctrine of riparian rights, which held that the right to use water depended upon the user's proximity to the water. Landowners who had water running through their property could use that water as long as they owned the property and did not seriously diminish the availability of water to other property owners downstream. However, as American settlers began to move into the more arid parts of the country they found that eastern laws did not work well in the western landscape. This disparity between the law and reality led to the development of a new water doctrine known as appropriative rights.[4]

This doctrine first evolved in California during the Gold Rush, when prospectors created mining districts and staked their claims based on the "first in time, first in right" rule, which stated that whoever arrived first was entitled to use the land. As gold mining grew and began to require greater quantities of water, miners began applying this rule to the water as well. Thus, in sharp contrast to riparian rights, a miner could now dam up and divert an entire stream flow for use in hydraulic mining. As long as he had the senior claim to use that water and continued to use the water in a "beneficial" way, the other users downstream could not challenge his actions. The requirements for continual and beneficial use did put some restrictions on the senior claimant. If the water use stopped for a significant period of time, the other miners could consider the water claim to be abandoned and appropriate the right to themselves. Additionally, if a claim holder only used part of his water allocation on a regular basis, then the right to use the remainder of the claim was forfeited. The same was true for water use not deemed beneficial by the mining district, although what exactly constituted a beneficial use remained a fluid, rather than fixed, definition combining the concepts of social utility and engineering efficiency.[5]

Diverting water out of a stream bed was not, in and of itself, a new practice in the West. Water had historically been diverted by Native American and Hispanic communities for irrigation and communal water supplies, and Hispanic water laws remained in use in some areas for a period of time after the arrival of Anglo settlers. The two major differences between those past practices and the usage that developed in the California gold fields were these: water could now be diverted and used solely for the benefit of one person rather than the community as a whole, and water usage rights were now detached from land ownership. No longer did a person have to own land next to a source of water in order to have the right to use it. Water had effectively become a commodity.[6]

Although the doctrine of prior appropriation arose in California, Colorado became the first state to adopt the doctrine to govern its system of water usage (California chose a hybrid appropriation/riparian system); as a result, prior appropriation became known as the Colorado doctrine.

The state formally adopted the doctrine as part of its 1876 constitution. Article XVI, sections 5–7 declare that the unappropriated water of every natural stream in the state is the property of the public, that it is subject to appropriation, and that the right to appropriation shall never be denied. The constitution further stipulates that the use of water for domestic purposes shall have priority over other uses; that irrigation shall have priority over manufacturing; and that any water project shall have the right-of-way across public or private property in return for just compensation.[7]

In addition to these explicit guarantees, the document also contains an important implied rule regarding water, namely that there is no geographical limitation to the appropriation right. Water may be freely diverted out of its basin of origin for use anywhere else in the state. The Colorado State Supreme Court upheld this interpretation in the 1882 case *Coffin v. Left Hand Ditch Company*. This possibility took on a special significance later when Denver and other Front Range cities began diverting water from the Western Slope, and Aspinall and other regional leaders tried to block their efforts.[8]

As these diversion projects indicate, Colorado's water development has often collided with the state's geographic and economic realities. One such reality is that Colorado has an extremely uneven distribution of water and people. The area west of the Continental Divide in Colorado, known as the Western Slope, occupies approximately one-third of the state's land mass, yet this region receives nearly 70 percent of the state's total precipitation.

The abundance of water on the Western Slope is the result of the region's topography. The western part of the state is dominated by the Rocky Mountains, which form the Continental Divide and include peaks between 10,000 and 14,000 feet high. These peaks serve as a moisture barrier capturing precipitation from the jet stream passing overhead. Farther to the west, near the border between Colorado and Utah, the mountains give way to a series of high mesas and plateaus, which receive little direct precipitation. Although there are numerous river valleys throughout the Western Slope, two major rivers dominate the region: the Colorado and the Gunnison. The rugged terrain of the Western Slope long served as a deterrent to settlement, and even today the region is sparsely populated.[9]

By contrast, more than 80 percent of Colorado's population currently lives in the 150-by-50-mile region just east of the Rockies known as the

The Western Slope of Colorado. (Map by Stephen Cox and Alexander Smith Design)

Front Range, a population disparity that shows no sign of abating. Between 1960 and 1970 alone, the population along the Front Range grew by 38 percent, while the population of the Western Slope grew by only 9 percent. As a result, what the Front Range may lack in water it makes up for in political power. Historically, the Front Range in general, and Denver in particular, has shown little reluctance to flex its political muscle in order to obtain water from the Western Slope. Denver's efforts to divert water began in 1913, and currently the city draws 56 percent of its water supply from the Colorado River Basin across the Continental Divide. Denver, however, is not the only Front Range entity actively to seek out

Western Slope water. Aurora, Colorado Springs, Fort Collins, and Pueblo have all developed diversion projects, oftentimes with other Front Range cities as partners.[10]

Despite growing municipal water demand, the two largest transmontane diversion projects in Colorado, the Fryingpan-Arkansas and the Colorado–Big Thompson, serve not urban but agricultural needs. In fact, currently 80 percent of all available water in Colorado goes to farming, compared to less than 3 percent for municipal and 4 percent for industrial needs. Just as there is a discrepancy between where people live in Colorado and where the water falls, so too the majority of usable farmland in the state is located east of the Continental Divide, far removed from plentiful water sources. Counting both agricultural and municipal efforts, a total of thirty-seven transmontane diversion projects (varying in size) have been built in the state of Colorado; together they divert approximately 650,000 acre-feet of water from the Western Slope to the Front Range. (One acre-foot is the amount of water needed to cover one acre of land with one foot of water—approximately 326,000 gallons, or roughly the amount of water an urban family of four uses in one year.)[11]

Although the people of the Western Slope are outnumbered by the people east of the divide, they have not acquiesced to the Front Range's water demands. Instead the residents of western Colorado, who believed water diversions posed a threat to the region's future economic development, actively fought these projects both in the courts and in the legislature. Organized efforts to block water diversions began during the 1920s with the founding of the Western Colorado Protective Association (WCPA), which represented the Western Slope during negotiations over the Colorado–Big Thompson project in the early 1930s.[12]

The WCPA ultimately did not succeed in stopping construction of the Colorado–Big Thompson, but it did succeed in gaining some compensation for the region's losses. As a result of the negotiations, supporters of the project agreed to construct a compensatory reservoir on the Western Slope, which would provide water storage in the same river basin in which the diversion was to occur. The reservoir would be built first and allowed to fill before any water could be diverted out of the river to the Front Range. Then the water would be released from the reservoir to help replace the water that was being diverted. The idea behind the reservoirs was to satisfy water claimants downstream from the diversion site, and to preserve future water options for the region.[13]

Even with the promise of compensation, the Western Slope continued to be suspicious of the Front Range. In the 1950s, a reporter for the *Rocky Mountain News* who investigated Western Slope attitudes toward water concluded that "Western Colorado citizens regard the Colorado River as their birthright and life blood." To be soft on water development was, in those days, the regional equivalent of being soft on communism. When, in 1954, the manager of the Glenwood Springs Chamber of Commerce made the mistake of calling for the "fair" sharing of the state's water between the Western Slope and Front Range, the Chamber immediately fired him.[14]

Despite the best efforts by the Front Range and the Western Slope to gain command of the state's water supply, both sides have to contend with the fact that the state actually controls less than half of its own water. The majority of Colorado's water is the legal property of other states. Four major rivers originate in the state: the South Platte in northeast Colorado, the Arkansas in the southeastern corner, the Rio Grande in the San Luis Valley, and the Colorado River in the western part of the state. Colorado receives almost no surface water from any other states, yet these four rivers directly deliver water to nine states and Mexico. Although Colorado may be a water exporter, it has achieved none of the clout that typically accrues to the source of an essential commodity (such as OPEC with oil). In fact, Colorado has lost nearly every court battle it has fought to keep exclusive control of its water supply. As a result, Colorado has been forced to enter into interstate water compacts with all of its neighbors except Oklahoma, plus all the states in the Colorado and Rio Grande river basins. (Compacts are the equivalent of treaties between states and are permitted under the federal Constitution with the consent of Congress.) Of the various compacts the state of Colorado has agreed to, there is no doubt that the most important, complicated, and confusing one concerns the Colorado River.[15]

The Colorado River starts its 1,440-mile journey to the sea at the base of the Never Summer Mountain Range, just inside the northwest corner of Rocky Mountain National Park. Efforts to use the river begin even before the Colorado River escapes the valley of its birth, with the Grand Ditch siphoning off part of the water to irrigate land east of the Continental Divide. The extent to which the river is used and overused (today experts calculate that every drop of water in the river is used seventeen times) in the course of its journey can be seen in the fact that the river no longer reaches its historic destination in the Gulf of California. Instead the river dries up a few miles across the U.S.-Mexican border, an ending that led environmental writer Philip Fradkin to describe the Colorado as "a river no more."[16]

While the state of Colorado might share its name with the river (and provide the river with 75 percent of its water flow), perhaps a more accurate name would be the California River, since California has dominated the river more than any other state. A basic theme in the Colorado River's history for the last seventy-five years has been California's efforts to use the river's water, and the attempts by other river basin states to curb that use as much as possible. California and the rest of the basin ultimately achieved a hostile peace by agreeing to develop the water together. The device that allowed this aquatic détente was the Colorado River Compact of 1922.[17]

The Colorado River Compact contains numerous requirements and technical specifications, but the crux of the agreement is that the river is divided into two administrative basin districts. The Upper Colorado Basin consists of the states of Colorado, Wyoming, Utah, New Mexico, and a very small portion of Arizona. The Lower Colorado Basin contains the states of California and Nevada, plus the bulk of Arizona. The dividing point between the two basins is designated as Lee's Ferry, Arizona. Each basin has the right to use 7.5 million acre-feet of river water each year, although what percentage each state receives is not determined under the terms of the compact.[18]

Although the Colorado River Compact of 1922 settled many of the issues that had divided the river basin states and allowed construction to start on massive reclamation projects like Hoover Dam, the agreement included two flaws which over time have threatened its viability. The most critical error in the compact concerns the amount of water, 7.5 million acre-feet (maf), allocated to each of the basins. This figure was based on the best scientific estimate in the 1920s that 16 maf flowed through the Colorado River each year. Unfortunately the negotiations for the compact occurred near the end of what had been a period of unusually high precipitation in the Southwest, and scientists now agree that the actual annual water flow in the river is closer to 13.5 maf, with frequent lengthy periods in which the annual flow is even lower. As a result, the compact is based on water levels the river rarely attains. This discrepancy represents a bigger threat to the upper basin than to the lower, since under the terms of the compact Colorado, Wyoming, Utah, and New Mexico promise

The Upper and Lower Colorado River Basin. (Map by Stephen Cox and Alexander Smith Design)

to deliver the lower basin's share of the water and, therefore, to absorb any shortfall.[19]

The second flaw in the compact is that two of the sections conflict with each other. The writers of the Colorado River Compact were concerned about the Supreme Court's decision earlier that same year, in *Wyoming v. Colorado,* to apply the doctrine of prior appropriations to interstate water disputes. This raised the prospect of endless litigation devoted to establishing senior claims on the Colorado River. To avoid this possibility, the compact established the 7.5 maf ceiling for each basin. However, the compact also states that any Upper Basin water that cannot be reasonably used for domestic or agricultural purposes must be allowed to flow into the Lower Basin, thus suggesting a "use it or lose it" right to the water. As a result of this ambiguity, Upper Basin water leaders (especially Aspinall) began to worry that unless they developed water projects as quickly as possible within their own states, they might permanently lose their water rights to the Lower Basin. Given California's aggressive tendency to try to block other states from building reclamation projects, this was not necessarily a paranoid assumption.[20]

When the Upper Basin states began to push for "their share" of the reclamation budget in the 1940s, however, they ran into a problem. The Bureau of Reclamation announced that it would not consider any projects for the Upper Basin until the water had been formally apportioned among the basin states. As a result, in 1948 Colorado, Wyoming, Utah, New Mexico, and Arizona negotiated the Upper Colorado River Basin Compact. One major difference between the Upper Basin Compact (UBC) and the older Colorado Compact was that the UBC assigned each state a percentage of the annual river flow, rather than a fixed amount, thus avoiding the dilemma of changing water levels in the Colorado River. The UBC gave Colorado 51.75 percent of the water, Utah 23 percent, Wyoming 14, and New Mexico 11.25. Arizona, due to the small amount of territory it has in the Upper Basin, received a fixed annual portion of 50,000 acre-feet.[21]

The fact that the Bureau of Reclamation could order the Upper Basin states to negotiate a compact indicates how powerful the agency was and how central its role in western water development. Congress had created the Bureau when it passed the Reclamation Act of 1902. The act authorized the Secretary of the Interior to help construct irrigation projects in seventeen western states. The cost of this assistance was to be paid for with the proceeds from public land sales in the West. Recipients of water from the federal projects would then reimburse the government over the course of ten years, and this money in turn would help pay the costs for subsequent projects.[22]

At least that was the plan. In reality, the Bureau of Reclamation quickly developed financial problems due to cost overruns, unexpected expenditures, tardy repayments, and the fact that the sale of public lands was not raising as much revenue as had been anticipated. Additionally, some reclamation projects produced water so expensive that the cost of paying for it threatened to bankrupt the very farmers the projects were intended to help. In response, Congress began the ongoing practice of extending the repayment period for some projects, and simply writing off the costs of others. The Bureau remained in poor fiscal health until the 1930s when, under the New Deal, the government embarked on a series of massive, subsidized public works projects. The Bureau also began at that point to benefit from the profits generated by the sale of hydroelectricity from Hoover Dam, which provided a cash subsidy that allowed reclamation officials to worry less about whether individual projects could pay back their costs.[23]

The Bureau's newfound prosperity continued after the Second World War when the federal budget for reclamation skyrocketed. During the Truman administration the annual expenditures for reclamation equaled 61 percent of the total budget for the Interior Department, the highest level of appropriations ever achieved by the Bureau. Thus by 1948 the Bureau of Reclamation was in a strong enough position to order the Upper Basin states to negotiate a compact before they could receive any federal water projects.[24]

In evaluating the Bureau of Reclamation's impact in shaping the development of the West, some historians have argued for a very critical interpretation, one in which the Bureau is seen as the occupying force for an imperial government that props up a wealthy, taxpayer-subsidized agricultural elite. This image, however, would undoubtedly strike the people of Colorado's Western Slope as odd, since, in fact, they saw the Bureau's projects as a way to free themselves from the perceived economic and territorial tyranny of the federal government. In the state of Colorado the federal government owns 36 percent of the land, a relatively low amount for a western state. Yet approximately 75 percent of that federal property is located on the Western Slope, and some counties have close to 100 percent federal ownership. As a result, residents of the Western Slope frequently feel that their economic fate is controlled by faceless federal bureaucrats located hundreds of miles away.[25]

This perception of victimhood has been a perennial theme in the region's history. Local people have routinely expressed frustration about the flow of their water to Los Angeles, their taxes to Denver and Washington, and their money to companies that provide limited or poor service to the Western Slope. One writer argues that given its hostility toward the rest of the state, the Western Slope is the Quebec of Colorado. A recent history of the area reflected this point of view in its title: *A Land Alone.* This mistrust, according to the historian and Western Slope native David Lavender, is the result of "a regional schizophrenia" brought on by the boom-and-bust cycles of the local economy. Local residents remember the peak economic years, but they also recall how booms collapsed, sometimes overnight. The most recent villain in this saga was Exxon, whose sudden decision to close its oil shale operation in 1982 plunged the area into an economic depression.[26]

Despite, or perhaps because of, the Western Slope's economic difficulties, regional leaders have attempted to achieve a level of autonomy and stability by developing local resources such as water. The initial local irrigation systems constructed in the late nineteenth century were quite modest in size, usually only big enough to water five or ten acres; frequently the ditches did not even survive the rush of water during the spring snow melt. Subsequent efforts grew in scale, particularly as towns began to develop. The historian Kathleen Underwood writes that in Grand Junction "[w]ater . . . became an even more hotly debated issue than prohibition. From the outset, water aroused great concern among Grand Junction's residents, dominated aldermen's meetings, and eventually became the subject of a dozen special elections." Grand Junction was not the only Western Slope town with an active interest in irrigation. Similar community-based irrigation projects were also developed in the southwest corner of the state, including one instance where a whole town relocated in order to be closer to the finished irrigation system.[27]

Water became such an important issue because town boosters believed that people would never settle in a dry area unless they knew there was a dependable water supply. Thus water became as important for its promotional value as for economic development. In that sense, the effort to develop irrigation systems did not really differ in motive and intent from other efforts by regional boosters to lure a railroad to town or to have their community designated the county seat. The chief stumbling block to developing irrigation projects on the Western Slope was money. Even the larger towns, like Grand Junction, simply did not have the capital available to help farmers develop local projects. As a result, promoters had to look outside the region for the money to pay for these projects. The amount of time needed to construct these projects, and the paltry financial return they offered, however, deterred investors, and many of the projects that did start ended up abandoned or bankrupt. Local attempts to get the state of Colorado to invest money also failed due to the state's own lack of capital.[28]

A crucial breakthrough for the Western Slope was the passage of the federal Reclamation Act in 1902. There were two main advantages to having the federal government pay for reclamation projects: one was that the federal government had sufficient capital to underwrite the projects, and the other was that federal projects did not have to make a profit, just break even. As a result, reclamation projects that had failed with private-sector funding were revived and finished with government support. The first Western Slope project completed with reclamation money was the Uncompahgre Project in 1909, which diverted water from the Gunnison River through a six-mile tunnel to irrigate the Uncompahgre Valley.[29]

With the advent of federal involvement in reclamation funding, the role of the local boosters shifted from recruiting outsiders to invest in a project to lining up politicians to support it. In this regard the Western Slope was particularly fortunate during the first half of the twentieth century to have a congressional representative who held a powerful position in the federal government. Representative Edward Taylor was elected to Congress in 1908 and served until his death in 1941 at the age of eighty-one. During his time in the House of Representatives, Taylor became one of the ranking Democratic members and served as chair of the House Appropriations Committee, which had financial oversight of all government operations. Although best known for the Grazing Act of 1934 that bears his name, Taylor also worked to secure funding for Western Slope reclamation projects, while at the same time opposing efforts to divert water out of his district. In addition to his involvement in the fight over the Colorado–Big Thompson project, Taylor also successfully blocked another transmontane diversion, the Gunnison–Arkansas Project.[30]

There is a striking resemblance between the lives of Ed Taylor and

Wayne Aspinall. Both moved from the Midwest to Colorado, both were lawyers who had also worked in public schools, both served in the state legislature, both became chairmen in the House of Representatives, and both were elected to Congress while in their fifties. Together they provided the Western Slope with nearly sixty years of powerful and prominent congressional representation. When Aspinall became the Western Slope's congressional representative in 1949 he inherited not only Ed Taylor's political mantle, but his mind set as well. He shared Taylor's suspicion of the Front Range and its interest in appropriating the Western Slope's water. Aspinall also shared Taylor's belief that the key to economic success for western Colorado was the development of its water resources, a development both men believed should be paid for by the federal government.

2

The Accidental Congressman

By my mid-50s, I had concluded that my responsibility in life,
my destiny's own demand, was to be a congressman.
— Wayne Aspinall[1]

PERHAPS THE BIGGEST IRONY of Wayne Aspinall's congressional career
is the fact that he did not want to be a congressman in the first place.
Throughout his early political life, and even after his "accidental" election to the U.S. House of Representatives in 1948, Aspinall's chief political
goal was to become governor of Colorado. Only after serving in Congress
for several terms, and rapidly gaining seniority on the House Interior
Committee, did Rep. Aspinall abandon his long-held goal and instead
decide that he could better serve his state and district by pursuing a congressional career.[2]

Aspinall's interest in the governorship was logical given his lengthy
political service in state government. By the time he won election to
Congress, Aspinall had already served ten years in the Colorado Senate
and six years in the state House of Representatives, two of these as Speaker
of the House. While Aspinall protested that he was a public servant who
did not pursue a political life merely to hold office, it is clear from the
length of his career that he did not actively embrace the philosophy of
Cincinnatus. Aspinall often reminisced that he had first run for office as a
student in the seventh grade, and except for a few short breaks he continued to hold some sort of elected position for the next seventy years.
Exactly what motivated Aspinall continually to seek public office is unclear; what is clear is the role regional expectations played in shaping his
political opinions and agenda.[3]

Born in Middleburg, Ohio, on April 3, 1896, Wayne Norviel Aspinall
moved with his family in 1904 to Palisade, a small farming town in western
Colorado, not far from Grand Junction. There Aspinall's father, Mack,
bought a newly established ten-acre peach orchard that depended on irrigation water from the Colorado River. Mack Aspinall profoundly influ-

enced his son's view of the world by continually stressing that they were outsiders and that other people made the decisions that shaped their lives. This circumscribed view of the world led Wayne to grow up convinced that he was always in the political and economic minority of society. As Aspinall later put it, "When I was young . . . I lived outside the little town of Palisade, and the townspeople always seemed to call the shots. Then I moved to Palisade, and the bigger town of Grand Junction always seemed to call the shots. Then I went to the state Legislature, and the Eastern Slope . . . seemed to call the shots. And in Congress, the big metropolitan areas seemed to hold all the marbles." This world view may help to explain Aspinall's later quest for political power. He always insisted that he was a servant of the people who was merely trying to protect the economically and politically weak Western Slope from outside threats (Front Range cities, California water interests, and environmentalists). While this was, in part, a self-serving justification, Aspinall did seem sincerely to believe it.[4]

Wayne Aspinall spent much of his youth exploring the outdoor environment around Palisade, but not all of his encounters with nature were positive. When he was fourteen, he attended a Sunday school picnic on the banks of the Colorado River. While playing in the water, Wayne got caught in the undercurrent and started to drown, and the "town bully" jumped into the river to save him. Aspinall maintained afterward that the incident had taught him not to prejudge individuals based on generalizations. It also gave him a profound respect for the river whose fate he would one day help control. Aspinall never played in the Colorado again, nor did he ever learn to swim. For the rest of his life he remained afraid of water.[5]

After graduating from high school, Aspinall attended the University of Denver. The Methodist-affiliated school was a logical choice given Aspinall's own lifelong association with the Methodist Church. As an adult Aspinall would remain active within his church, but he was not evangelistic and expressed a fairly tolerant view of other religions. Aspinall's own religious credo could best be summarized as belief in a supreme being, in the inspired nature of the Bible, and in the notion that God had created the natural world for man's full use.[6]

During his college years Aspinall did break with one family tradition— he opted to join the Democratic Party. Raised in a family of staunch Republicans, Aspinall became disillusioned with the internal fighting that developed within the Republican Party in 1912 between supporters of

Theodore Roosevelt and of William Taft. Instead, young Aspinall became a supporter of Woodrow Wilson and the Democrats. He kept this political affiliation for the rest of his life, although he frequently bragged that he never voted a straight ticket and in fact publicly endorsed Gerald Ford for president in 1976.[7]

Aspinall graduated from the University of Denver in 1919, but he returned a couple of years later to earn a law degree, which he completed in 1925. He opted to specialize in irrigation law (perhaps influenced by the large amount of water litigation taking place in the irrigation districts of the Western Slope) and studied under L. Ward Bannister, an expert in Colorado water law. After graduating, Aspinall received two job offers to work on water law in Denver, but he rejected these more lucrative opportunities and moved his wife and four children back "home" to Grand Junction to practice law.[8]

Soon after returning home, Aspinall decided to run for the Colorado General Assembly, but his initial attempts to do so in 1926 and 1928 ran afoul of the local "political boss," Walter Walker. Walker was the longtime publisher of the Grand Junction *Daily Sentinel* and a staunch conservative Democrat. His control of the dominant newspaper on the Western Slope made Walker the *de facto* local political gatekeeper, the man with the power to determine who would be the local party nominees, what positions they could seek, and when they would be allowed to run. Candidates could choose to run for party nominations without Walker's blessing, but they simply did not win, a barrier Aspinall ran into during his initial bids for the state legislature.[9]

Walker finally dropped his opposition when Aspinall decided to run for the Colorado House of Representatives in 1930. When Aspinall won the race, Walker helped the freshman representative secure a party leadership position in the chamber as the Democratic caucus chair (or whip). By all accounts Aspinall's four years as Democratic whip and subsequent two years as House Speaker were successful. One reason for his success was Aspinall's self-taught mastery of parliamentary procedure. Another reason was that he always insisted on knowing exactly how the Democratic House members were going to vote before submitting a measure for consideration, a pattern that he repeated later in the federal House of Representatives.[10]

In 1938 Aspinall decided to run for the state senate. Following his election, Aspinall again received help from Walter Walker to secure an appointment as whip in the chamber. Aspinall served in that position for the first two years of his four-year term, and in 1941 he continued his fast rise in the legislature by becoming the majority leader. After the 1942 elections, however, the Democrats lost their majority in the state senate and Aspinall became the minority leader, a position he held for the next six years until his election to Congress in 1948.[11]

As a state legislator from western Colorado, Aspinall spent a great deal of his time and efforts on farming and water-related issues. During his senate years, Aspinall served as a key member of the agricultural and the irrigation committees, and he also served a two-year term on the state water board in 1937 and 1938. The biggest reclamation issue the state legislature had to decide during those years was whether or not to approve the federal Colorado–Big Thompson water project, which called for diverting water from the headwaters region of the Colorado River through a tunnel underneath Rocky Mountain National Park to a reservoir near Fort Collins.[12]

By the mid-1940s Aspinall had begun to think seriously about making a bid for the governorship. In addition to serving in the state senate, he had also been active in the state Democratic Party, first serving as the Mesa County chair, then as Democratic chair of the fourth congressional district, and finally as chair of the state party. Aspinall flirted with the idea of running for governor in 1946, but he ran for reelection to the state senate instead. Aspinall's visions of seeking higher office were not strictly his own; other state Democratic officials were encouraging his plans as well. Former governor, and then U.S. Senator, Edwin "Big Ed" Johnson, a longtime friend, said of Aspinall that he "would eventually if not sooner hold any office in Colorado to which [he] might aspire."[13]

In 1948 Aspinall considered running for lieutenant governor, which would be a logical stepping-stone to pursuing the governorship in 1950 (prior to 1958 executive-branch officials in Colorado served two-year terms). Aspinall hesitated, however, because he would have had to run in the primary against his friend Walter Johnson of Pueblo, and also because he realized that someone from the Western Slope would be at a disadvantage when competing against a Front Range politician. As a result Aspinall concluded that "[i]t just didn't appear to be in the cards" that year.[14]

Instead Aspinall became the reluctant Democratic candidate for the fourth congressional district seat, a position for which he had actually made an abortive bid seven years earlier when the seat became vacant on the death of thirty-year Democratic incumbent Edward Taylor. As in the past, however, Aspinall's desires in 1941 had run afoul of Walter Walker. When Aspinall had asked Walker and other local party officials to support his bid to succeed Taylor, they responded by asking him if he "had $7,500 [of his own money] to gamble on the job." Aspinall responded that "I wouldn't bet that much on a regular election, let alone a special election," and, lacking any potential funding from the party, Aspinall abandoned his bid for the nomination. Ultimately Robert Rockwell, a Republican former state legislator and lieutenant governor, won the congressional election to succeed Taylor and served for the next six years.[15]

By 1948, however, the roles had reversed, and it was Walker and others who asked Aspinall to challenge Rockwell. Even though Aspinall, who was now the state chair of the Democratic Party as well as a state senator, was more interested in being governor, he decided to enter the race to help local Democrats on the Western Slope. Aspinall entered the race not expecting to win (in fact he thought that no Democrat could beat Rockwell) but convinced that running would further strengthen his political base for a statewide race for governor in 1950. In addition, Aspinall had nothing to lose politically, since he was only halfway through his state senate term.[16]

The election year of 1948 was not one of high optimism for Democrats, particularly given the apparent unpopularity of President Truman. State political observers, however, felt that Aspinall, whom they considered to be the most widely known politician in western Colorado, had the best chance of any Democrat to unseat Representative Rockwell. While fretting that the wealthy Rockwell could spend up to five times more on the election than he could, Aspinall did take comfort from the public criticism Rockwell had recently received in *Harper's Magazine* regarding his opposition during House hearings to public land grazing fees increases. Although Aspinall had the endorsement of the local Democratic establishment, he was not the only party candidate seeking to challenge Rockwell. Thomas Matthews, the Democratic nominee for Congress during the 1946 election, was also running, but Aspinall beat him handily at the state Democratic convention. As it turned out, this was the last time Aspinall would face a primary opponent for the next twenty-two years.[17]

Despite his pessimism about the likelihood of winning the race, Aspinall launched an active campaign based on the "door-to-door" style of his legislative races. As he toured the district Aspinall stopped in each town

The Fourth Congressional District, 1948–1964. (Map by Stephen Cox and Alexander Smith Design)

to shake hands with people at the post office or courthouse, a campaign style he would continue throughout his congressional career. Although he was not known for a warm personal style, the key to Aspinall's campaigning success was his phenomenal memory for faces and names, which enabled him to greet people personally at each campaign stop and ask them about members of their families.[18]

As the campaign wore on, Aspinall began to consider the possibility that he might win. The high point of the race came when Aspinall joined Harry Truman aboard the president's train for a high-visibility, whistle-stop tour of the district. When Aspinall left the campaign train in Salida he thought to himself that while "I might have a chance, that poor devil doesn't have a chance in the world." In fact, Aspinall ended up beating Rockwell by 3,000 votes, and Truman won 1,000 more votes in the district than Aspinall did—the only time in Aspinall's congressional career that a Democratic president won more votes than he did. Aspinall later conceded that he probably won the election because of the last-minute surge of public support for the president.[19]

When Aspinall arrived in Washington, D.C., in January 1949, he was part of a new generation of representatives, many of whom would go on to become national political leaders in the following decades. Aspinall's fellow freshmen congressmen included Lloyd Bentsen and Gerald Ford. (Over time Ford would become one of Aspinall's closest political friends.) Two sophomore members of the House were Richard Nixon and John Kennedy. Kennedy had an office across the hall from the one assigned to Aspinall, and over time the two representatives got to know each other quite well.[20]

Throughout his congressional career Aspinall was well known for his long hours at the office. Shortly after becoming a congressman, the then fifty-three-year-old Aspinall had to reduce his work-day schedule from 14–18 hours to 10–12 after his doctor warned him that he was risking his health. Even then, Aspinall was almost always one of the first congressmen to arrive at the House office building in the morning; he considered 8:30 a.m. a late-morning arrival. As Aspinall later remarked, "I've always been a person who loved to work, and hours didn't mean anything to me, days didn't mean anything to me. Go to church on Sunday and relax—the rest of the time was for work."[21]

Aspinall also soon developed a reputation for his strict expectations concerning office visitors. During his career, the congressman became notorious for his fanatical obsession with punctuality. As one person recalled, "[Aspinall] had very little patience for people who made an appointment and then didn't keep that appointment right on time. . . . He was pretty insistent upon it, he would always look at his watch if you were a few minutes late." Chuck Henning, a lobbyist from Colorado, remembers the extremes Aspinall would exhibit regarding punctuality:

> I was with the Savings and Loan League at the time and Washington got hit by the biggest blizzard in something like forty-five years, about 15 inches. Nothing moved. Had to shovel our way out. I think we showed up in his office . . . about three minutes after nine, after commandeering taxicabs and everything else, and there he was sitting in his office, none of his staff was there, the corridors were empty—"you're late," and that's the way we got the meeting off to a start. He let it be known that it was not right that we had been three minutes late. You know how Washington is when it snows, but Wayne was on duty.

The congressman sometimes used his appointment schedule as a way to test how serious someone was about meeting with him. Bill Cleary recalls that Aspinall "would say let's see how interested they are when he'd set a meeting for six in the morning—'if they can't be here on time, they're not going to find me here.'" Aspinall would also schedule appointments at odd times, such as 9:37, and for unusual lengths. Two-minute meetings with constituents and lobbyists were not atypical until his secretary convinced him to discontinue the practice.[22]

Unlike his rapid political ascent in the Colorado General Assembly, Aspinall's arrival in Washington went largely unnoticed. As Newton Drury, President Truman's Director of the National Park Service, later remarked, "When I was in Washington, he was just a freshman congressman and nobody paid much attention to him." (One agency that did pay attention to Aspinall was the Federal Bureau of Investigation, which started a file on the congressman in 1949.)[23] Certainly there was nothing about Aspinall's political views that made him noteworthy. Although one historian has written that Aspinall "was a little to the left of center when he entered Congress, a little to the right when he left," and Aspinall himself claimed that he was a "progressive moderate and not a blue-eyed liberal," the record suggests that the congressman was far more economically liberal at the start of his congressional career than he was at the end. By the 1960s, however, Aspinall had abandoned these liberal views and had begun criticizing government efforts to solve problems concerning economic disparity, a shift driven in part by his belief that economic and social spending competed with funding for reclamation.[24]

While Aspinall's attitudes on some issues changed over the years, his attitude toward nature and the "wise use" of natural resources remained static. The congressman firmly believed that the future of the Western Slope depended on developing local natural resources. When Aspinall became a congressman, he believed he had a mandate from the voters to work aggressively to promote water development in his district. In so doing, Aspinall saw himself as following in the footsteps of his predecessor, Congressman Ed Taylor, who had worked vigorously to protect and develop the water interests of the Western Slope. Unlike Taylor, who served as chair of the House Appropriation Committee, Aspinall made it his goal to become a member of the House Interior Committee (then known as the Public Lands Committee), which had direct oversight of the federal reclamation program. With the help of Rep. John Carroll, a fellow

Coloradoan, Aspinall received a seat on the Interior Committee as soon as he took office. In addition to his key committee assignment, Aspinall also developed a friendship with a minor Bureau of Reclamation official named Floyd Dominy, which eventually would prove useful when Dominy became the Commissioner of Reclamation.[25]

Although he had secured the committee appointment he wanted, Aspinall continued to express an interest in the governorship of Colorado. It was only after being in Congress for several years and rapidly gaining seniority on the Interior Committee (he moved from fourteenth in seniority in 1949 to fourth in 1953) that Aspinall finally, and somewhat reluctantly, gave up his dream. Aspinall did express sporadic interest during the 1950s in running for the U.S. Senate, but he never seriously pursued the option, and by the 1960s, when he had become a power broker in the House, the congressman had ruled out the possibility. Aspinall's commitment to remaining on the Interior Committee was so strong that he declined the chance to serve on the more visible and politically powerful House Ways and Means Committee. Claiming a sweeping regional mandate, Aspinall said in declining, "I believe I owe it to the voters of Colorado and the West to stay on the committee where my personal and legislative knowledge would do the most good."[26]

Aspinall's congressional career almost came to an early end in 1952 when he was reelected by only 29 votes out of 85,000.[27] While a variety of factors contributed to his ultra-narrow margin of victory, the chief reason was that Aspinall was a Democratic politician in a district where a majority of the voters were Republican. In 1969 two political scientists examined Aspinall's district and concluded that, despite the fact that the congressman had by then won ten elections, his seat could not be classified as a "safe" one for the Democrats. The fact that Aspinall managed to remain in office for twenty-four years undoubtedly was due to his active attention to local concerns, particularly reclamation.[28]

Many of the local water issues Aspinall had to deal with involved existing reclamation projects. One of the first crises he had to contend with while in office occurred in March 1950 when a tunnel on the Government High Line Canal collapsed. This canal was part of the Grand Valley Project that provided irrigation for the farmlands surrounding Grand Junction. Aspinall rushed an appropriation bill through Congress, and a new bypass tunnel was built before the irrigation season began.[29]

Aspinall also worked to secure legislative approval for new reclamation projects in his district. One of the first major bills he sponsored was the Collbran Project, which authorized the Bureau of Reclamation to build a storage facility (Vega Reservoir) near the town of Collbran, Colorado. The primary aim of the project was to irrigate 21,000 acres of cropland, but it also included the construction of two hydroelectric plants and several smaller reservoirs to augment the water supply for Grand Junction. Two things made the Collbran Project different from previous water projects: the way the project was financed, and the way the project was sold to Congress.[30]

When Aspinall became a member of the House of Representatives, the federal reclamation program was facing a financial crisis. Although the costs of building reclamation projects were supposed to be reimbursed by the farmers and others who used the projects, many of these users were defaulting on their repayment schedules. As a result, Congress had to grant long-term extensions to the length of time project-users had to repay the costs. One Colorado project Aspinall bailed out early in his congressional career was the Uncompahgre Project near Delta. Constructed in 1904, the project was one of the first federal reclamation efforts in Colorado, and it originally had a repayment period of 10 years, which the government then extended to 20 and later 40 years. Despite the extensions, however, farmers proved unable to meet the repayment schedule. As a result, Aspinall secured passage of an extension for the project that spread the repayment period out over 106 years (a period of time which even he later admitted was too long).[31]

Eager to avoid any more financial embarrassments, the Bureau of Reclamation started adding features that would help new projects produce revenue, but which frequently had nothing to do with the supposed "agricultural" purpose of the project. In the case of the Collbran, the Bureau added hydroelectric plants and municipal water supplies to the project as revenue sources that would help to offset the costs of the irrigation part of the project. In addition, the repayment period for the project was set at fifty years. This combination of revenue producers and long repayment periods became known as the "Collbran formula" and was later used by the Bureau as a way to secure congressional support for much larger projects on the Colorado River.[32]

The other element that made the Collbran Project different from other water projects was the way supporters sold it to Congress—not simply as a reclamation project that would benefit the local economy but as one that would benefit the nation's security. Although the Bureau of Reclamation's documents on this project contained barely any reference to defense concerns, Aspinall made those concerns the centerpiece of his successful congressional lobbying effort. Speaking before the House of Representatives, Aspinall reported, in part, that

> The project has been approved by the Committee on Interior and Insular Affairs because, it would definitely assist the national-defense program. The primary reason for the urgency of the project is that it would provide a much-needed water supply in an area that has been described recently as the uranium center of the world.
>
> The Congress has appropriated huge sums of money for the nation's atomic-energy program. It would seem logical that the Congress would be equally interested in approving an authorization for $16,800,000, a relatively small amount of money, to assure continued and unburdened production of the raw materials for our atomic-energy program.
>
> Again, I wish to emphasize that the primary purpose of the bill is to authorize a cooperative enterprise . . . which is vital to the defense program.

Aspinall's sales pitch was rather disingenuous, since increased uranium production itself was not dependent upon an expanded water supply. The water *would* be needed by the large influx of people Western Slope boosters expected to move into the area to work in the uranium-processing industry, an influx that never actually occurred. Other members of Congress, however, did not question the logic of Aspinall's argument, and the project passed on July 3, 1952.[33]

Aspinall, however, did not restrict himself merely to promoting local water projects; he also became a national spokesman for reclamation issues. The National Reclamation Association began inviting Aspinall to address their annual meetings, and soon these addresses became the equivalent of a "state of the union" address for the reclamation field. In his first address to the association in 1950, Aspinall warned the group that Congress would not allow the Bureau of Reclamation to continue to have massive cost overruns on its projects. Additionally, the congressman criticized the mentality in the Bureau that led it to favor large projects at the expense of smaller ones—a hypocritical comment in light of his own subsequent support of larger regional projects. Aspinall also warned his audience, comprising mainly water lobbyists and state reclamation officials, about the "nature-lover contingency" that "now appear to desire to have the West left as a wilderness."[34]

Aspinall's rhetoric, however, really began to flow following the election of Dwight Eisenhower as president in 1952. Whereas the Truman administration supported reclamation programs, Eisenhower embarked on a go-slow approach to water projects, which in general he tended to view with fiscal suspicion. This strategy brought out Aspinall's ire, and he repeatedly criticized Eisenhower's reclamation policies. The congressman particularly resented the president's actions because he felt it was an encroachment by the executive branch on the legislative prerogative to determine federal spending priorities on matters such as water projects.[35]

Aspinall's decision in the 1950s that his destiny was to be a congressman represented the logical culmination of various beliefs that had shaped him throughout his life. The congressman saw himself as the literal representative of a forgotten backwater region rich in natural resources but at the economic mercy of outside forces. Aspinall decided to remain in Congress because his seat on the Interior Committee allowed him to help shape federal policies regulating natural resource development in western Colorado. His position also enabled him to promote federal programs, particularly in reclamation, that would actively assist the economic development of the Western Slope. It was with this objective in mind that Aspinall began working to secure congressional approval for a massive integrated reclamation project on the upper Colorado River.

3

This Is Dinosaur

> [Americans] will habitually prefer the useful to the beautiful,
> and they will require that the beautiful should be useful.
> —Alexis de Tocqueville[1]

THE SIGNING OF THE Colorado River Compact in 1922 solved many old problems and created a variety of new ones. The upper basin states (Wyoming, Utah, New Mexico, and Colorado) had agreed to the Compact in the hopes of limiting the amount of river water that lower basin states, particularly California, could claim or use. The states in the lower basin (Arizona, Nevada, and California) agreed to the Compact because the lack of an interstate agreement had caused Congress to stall on approving new reclamation projects for the lower half of the river.[2]

Following passage of the Compact, a flood of federal reclamation projects in the lower basin received congressional authorization. Among those projects were the All-American Canal, Imperial Dam, the Colorado River Aqueduct, and Parker Dam. In comparison to the massive reclamation construction in the lower basin states, during the first half of the century only one major (the Colorado–Big Thompson) and three minor (the Uncompahgre and Grand Valley in Colorado, and Strawberry Valley in Utah) federal projects were built in the upper basin.[3]

In 1946, however, the Bureau issued a report that identified 100 possible reclamation projects for the Colorado's upper basin. The report was more of a laundry list than an actual plan for development, since the Bureau also noted that full construction of all the projects would require more water than the river held. The report also contained an ominous recommendation. The Bureau advised that no further investigation of these projects be made until the upper basin states agreed on a formal apportionment of their share of the Colorado River's water.[4]

Within four months of the report being issued the governments of the upper basin states responded by forming the Upper Colorado River Compact Commission, which spent the next two years negotiating a formal distribution of the water among Wyoming, Utah, Colorado, and New Mexico. (Arizona, which had a small section of land in the upper basin, was a limited participant.) The negotiators, seeking to avoid one of the chief flaws in the 1922 Colorado River Compact, decided to allocate their water on an annual percentage basis rather than a fixed acre-feet amount, except for Arizona, which was awarded 50,000 acre-feet annually.[5]

Initially the commission members from Colorado argued that the annual flow should be divided based on the amount of water each state contributed to the river. Under this scenario, Colorado would have received 70 percent, since that was the amount of river water that originated in the state. Ultimately, however, Colorado backed down in the face of opposition from the other upper basin states and agreed to the following distribution: Colorado 51.75 percent, Utah 23 percent, Wyoming 14 percent, and New Mexico 11.25 percent. A key part of the agreement was Utah's demand that it receive 500,000 acre-feet annually from the Yampa River, even though the river flowed through Colorado rather than Utah. The only way for Utah to use this water effectively would be to build a dam at Echo Park, inside Dinosaur National Monument, a proposal that would later become a focus for controversy.[6]

One politician who took an immediate interest in the commission's efforts was Rep. Aspinall, who in 1949 introduced the legislation that secured federal ratification of the Upper Basin Compact. Despite concerns that California might view the Compact as a threat to its own water interests and try to block approval, the bill received unanimous support in the House and was quickly passed by the Senate and signed by President Truman. Aspinall's support of the Compact was not merely an attempt to win votes back home; rather, it grew out of his long-term interest in water matters. Years later Aspinall wrote, "My ambition has been to secure all of the reservoir capacity in western Colorado to take care of the share of the Colorado River waters to which Colorado is entitled." The best way to achieve his goal, Aspinall believed, was through the passage of an integrated, upper basin–wide reclamation project.[7]

Following approval of the Upper Basin Compact, the Bureau of Reclamation resumed its study of water projects for the region, and the plan that began to emerge quickly attained epic proportions. Unlike earlier Bureau efforts to develop specific projects for a particular area, the plan for the upper basin called for the development of numerous individual projects over a vast region. The Bureau released the first draft of what came to be

Wayne Norviel Aspinall, 1896–1983. (Courtesy of the University of Denver Special Collections; photograph by Fabian Bachrach)

known as the Colorado River Storage Project in 1950, calling for the construction of ten major dams and reservoirs on the Colorado and its tributaries. These major reservoirs, however, would not serve any irrigation or flood control purpose. Instead they would regulate the flow of water in order to help maximize the production of hydroelectricity. In turn, the profits from the sale of this electricity would help offset the cost of building a dozen smaller regional reclamation projects.[8]

These "cash register" dams were a recent reclamation innovation, designed to help achieve the often difficult task of making water projects pay for themselves—the ostensible goal of all federal reclamation efforts. The method used to judge the economic viability of a project is called benefit-cost analysis, which attempts to predict whether the cost of a given project (in this case, construction and maintenance of an irrigation system) will exceed the benefits derived (bringing new farmland into production). In theory all water projects were subject to this strict analysis, and only those that promised to yield a profit, or at least to break even, could be considered for government approval. In practice, however, benefit-cost analysis reports have historically been vulnerable to manipulation intended to insure that congressional pet projects met the criteria for approval.[9]

The proposed Colorado River Storage Project (CRSP) comprised numerous reclamation projects that were not economically viable on their own. Supporters devised two ways to finesse this problem. One involved using the future profits from hydroelectricity to cover the potential losses on other projects. The other strategy was to establish a link, for purposes of congressional authorization, between the individual reclamation projects and the hydroelectric dams. Rather than sell projects on their own merits (or lack thereof), supporters argued that Congress should evaluate water projects as part of a larger whole, which tended to obscure the economic difficulties of any particular component. Aspinall himself acknowledged the effectiveness of this legislative technique.[10]

Supporters of the Colorado River Storage Project also touted it as necessary for other, nonfinancial reasons. Some pointed to predictions of explosive economic growth in the upper basin region, though it was not always clear whether the project would foster this growth or benefit from it. Supporters also rejected the argument that the reclamation parts of the project would contribute to further agricultural overproduction, countering that the rapid growth in the U.S. population would eliminate such surpluses. At times proponents even tried to argue that the project was necessary for defense purposes in that it would help to develop the interior region of the United States and thus make the country more competitive with the Soviet Union.[11]

Although the Truman administration gave its full support to the Colorado River Storage Project, the Department of Interior delayed congressional consideration of the proposal for several years. This delay was caused in part by political infighting between the Bureau of Reclamation and the Army Corps of Engineers over who would control the development of water projects in the United States. The delay began to test the patience of some upper basin congressional representatives, who felt they had met all the prerequisites for the plan. Aspinall, however, was troubled by the fact that the costs and the water amounts necessary for the proposed CRSP were not equally distributed among the upper basin states. As Aspinall later remarked, the initial plan "was most unfair," and seemed "to develop water and lands in Utah to the disadvantage of like development in the other states."[12]

Aspinall's concerns about the CRSP deepened even further following the 1952 election. Having barely won reelection, now Aspinall (along with other supporters of the project) was confronted with the difficulty of working with a new Republican presidential administration that advocated fiscal conservatism in federal spending.[13] Upon taking office, President Dwight Eisenhower embarked on a natural resource policy that called for reduced federal control of natural resources and less federal spending on their development. This led Eisenhower and his Secretary of the Interior, Douglas McKay, to call for a "no new starts" policy for reclamation projects. Despite this policy, however, the Eisenhower administration also soon endorsed the CRSP.[14]

While pleased with the president's backing of the Colorado River Storage Project, Aspinall remained sharply critical of Eisenhower and his administration's reclamation actions. The congressman had warned in 1952 that under Republicans, "the West will get lots of talk about reclamation, but can expect little in the way of dams." Not surprisingly, Aspinall was a vocal opponent of the administration's "no new starts" policy for reclamation projects. In a 1955 speech to the House of Representatives, he warned that if the Congress decided to do nothing on reclamation, "the Nation will not soon regain the ground lost." When in 1956 the Congress rejected Eisenhower's reclamation program and approved several new starts, Aspinall praised the "reversal of a trend of the last few years which was bringing the federal reclamation program to a virtual halt."[15]

A year later, however, Eisenhower vetoed a public works bill that contained several reclamation projects, claiming that they were "pork barrel" projects that would lead to "overspending." Aspinall responded by asking, "Who determines at what level we are overspending? I believe that it is the responsibility of Congress to determine an orderly program and the appropriate level of spending." The representative then helped lead the successful effort to overturn Eisenhower's veto of the bill—the first veto override the president suffered.[16]

Although the concern that CRSP supporters had about possible active opposition from the Eisenhower administration turned out to be largely unfounded, opposition was building on another front and to a degree that was completely unexpected by advocates of the project. Reclamation supporters at first dismissed as a minor protest the objection by conservationists to the proposed building of a dam inside Dinosaur National Monument. Over time, however, this minor protest gained such strong public support that it threatened the passage of the entire Colorado River Storage Project.[17]

By all accounts, Dinosaur National Monument was an unlikely focus of attention for a national controversy. President Woodrow Wilson had created the monument near Vernal, Utah, in 1915 as an eighty-acre preserve for a quarry full of dinosaur bones. President Roosevelt in 1938 annexed an additional 200,000 acres, including the scenic river canyons at the confluence of the Green and Yampa Rivers. As a result, the monument now straddled the Utah-Colorado border. Due to the remote location of the 320-square-mile monument and the poor local roads, few people other than paleontologists had visited the place prior to the 1950s or even knew of its existence. As one national conservation leader later remarked, "No one had ever heard of Dinosaur National Monument."[18]

The relative "anonymity" of Dinosaur National Monument proved to be a bonus to the Bureau of Reclamation as it considered the possibility of building a dam inside the preserve. When the Bureau announced its plans for the Colorado River Storage Project, they declared the Echo Park Dam, along with the proposed Glen Canyon Dam in Arizona, to be the centerpieces. Without these two cash register dams, the Bureau insisted, the entire project would not be economically viable. The scope of the Echo Park Dam and reservoir was massive. Located just below the confluence of the Green and Yampa Rivers, the 525-foot-high dam would create a Y-shaped, 43,000-acre lake, which would flood the Green River Canyon for sixty-three miles and the Yampa River Canyon for forty-four miles.[19]

During the initial phases of the discussion over Echo Park Dam, the conservation movement raised no objections. This silence was due in part to conservationists' lack of familiarity with the area. It also, perhaps, arose out of a form of conservationist snobbery, which deemed the area not scenic enough to worry about—"just rock and sagebrush," as a former Sierra Club president told his group. This indifference soon changed, however, as conservationists began to explore the canyons that would be affected by the dam and began to realize that to do nothing would allow another "Hetch Hetchy" to occur.[20]

To conservationists the memory of Hetch Hetchy served as a rallying cry and a reminder of the movement's symbolic "loss of innocence." In 1911 the city of San Francisco had requested permission to build a dam in Hetch Hetchy Valley, located inside Yosemite National Park, to provide the city with water and electricity. John Muir, the founder and head of the Sierra Club, launched a vigorous grass-roots campaign to block the project, arguing that building the dam would violate the sanctity of Yosemite and the integrity of the national park system. Ultimately Muir's efforts failed, and Congress approved the dam in 1913. In the aftermath of the defeat, conservationists vowed they would never again allow such an "invasion" of a national park. Although conservationists initially chose not to challenge the proposed Echo Park Dam, the realization soon emerged that the similarities between Hetch Hetchy and Echo Park were too strong to allow for inaction. As one conservation leader remarked, "[T]he two situations are so much alike that the campaign literature on both sides, might be interchanged, with the appropriate names added."[21]

In response to the Echo Park Dam proposal, national conservation organizations launched an effective public relations campaign challenging the proposed dam and raising questions about the larger Colorado River Storage Project. The first salvo in this effort was fired in July 1950 when writer Bernard DeVoto published an article in the *Saturday Evening Post* titled "Shall We Let Them Ruin Our National Parks?" in which he sharply criticized both the Bureau of Reclamation and the Army Corps of Engineers for their plans to build dams at various sites in the national park system. He specifically criticized the proposed Echo Park Dam, saying that it would reduce the Green River to "a mere millpond" and that as a result, "Dinosaur National Monument as a scenic spectacle would cease to exist." The article served as an alarm call to conservation supporters throughout the country, many of whom had never heard of Dinosaur National Monument or the proposed Echo Park Dam.[22]

The next few years saw the appearance of other anti–Echo Park Dam articles in such major publications as *Life, Collier's, Newsweek, Reader's Digest,* and the *New York Times.* In addition to the friendly press coverage, the conservation movement launched its own public relations efforts, including mass printings of pamphlets and the nationwide screening of a movie about the dam. Perhaps the best-known result of this publicity effort was the book *This Is Dinosaur.* Edited by Wallace Stegner and published by Alfred Knopf, both strong supporters of the conservation movement, the book contained essays and photos focusing on the scenic beauty that would be lost if the Bureau of Reclamation built the Echo Park Dam. Conservationists gave a copy of the book to every member of Congress.[23]

Ultimately, conservation leaders felt the best way to impress upon the public what exactly would be lost if Echo Park Dam was built would be to take people to see Dinosaur National Monument. Beginning in 1952 both the Sierra Club and the Wilderness Society organized rafting trips down the Green River inside the Monument. The trips led to a sharp increase in the number of visitors to the area. Whereas approximately 13,000 people visited Dinosaur National Monument in 1950, more than 70,000 visited it in 1954.[24]

While many of these visitors were ordinary tourists, conservation leaders also made it a point to try to lure VIP visitors as well. Perhaps one of the most unusual guests was Aspinall himself. His August 1953 rafting trip was organized by Joe Penfold, western representative for the conservationist Izaak Walton League, and included Rep. John Saylor, a Republican member of the House Interior Committee and an active conservation supporter, as well as the Superintendent for the Monument. In a confidential report to his supervisor after the two-day trip was over, Penfold said that the trip had gone well for the most part, but that he had been worried about Aspinall "as he can't swim and is scared to death of the water. The first day I believe he was somewhat nervous but had more confidence the second day and enjoyed it as much as any of us. He was a thorough-going good sport."[25]

As far as the lobbying part of the trip, Penfold states that "I made it a point not to do any arguing, lecturing, speech making, or whatnot. I did not discuss the dam or the future of the Monument except when Mr. Saylor or Aspinall brought up the subject." Penfold did note, however, that "I don't think there is any question but that Aspinall was very much

impressed with the beauty of the canyons and the great recreation potential which they offer." Ultimately, though, Penfold expressed a certain
resignation concerning Aspinall's support of the Echo Park Dam:

> I wish we could count on Aspinall, but I'm afraid he is too much
> committed to the Upper Colorado Project to be of much help. On
> the other hand, Aspinall is a fair man. I think his efforts in helping to
> get Saylor out here, whom he recognizes as his most difficult opposi-
> tion, would certainly indicate that. I think it would be safe in saying
> that Aspinall's statement to me last Spring that if the Bureau could
> come up with a revised project leaving out Echo Park that would do
> the job, that he would certainly lend his every influence to the au-
> thorization of such a revised project . . . has been strengthened by
> this trip.

When Penfold suggested that the Bureau of Reclamation could quickly
devise a plan without Echo Park if it spent as much energy looking for
alternatives as it did promoting the dam, "Aspinall just laughed and said
maybe so."[26]

Although Aspinall did not experience a conservation conversion after
his trip through the monument, other visitors came away convinced that
building the Echo Park Dam would be a mistake. When these new con-
verts returned home, many began writing letters to government officials
expressing their opposition to the Echo Park Dam. In addition, members
of conservation groups and people who read about the dam proposal also
started writing letters. The result was an avalanche of correspondence (in
1954 alone the Department of Interior received a record 20,000 pieces of
mail on this topic), the vast majority against the plan. One estimate was
that the letters were running 80 to 1 against the Echo Park Dam. Even
more worrisome to supporters of the Colorado River Storage Project was
that many of these letters criticized not just the dam, but the entire upper
basin plan.[27]

Aspinall received his share of these letters, many of them from constituents. Despite his claims that "I am too busy to take part in such a controversy," the congressman often wrote lengthy responses. In these replies he
outlined his position of support for the Echo Park Dam. Aspinall insisted
that he did not doubt the sincerity of dam opponents, and in fact shared
their aesthetic appreciation for the area. "I can tell you in all frankness that

there is no one in the United States who loves these canyons and beautiful primitive areas more than I. I have the most sincere appreciation of the efforts . . . to protect them in all respects."[28]

Ultimately for Aspinall, however, economic concerns outweighed environmental ones. "I continue to be of the opinion that a storage and power reservoir at Echo Park would bring more [economic] values to the Upper Basin than the retention of the area in its present condition." The congressman was in favor of the Echo Park Dam in particular since it would be a major producer of electricity for his district. In defending the Echo Park Dam, though, Aspinall sometimes inadvertently raised economic questions about the Colorado River Storage Project as a whole. "The main reason for the storage units is to use . . . the net power revenues not needed for payment of . . . the cost of [the] storage units for payment of costs allocated to irrigation, which . . . users themselves are unable to pay." What Aspinall was essentially admitting was that the hydroelectric dams were necessary to underwrite the cost of the reclamation projects in the CRSP, since they could not pay for themselves.[29]

Aspinall tried to offer a counter-argument that the damage to the Dinosaur National Monument caused by the dam would be offset in the CRSP bill by "generous appropriations [for new facilities in the Monument] which I doubt the Park Service would be able to get by its own efforts during the next 25 or 50 years." However, Aspinall realized that such offers would not stop the opposition to the Echo Park Dam and that the growing controversy could threaten the CRSP bill. He complained to a friend that "I have . . . mentally kicked the Bureau of Reclamation many times for bringing [the Echo Park Dam] up as it has."[30]

Eventually the sheer physical volume of correspondence on this issue overwhelmed Aspinall and he gave up trying to answer all of it. He frequently had his staff send out a stock response letter, and he stopped responding entirely to almost all letters from outside Colorado. Even when responding to "local" letters, the congressman sometimes wrote with a tightly clenched pen. In a reply to a letter from a conservationist in Colorado Springs, Aspinall concluded, "I regret that we do not agree, but I do appreciate receiving your viewpoint." However, in a handwritten note on the original letter, Aspinall instructed his staff to write a response which "[i]n polite words tell him to go to hell." Despite his frustration with these letters, the congressman did recognize their effectiveness. Aspinall later remarked on how "[a]ll of a sudden, members [of Congress] from all over the country began to receive letters (and I received letters from all over the country) from their home districts in opposition to the Echo Park unit of the project." The correspondence campaign clearly was having an impact.[31]

While acknowledging the sheer volume of the letters, Aspinall did raise questions about the "real" motive for the campaign. He claimed that the letter writers "were contacted from some central headquarters and urged to stop some terrible thing." This "headquarters" Aspinall referred to was not the conservation groups themselves; in fact, the congressman (who was not the only one to suggest a larger conspiracy) believed that these groups merely served as a front for Southern Californian interests who were actively trying to defeat the Colorado River Storage Project. As Aspinall remarked in a letter to conservation leader Horace Albright, "Personally, I have thought that at times some Southern California interests were using a number of those who expressed . . . opposition to . . . the Echo Park Project."[32]

Conservation officials did take these charges seriously. Richard Leonard, the president of the Sierra Club, remarked in a letter to Joe Penfold that "All of us fully agree with your strong warnings that the Sierra Club and other conservation groups in California have to be extremely careful not to give the slightest impression that we are fighting the Upper Colorado Project in order to get more water for southern California. That actually is one of the reasons I feel it is not wise for the Sierra Club to get into the argument over the basic economics of the Colorado River Project as a whole." Another Sierra Club official publicly tried to stress the fact that the San Francisco–based organization had no vested interest in Colorado River water.[33]

Reclamation supporters did not merely criticize the actions of the conservation movement; they also launched their own campaign to try to salvage public support for the whole Colorado River Storage Project, if not for the Echo Park Dam. These efforts imitated many of the conservationists' own tactics, including articles, pamphlets, and films, and tried to emphasize the local, grass-roots support for the CRSP in the upper basin region. One such effort recruited thousands of schoolchildren into special clubs to serve as "Aqualantes" in support of the project. In return for their one-dollar membership fee, students received star-shaped badges emblazoned with a message indicating they supported the CRSP. Ultimately, though, the public relations effort by the reclamationists was too little and too late to thwart the conservationists' attack on Echo Park. The dam's opponents had discovered a new weapon—the Bureau of Reclamation's numbers did not add up.[34]

Ostensibly, the congressional hearings that opened in January 1954 were intended to examine the entire Colorado River Storage Project. The debate over Echo Park, however, soon came to dominate the whole proceedings, much to the frustration of reclamation supporters. The House Subcommittee on Irrigation and Reclamation, of which Aspinall was a member, held ten days of hearings on the CRSP, January 18–28, with the first six days reserved for testimony from supporters of the project. When the time came for the conservationists to testify they met with a hostile reception from the subcommittee, especially from Reps. Aspinall, William Dawson, and Arthur Miller, all of whom supported the project. Most of the testimony repeated the arguments against the Echo Park Dam that had already received extensive coverage in the media: how it violated the integrity of the park system, what great scenic beauty would be lost, and how the Bureau of Reclamation refused to explore other options. A crucial development occurred, however, when David Brower, the Executive Director of the Sierra Club, gave his testimony.[35]

While the first part of Brower's testimony repeated many of the themes that other conservationists had stressed, at the conclusion Brower took a risky gamble—he attacked the engineering calculations that the Bureau of Reclamation had used to claim that Echo Park was a superior reservoir location when compared with other alternative sites. Using what he described as "ninth-grade arithmetic," Brower demonstrated on a blackboard before the committee that the Bureau's figures on the amount of water loss due to evaporation from the Echo Park reservoir were wrong, and that in fact the Echo Park site would have a higher rate of evaporation than other dam sites proposed in the CRSP. Brower's testimony was a stunning blow against the Echo Park Dam because it challenged the economic and engineering justifications for the project, and brought into question the very credibility of the Bureau of Reclamation.[36]

Congressional supporters of the dam quickly tried to discredit Brower. Aspinall in particular, despite being a minority member of the subcommittee (the Republicans controlled the House of Representatives in 1953 and 1954), was active during the hearings, and seemed incredulous at Brower's claims. The congressman pointedly asked, "[Y]ou are a layman and you are making that charge against the engineers of the Bureau of

Reclamation?" Brower replied that he was merely using the Bureau's own numbers. Aspinall then insisted that the Sierra Club leader submit his figures to the Bureau to confirm their validity. (Undersecretary of the Interior Ralph Tudor later admitted that the Bureau had made an error in its calculations.)[37]

The congressman also tried to challenge Brower's expertise on the aesthetic uniqueness of Green River Canyon in Dinosaur by mentioning a long list of other river canyons in Colorado and asking Brower whether or not he had visited them. When the Brower replied that he hadn't, Aspinall replied, "All I can say is that if you give these other places in my district . . . the same publicity you are not going to find people falling all over themselves to get down into this Dinosaur National Monument to get to this beauty, because it has no corner on it." Aspinall then complained that a person from outside the region was trying to lock up local areas. "[H]e does not live there, he does not know the ambitions and wishes and the desires and the longings of the people of the area. I can understand when a person lives away from anything and he just wants to use it as a playground—I can understand how he would say, 'We will keep it undeveloped. Let us go there and play.' "[38]

The attempt by Aspinall and other committee members to undermine Brower's testimony was ultimately unsuccessful. The conservation movement had publicly undermined the rationale for Echo Park Dam. Howard Zahniser, the Executive Secretary of the Wilderness Society, sent a congratulatory telegram to the Sierra Club. "I have not seen Goliath today but David is on his way to what should be return in triumph. Salute him well. He certainly hit the giant between the eyes with his five smooth stones."[39]

While the debate over Echo Park garnered national headlines, other less well-known issues and groups were also hindering passage of the CRSP. Perhaps the second most aggressive group (after conservationists) working to block the Colorado River Storage Project was an informal alliance of Southern Californian interests that opposed any upper basin water development as a threat to the lower basin. A more amorphous opposition to the CRSP came from fiscal conservatives who claimed that the ends did not justify the means. Yet another source of difficulty for the project was, oddly enough, the alliance that supported it. Different states and regions in the upper basin continually jockeyed to receive the maximum benefit from the bill, often at the expense of other supposed allies. As the battle for approval dragged on, this alliance began to show signs of unraveling.[40]

Just as he actively attacked conservationists, Aspinall also battled these other CRSP opponents. The congressman took particular exception to California's attacks on the Colorado River Storage Project. He repeatedly denounced the state's position as selfish and hypocritical. Perhaps his strongest attack on California came in a speech to the House of Representatives on August 16, 1954. Aspinall began by saying that "I have been somewhat irritated and angered by the activities of some of my colleagues, especially those from the southern part of the great State of California." Dismissing any claims of merit in California's case, Aspinall was quick to note the irony of California's opposition to reclamation spending given that "[t]he sovereign State of California has received more benefits from Federal expenditures for reclamation than any other State in the reclamation West."[41]

Aspinall concluded his speech by claiming that California's opposition to the CRSP was part of a larger plan to deprive other Colorado River states of the opportunity to use the river's water. In a burst of hyperbole, Aspinall warned:

The hungry horde in the lower basin wants every possible drop and they want to get this clamp of first beneficial use on it. That explains this proclivity to take one's near neighbors to court, to oppose by all available means one's neighbor's development—and at the same time fatten one's own political nest irrespective of party so that one can move on to a small and possibly more select body—and the proclivity to hide as much of this as possible behind the cleanest possible skirts that can be prostituted for this end. We in the upper basin are reaching the limit of our endurance of such machinations.

Despite the rhetorical excess, there was some merit to Aspinall's view. California had for several decades been trying to prevent other states from developing their water rights. In light of the harshness of his views, it is not surprising that Aspinall expressed little hope of reaching a compromise with California interests. "[A]ny compromise . . . to which [California] would agree and which would have my consent would be something which they more than likely would consider to be unfavorable."[42]

Aspinall also attacked the criticisms by fiscal conservatives that the Colorado River Storage Project's $1.5 billion price tag was too high. The chief fiscal critic of the CRSP was Sen. Paul Douglas of Illinois, a former professor of economics at the University of Chicago. Douglas described the CRSP as "the greatest boondoggle project ever." He criticized the fact that the government would spend nearly $2,000 per acre to bring new irrigated farmland into production when farmland in his home state sold for a tenth of that amount. He also criticized the fact that the chief use of this land would be to produce low-value crops such as hay and alfalfa. Additionally, Douglas argued that the CRSP would result in "high cost hydroelectricity, almost as high as the Rocky Mountains themselves."[43]

A month after Sen. Douglas's criticisms of the CRSP, Aspinall read into the House record a rebuttal prepared by Morris Garnsey, a University of Colorado economist, which challenged several of Sen. Douglas's claims. Aspinall himself spoke about the economic aspects of the CRSP in a June 1955 letter to fellow House member John Dingell. Echoing many of Dr. Garnsey's comments, Aspinall freely admitted that developing the upper basin would be expensive, but he argued that the nation as a whole would benefit from the creation of the new wealth produced by the Colorado River Storage Project: "Such has always been the story of progress." Ultimately, Aspinall dismissed the economic criticisms of the project: "[T]his is largely a numbers game and is utilized primarily by those who would oppose the project even if it would make a gleam rise in a banker's eye (and how I wish it would). If it is remembered that this program will take many years to build so that each annual appropriation will be small and . . . that repayment will be made, these slippery numbers come into focus." Aspinall's comment is interesting because he basically concedes that from a strict financial point of view the CRSP did not make sense, but since the cost would be spread out over a long period of time and would be repaid eventually, it is still a good idea.[44]

It should be noted that Aspinall accepted, and did not seem troubled by, the criticism that the irrigation projects were financially dependent upon the revenue from the hydroelectric plants in the CRSP. In his letter to Dingell, Aspinall did admit that "[i]n some cases this assistance will be rather substantial." However, he also said that "the only actual subsidy is that money advanced for the irrigation segments, while it will be returned, bears no interest. . . . As you can see, this latter crutch asks nothing of the general taxpayer. The users of power—that is, the people of the area—will pay this differential as they buy power."[45]

In many ways Aspinall's strategy for handling economic criticisms of the

Colorado River Storage Project followed a trajectory opposite the one conservationists had used in their attack on the Echo Park Dam. Whereas dam opponents had switched from moral outrage to economic criticisms, Aspinall shifted from economic defenses to emotional appeals. In his letter to Rep. Dingell, Aspinall appealed to a sense of fairness, noting that the lower basin had received their share of federal reclamation projects. "The States of the Upper Basin gave strong support to this Lower Basin development but the long expected return of support is not now forthcoming." "If this program fails, then the Upper Basin area will be condemned to its under-developed status while its most precious resources flow down without use." Aspinall also offered a sharp apocalyptic/utopian contrast between a waterless and a watered West. "[S]tand on a canal bank as it winds its way over the land. On the uphill side, you have virtually a barren desert with but scrub growth and little green. On the downhill side you have green and growing crops, houses, cities and life. That is the choice in the West, irrigation or desolation; abundance or scarcity."[46]

Although his contemporaries thought of Wayne Aspinall as a dull speaker, the topic of water and the Colorado River Storage Project seemed to inspire him to flights of passionate prose. In a speech to his House colleagues Aspinall tried to change the case for the CRSP from abstract ideas to human realities.

We are dealing, gentlemen, with the lives of human beings. If you and I are to do what is *right* in this matter, we must go beyond the cold facts, the lifeless figures.

Put yourself in the position of a western farmer, watching your crops wither and die . . . because the irrigation ditches along your fields are dried up and split open from the heat of the sun. You have paid for water, but it is not there. It has gone downstream. And now your crops are gone and with them your hopes for a good year for your family.

Can you say to that man, "Sorry, but I refuse to do anything for you"? All this man asks is the right to work hard. . . . Can you *deny* him that opportunity?

Can you *deny* any further progress in 110,000 square miles of the United States?

These people want no "handout." They are Westerners, strong in the traditions of the frontier—self-reliant, standing on their own feet, willing to work for what they get, and ready to pay for whatever they get . . . not accepting a "something for nothing" philosophy.

These are the people with whom we are dealing, gentlemen. Farmers already on the land, fighting the forces of nature . . . people of the cities, ready to move forward. But, above all, *people*.

Search in your hearts, gentlemen. Can you deny these people the right to live and work and realize the opportunities of a frontier land? I cannot.

This House of which we are members has many traditions. It has a tradition of greatness and a tradition of humanness. . . . I have faith that its present members will carry on today in the great traditions of this House and be men of clear vision who are not afraid of the future.[47]

Aspinall's remarks reveal the strange tension that existed in the rhetoric supporting reclamation programs. The image he painted is of hearty, independent farmers who are simultaneously victims of forces beyond their control. The solution Aspinall demands is for the government to build a massive project to help save these victims. Since they promise to repay the money someday, this bailout does not taint their self-reliant image.

While westerners might be self-reliant, they could also be extremely difficult to deal with, as their infighting over the Colorado River Storage Project showed. At times the upper basin states were their own worst enemies when it came to securing approval for the CRSP. It was one thing to reach agreement in general about the concept of developing the water resources in the upper basin; the difficulty came in reconciling sometimes divergent agendas in order to have a single plan with unified support. Each state tried to maximize the number of projects it would receive under the bill, while at the same time trying to address often competing water claims within the state itself.[48]

Colorado, perhaps more than any other state in the upper basin, had to deal with sharp internal divisions over proposed elements of the CRSP. This fighting, particularly between the Western Slope and the Front Range, at times threatened to completely undermine Colorado's support for the CRSP, and in fact led Secretary of the Interior Douglas McKay in 1953 to omit any Colorado projects from the first version of the bill. When officials from the Colorado Water Conservation Board protested this deci-sion, the Bureau of Reclamation replied that "if Colorado had been able to make up its mind earlier, Colorado could have received better treatment in the initial phase." (The omission was reversed when the bills were intro-duced in 1954.)[49]

Aspinall managed to avoid being drawn into most of this intrastate squabbling. The one exception was the fight between supporters of the CRSP and supporters of the Fryingpan-Arkansas Project. Residents of the Western Slope adamantly opposed the transmontane diversion of water out of the Colorado River basin and into the Arkansas River valley in the southeastern corner of the state. Aspinall also opposed the project, par-ticularly because he did not think Congress would be willing to pass two major reclamation projects for Colorado simultaneously. As a result As-pinall successfully lobbied to have the Fryingpan-Arkansas Project shelved until Congress passed the CRSP.[50]

Given the numerous groups who, for various reasons, were opposed to the passage of the Colorado River Storage Project, and given the divisive-ness among supporters, it is not surprising that the legislation eventually ran into trouble in Congress. On June 9, 1954, the House Interior Com-mittee voted to send the CRSP bill to the full House of Representatives. The bill, H.R. 4449, called for the construction of eleven participating irrigation projects and three large storage projects, including the Echo Park Dam. The committee was sharply split, however, voting only thir-teen to twelve in favor of recommending the bill.

Both sides issued lengthy reports outlining their support for or opposi-tion to the bill. The majority report argued, in part, that the CRSP was necessary for the economic and agricultural well-being of the nation, and that building the project would help the upper basin states to meet their water obligations to the lower basin and would foster economic develop-ment in the Interior West. The minority report criticized the bill, in part, for providing a "grossly excessive" subsidy for the region, developing marginal agricultural land, and undermining existing federal water and power policies. This report also stated that the plan violated the integrity of the National Park System with the recommended construction of Echo Park Dam. Given the close vote in the Interior Committee, and the con-tinuing public controversy over Echo Park, the House leadership opted to let the bill die without further consideration rather than have the bill be formally defeated, which would make it harder to revive later. Upon learning of the House's action, the Senate also dropped further consideration of its version of the CRSP bill.[51]

New legislation for the Colorado River Storage Project was introduced in both chambers in 1955. The House Subcommittee on Irrigation and Reclamation held two weeks of hearings in March and April. Aspinall, in his new capacity as chairman of the subcommittee, initiated the hearings with a statement arguing that there was a vital need to begin construction of the CRSP. "We have reached the point . . . where we cannot consider any substantial development of the waters of the Colorado River unless and until we have achieved a measure of regulation of the erratic flow of the Colorado River." He continued his argument by saying "The down-rush of the waters of the Colorado will provide the bootstraps by which this area can pull itself up, paying its own way as it goes and adding presently incalculable values to the nation generally."[52]

While the bulk of the hearings again focused on the Echo Park Dam issue, some of the more heated moments dealt with California's opposition to the CRSP. Southern Californian House members focused much of their criticisms on the massive cost of the project, arguing that other parts of the country would be unfairly burdened with subsidizing the economic development of the region. Supporters of the project tried to attack the credibility of witnesses from Southern California by arguing that they were paid lobbyists. This strategy backfired, however, when Rep. Craig Hosmer of Long Beach pointed out that witnesses from the upper basin were also paid for their work on behalf of the project but were not, unlike the California witnesses, registered as lobbyists as federal law required.[53]

Although the testimony from California's witnesses presented some sharp challenges to the Colorado River Storage Project, the most ominous threat, from the point of view of reclamation supporters, came from the testimony of a conservationist opposed to the Echo Park Dam. Dr. David Bradley, who had coordinated his testimony with the Sierra Club's anti-dam efforts, announced he was appearing before Congress not simply to testify against the Echo Park Dam, but to call into question the "entire project as presently conceived." His comments suggested that if Congress did not drop the Echo Park Dam, conservationists might be ready to broaden their attack to oppose any new dams on the Colorado River. Given the public support conservationists had mobilized against the Echo Park Dam, CRSP supporters worried that conservationists might be able to kill the entire bill. At the same time, the Bureau of Reclamation back-tracked on its earlier argument that it would be impossible to build the CRSP without Echo Park Dam. Reclamation Commissioner Wilbur Dexheimer testified that omitting the dam would merely "impair full development in the 'upper reaches.' "[54]

At the end of the House hearings, Aspinall faced a dilemma. He ardently supported the proposed Echo Park Dam, not just because his district stood to benefit from the project, but out of a fear that a defeat would set a precedent against other reclamation projects. The previous year Aspinall had even warned that any attempt to delete the dam would "give conservationists a tool that they will use against us for a hundred years." However, the congressman had a stronger commitment to the Colorado River Storage Project than he did to the dam, and he knew the CRSP could not pass as long as the Echo Park Dam remained in the bill. Reluctantly, he concluded that the dam would "have to be sacrificed on this altar of opposition." Fortunately, the commissioner's statement provided the congressman with the "wiggle" room he needed in order to salvage the CRSP legislation. On June 9, 1955, Aspinall announced his change in position to an executive session of the House Irrigation and Reclamation subcommittee. For the good of the larger CRSP bill, Aspinall said, the Echo Park Dam would have to be dropped.[55]

Aspinall's strategy initially failed when his motion to delete the Echo Park dam was defeated on a twelve to eight vote. Members of the subcommittee from Southern California refused to remove Echo Park in the hopes that retaining it would kill the entire CRSP bill. After three days of lobbying, Aspinall managed to reverse the vote, and the subcommittee formally dropped the Echo Park Dam from further consideration. The full Interior Committee then voted, twenty to six, to report the bill favorably to the full House.[56]

Removal of the Echo Park Dam did not, in and of itself, solve all of the problems facing the CRSP bill. Despite the fact that the Senate had passed its own version of the Colorado River Storage Project (which included Echo Park) by a wide margin, Aspinall quickly determined that the version his committee had approved would lose if brought to a vote in the House. There were several reasons for the lack of support in the House—cost concerns, regional rivalries, disputes over power revenue sharing, and lingering suspicions from conservationists. Despite the fact that the opposition was not unified, Aspinall concluded that bringing the measure up for a vote during the current session of Congress would doom it to failure. Instead he lobbied for a delay and the House formally postponed consideration of the bill on July 26, 1955. In an appearance before the Upper Colorado River Commission in September, Aspinall warned that if CRSP supporters pressed ahead the following year with the current bill, "and we are defeated, we will be set back ten years."[57]

Aspinall and other congressional supporters of the Colorado River Storage Project spent the congressional recess trying to broker a deal with opponents of the project. Most of their effort was spent trying to address the continued opposition of conservationists to the Echo Park Dam. Although the House had deleted the dam from its bill, it still remained in the Senate bill, and conservationists had publicly speculated that Echo Park supporters would try to have the project reinserted during the House-Senate conference negotiations. Supporters of the CRSP worried that if conservationists succeeded in delaying the bill much longer, the entire effort would collapse due to the strain that was developing among project proponents. As a result, on November 1, 1955, forty key supporters of the CRSP (governors and congressional members) met in the Brown Palace Hotel in Denver to devise a strategy for ending the impasse.[58]

Upon arrival in Denver, the delegates found a full-page "open letter" in the *Denver Post* from the conservation lobby. In the letter conservationists outlined their "demands" for dropping opposition to the Colorado River Storage Project, the chief one being the permanent removal of Echo Park Dam from the bill. The ad did offer an olive branch when it stated that conservationists were not automatically anti-reclamation. After two days of meetings, the CRSP supporters passed a resolution formally calling for removal of the Echo Park Dam from the legislation pending before Congress. On November 29 Secretary of the Interior Douglas McKay, who just prior to the Denver summit had expressed continued support for the Echo Park Dam, announced that the Bureau of Reclamation was formally dropping the dam from its CRSP plans.[59]

One person strangely absent from the Denver meeting was Rep. Aspinall, who had announced more than a week prior to the summit that he had not been consulted about the meeting date and had prior commitments. Apparently Aspinall and others from the Western Slope viewed the meeting, which had been scheduled by the chair of the Senate Interior Committee, Clinton Anderson, as an example of that committee ignoring the interests of western Colorado. For his part, Senator Anderson viewed

Aspinall's absence as evidence that the congressman, and other Colorado politicians, did not support the effort to reach a compromise. Conservationists also noted Aspinall's absence and worried that he would not honor the agreement reached at the meeting.[60]

In December conservation leaders announced that they would no longer be satisfied with a simple promise from Congress not to build the Echo Park Dam; instead they now wanted a provision added to the legislation reaffirming the integrity of the National Park System and prohibiting the construction of any CRSP reclamation project inside a national park or monument. The fact that negotiations were happening at all represented a victory for the conservation movement, since it meant that congressional leaders now viewed them as a political force that could not be ignored.[61]

It was not immediately clear whether Aspinall, whose approval was critical, would accept this latest demand. David Brower noted that the congressman had earlier expressed opposition to the idea of a blanket statement but had expressed a willingness to include wording in the bill to protect Rainbow Bridge National Monument from being flooded by water from the reservoir formed by Glen Canyon Dam. Despite his doubts, the Sierra Club's executive director and Aspinall held several meetings in January 1956 in which the congressman finally agreed to accept two new provisions in the CRSP bill: one specifically calling for the construction of a small dam to protect Rainbow Bridge National Monument, and the other restating the integrity of the park system in general.[62]

In mid-January Aspinall met with several other congressional supporters of the Colorado River Storage Project to consider the revisions in the bill. They all agreed to accept the conservation provisions and to allow Aspinall and Rep. William Dawson of Utah, a Republican co-sponsor of the bill, to handle the matter of revising the bill and taking the parliamentary steps necessary to arrange quickly for a vote by the full House of Representatives. By late January Aspinall felt sufficiently confident that a deal was at hand that he began to leak the details to the press.[63]

On January 26, Aspinall and Dawson formally sent a letter to Edgar Wayburn, the president of the Western Outdoors Clubs, one of the umbrella conservation lobbying groups, stating that Echo Park Dam had been formally dropped from the CRSP bill, and that "in order to show our good faith," a clause has been added, stating "It is the intention of Congress that no dam or reservoir constructed under the authorization of this Act shall be within any national park or monument." They further added, "We have also agreed to an amendment specially designed to protect Rainbow National Bridge." The letter closed with a request from the congressmen that they receive a formal assurance that all opposition by conservationists to the Colorado River Storage Project would now be withdrawn. Conservationist groups obliged and began publicly to announce that they were withdrawing their opposition to the CRSP bill.[64]

After a brief series of meetings, the House Interior Committee voted on February 8 to send the revised Colorado River Storage Project bill to the full House with a favorable report. Its fate in the House of Representatives, however, remained uncertain due partly to lingering opposition from Southern California's representatives and from fiscal conservatives. In an attempt to further shore up support for the bill and to extinguish any lingering questions about the Echo Park Dam, both Aspinall and Rep. Clair Engle, the chair of the Interior Committee, stated publicly that when the bill reached the House–Senate conference committee they, as the delegates from the House, "would let the bill die . . . before agreeing to authorize Echo Park Dam in this bill."[65]

The House considered the final bill for three days (February 28 and 29, and March 1). In his speeches to the House Aspinall stressed the long history of the CRSP bill, the resolution of the conservation challenges to the legislation, the national economic benefits to be derived from the measure, the compliance of the bill with existing water laws, and the bipartisan nature of the proposed legislation. In the end the House leadership for both parties formally endorsed the bill, and supporters of the Colorado River Storage Project received the supreme blessing when, at a March 1 press conference, President Eisenhower simultaneously announced his bid for reelection and his full endorsement of the current CRSP legislation. That same day the House formally approved the bill with 256 votes in favor and 136 against.[66]

The Colorado River Storage Project was one of the largest reclamation projects ever constructed in the United States. Even today, more than forty years later, the CRSP still inspires debate and controversy. The political history of this project shows that Aspinall played a critical role in its passage. While the story of how conservationists battled the Echo Park Dam is a familiar one, what has not been as thoroughly examined is the larger story of how the CRSP bill managed to pass despite the controversy surrounding it. As a result, Aspinall's role in the passage of this bill has often been overlooked. Understanding his role helps provide insight into western politicians' convictions regarding the importance of federal economic development of the region.

Perhaps the strongest evidence, though, of Aspinall's central role in the CRSP legislation came from one of its strongest opponents, Northcutt Ely, the attorney who represented Southern Californian interests before Congress. After the bill passed, Ely came to Aspinall's office and told him that the best man had won. The congressman also received praise, albeit more restrained, from David Brower, who wrote, "Someday, somebody is going to write a book about the . . . history of Dinosaur and you're going to have an important part in it unless I miss my guess." Although Brower would have less positive things to say about Aspinall later, other people continued to praise the congressman's crucial role in passing the Colorado River Storage Project. Stewart Udall, who during his years in the House served on Aspinall's committee, later remarked that the congressman had provided decisive leadership in securing passage of the CRSP bill, "acting as our captain and quarterback." Aspinall's achievement was particularly impressive given his still relatively junior political status in the House at the time the bill was passed. Although the congressman himself never felt there was a single "Father or Mother to the . . . Colorado River Storage Project," he did look back on his role in passing the bill with a great deal of satisfaction, and even had it listed on his gravestone as one of his legislative achievements.[67]

Aspinall's major role in passing the Colorado River Storage Project helped to enhance his political stature with other members of Congress. He was no longer seen as simply a local congressman interested in water projects; instead he was recognized as a national advocate for reclamation. Other western officials, in particular, now viewed Aspinall as a key promoter for water projects. This perception, however, was not completely accurate. While Aspinall spoke publicly in favor of reclamation, he always based his support for a particular project on whether it would benefit his district, or at least not harm its water interests. This dichotomy between words and actions would later lead some Western politicians to feel betrayed when Aspinall failed to support, or even actively hindered, the passage of their own reclamation projects.

Aspinall was not the only one to gain clout from his involvement with the CRSP bill. The conservation movement also gained national prominence from its successful opposition to the Echo Park Dam. The emergence of the conservation movement as a powerfully lobbying force represented a new complication in reclamation legislation. Whereas in the past the debate over a particular water project typically only concerned the people living in the area the project would affect, now the conservation movement had the demonstrated ability to make a local project a national issue. The development of this new nationwide constituency represented a direct challenge to the traditional institutional power that Aspinall cultivated in the House. The enhanced stature and conflicting agendas the congressman and conservationists now had would lead to repeated clashes in the future.

The passage of the Colorado River Storage Project did have an immediate beneficial effect for Rep. Aspinall. It helped him to solidify his electoral hold on Colorado's Fourth Congressional District. During the 1956 election Aspinall actively ran on his reclamation record, making the CRSP the centerpiece of his advertising campaign and reminding voters that the CRSP included five reclamation projects and three major hydroelectric dams for the Western Slope. That November he won reelection by a 10,000-vote margin, his first decisive congressional election victory and one that helped establish his political base for the next sixteen years. This base would prove particularly crucial during the congressman's next major reclamation battle, when Aspinall gave his support to a reclamation project his district did not want: the Fryingpan–Arkansas.[68]

4

The River Went over the Mountain

And men shall fashion glaciers into greenness,
And harvest April rivers in the autumn.
—Thomas Hornsby Ferril[1]

IT IS DIFFICULT TO KNOW who the residents of the Western Slope mistrust more on water matters, the state of California or Colorado's
own Front Range. California historically has represented the potentially
greater threat; its congressional muscle allows it to treat any water project
affecting the Colorado River basin as a threat to the state itself. However,
the proximity of the Front Range to the Western Slope has made that area
more of an immediate threat, as various cities and agricultural interests in
Colorado have built new and ever larger projects to divert water across the
Continental Divide.

Despite the Western Slope's best efforts to resist water diversions over
the mountains, Colorado's constitution insured that, in the eyes of the law,
the Front Range's efforts would be almost unstoppable. The only thing
that prevented the wholesale diversion of water across the Continental
Divide was the Western Slope's congressional representatives. First Rep.
Ed Taylor (1909–1941) and then Wayne Aspinall used their positions of
political influence to curb, if not actually reduce, the extent to which the
Front Range could expropriate water from the Western Slope.

Large-scale Front Range diversions began when the city of Denver
started transferring water across the mountains in 1913. The federal government became involved in the process when Congress approved construction of the Colorado–Big Thompson Project in 1937, which diverted water across the divide to farmers in northeastern Colorado. By the
1950s the southeastern corner of the state was also demanding a share, a
possibility the Western Slope vehemently opposed. Initially Rep. Aspinall
had no political option but to try to block this latest diversion plan, even
though he realized that his opposition to the reclamation project was a
hypocritical one. As a strong proponent of water development (at public

expense) in his own district, it seemed contradictory for him to block reclamation projects that benefited others. Aspinall worried that if he completely blocked this plan, he would have a difficult time lining up support for his own reclamation projects in the future. Eventually Aspinall decided that he needed to secure passage of a water diversion project that would both placate the people back home, as well as help the people on the other side of the mountains.[2]

Commercial farming in the Arkansas River Valley of southeastern Colorado began in the 1850s. Even in the early days the relative scarcity of water limited the size and commercial viability of the farms, and by the 1890s many streams in eastern Colorado were already over-appropriated. As a result, by the 1920s regional boosters became convinced that a transmontane diversion of water would be the solution to their problem. The first plan, which supporters named the Gunnison-Arkansas Project, called for diverting 800,000 acre-feet a year out of the Gunnison River and transferring it across the Continental Divide into the Arkansas River. At the request of local boosters, the Bureau of Reclamation had began conducting studies for the plan in 1936, and the Gunnison-Arkansas Project remained under active consideration until the mid-1940s.[3]

Not surprisingly, opposition to the plan developed quickly on the Western Slope. In 1938 Rep. Ed Taylor denounced the Gunnison-Arkansas Project as "a bold, brazen, buccaneering fight to deliberately steal the summer water of Gunnison country." He vowed, "I will never permit any bunch of promoters to get away with it as long as there is a spark of vitality left in my body." Taylor warned, though, that "it is not at all an easy fight that I am up against in trying to protect our most priceless birthright." Many of the Western Slope critics of the project complained that it would divert more than half of the water from the Gunnison River and its tributaries, the loss of which they believed would hinder future local growth. Aspinall later pointed to the size of the diversion as the chief reason the Gunnison-Arkansas Project was never constructed, although he tended to blame the Bureau of Reclamation, rather than local promoters, for what he perceived as the excesses of the original plan: "Federal Government Agencies are usually more prone to human error and ambitions than are the persons whom they are supposed to serve." The congressman no doubt found it easier to criticize a faraway bureaucracy than a group of local boosters.[4]

By the late 1940s the Gunnison-Arkansas Project was dead, so diversion supporters in the Arkansas Valley adopted a smaller-scale plan, the Fryingpan-Arkansas Project. They hoped this plan would achieve part of their reclamation goals. The Fryingpan-Arkansas Project (or Fry-Ark for short) was originally conceived as the first phase of the larger Gunnison-Arkansas Project. The state of Colorado, however, formally requested in 1951 that the Bureau of Reclamation drop its plans for the Gunnison-Arkansas and treat the Fry-Ark as a completely separate project, in the hopes of increasing the likelihood that the latter project would be approved by Congress. The plan called for diverting water out of the Fryingpan and Roaring Fork Rivers on the Western Slope, sending it under the mountains, and then placing it in the Arkansas River. The plan also called for the construction of a 28,000-acre-foot reservoir on the Roaring Fork River near Aspen. The purpose of this reservoir was to compensate the Western Slope for the loss of its water by building a storage unit that, when full, would help provide a new, alternative source of water.[5]

Aspinall faced political difficulties over the project because, while the majority of his district was located on the Western Slope, part of it extended across the continental divide and stood to benefit from the Fryingpan-Arkansas Project. Thus Aspinall had constituents not only on both sides of the continental divide, but on both sides of this issue as well. As one of the congressman's staff members later put it, the Fry-Ark was "a real pain in the ass." Opposition to the Fry-Ark developed shortly after the Bureau of Reclamation released its report on the project in 1951.[6]

Part of the Western Slope's concern about the Fryingpan-Arkansas Project arose from the belief that congressional consideration of the plan deflected interest and attention away from the then pending Colorado River Storage Project. This concern caused Aspinall to withhold his full endorsement of the Fry-Ark bill in the House. Addressing his congressional colleagues in 1954, Aspinall stated that given his support of reclamation projects in general, he "could not be consistent and do other than support [the Fry-Ark Project] although I feel that its consideration . . . at the present time is unfortunate and untimely."[7]

The congressman further argued that projects such as the Fry-Ark, which diverted water out of a river basin, could eventually lead to the Colorado River's water supply being over-tapped. He also noted "that the Western Colorado residents of the immediate area from which the water will be taken are practically unanimous in their opposition to the project." Aspinall further complained that the previous major federal diversion project in the state, the Colorado–Big Thompson Project, "has taken practically all of Colorado's Federal Reclamation contributions for the past seventeen years." Finally, he criticized the project's anticipated $200 million price tag. Despite these concerns, though, Aspinall concluded that in the absence of any "supporting evidence" (which he did not define) to contradict Colorado's endorsement of the project, Congress should approve it.[8]

The Interior Committee did vote in 1954 to endorse the Fryingpan-Arkansas Project, but the bill had to receive approval from the Rules Committee before the House of Representatives would schedule a final vote. Aspinall took the opportunity when the Rules Committee was considering the bill to suggest that the House should consider the Colorado River Storage Project before it considered the Fryingpan-Arkansas Project. The congressman argued that it was necessary to first develop water usage within the basin of origin (in this case the Western Slope) before transferring water elsewhere—a belief that was a guiding principle throughout his career. Projects such as the Fry-Ark, Aspinall said, "alarm the people of Western Colorado greatly. It is difficult for them to see the equity and justice which make possible the diverting of large amounts of our most valued natural resource from our own originating Basin, while denying to them a like opportunity for development within the Basin itself."[9]

The congressman did acknowledge that he had supported the Fry-Ark Project before, and had even voted for it in the Interior Committee, but he said he had done so "with the understanding that the Upper Colorado River Project would come first." Aspinall worried that if the Fry-Ark passed first, not only would it divert water out of parts of his district, but it might also divert reclamation funds away from projects that favored his district. The Rules Committee did not heed Aspinall's plea, but the issue of which bill should go first became moot when the House, in a rush to reach adjournment, voted 195 to 188 not to consider the Fryingpan-Arkansas bill during the session.[10]

When Aspinall went home to campaign for re-election in the autumn of 1954 he realized that, despite the refusal of the House to vote on the Fryingpan-Arkansas bill, his own support for the project, no matter how limited, might become a campaign issue for those who completely opposed the Fry-Ark. In an attempt to forestall this criticism, his campaign ran numerous newspaper, radio, and television advertisements stressing the congressman's commitment to protect the Western Slope's water interests and explicitly stating that he favored construction of the Colorado River Storage Project before the Fryingpan-Arkansas Project. Aspinall's intent was to assure his constituents that they too would receive reclamation projects.[11]

Aspinall's Republican opponent, Charles Wilson of Glenwood Springs, based his campaign on the water issue and announced his total opposition to the Fry-Ark. Shortly before the election, Aspinall ran an advertisement in which he denounced the "published LIE" that he was "willing to barter away our most precious resource (water)." The congressman complained that it was the state of Colorado, and not he, who had decided to seek federal approval for the Fryingpan-Arkansas Project, and that he remained committed to seeking CRSP authorization first. Aspinall won re-election, but the margin of victory was only 4,000 votes. After the election Aspinall, who stood to become the chair of the Irrigation and Reclamation Subcommittee in the new Congress, announced that he would move the CRSP bill ahead of the Fry-Ark for first consideration, noting that "I was never in on the sponsorship of [the Fryingpan-Arkansas Project]," but he did concede, "I shall expect to co-operate with members of the Colorado delegation."[12]

While Aspinall promised to work with the other congressmen from Colorado, one segment of his own constituency had decided they no longer wanted to work with him: the voters in Pitkin County. The origin of this opposition to Aspinall in Aspen (the county seat) grew out of local criticism over plans to build a reservoir above the city on the Roaring Fork River as part of the Fry-Ark. Local residents complained that Aspinall was not actively trying to defeat the project. The congressman tried to explain his dilemma in a June 30, 1954, letter to the Democratic Chairman of Pitkin County. Aspinall stated his belief that it "would not be consistent if I . . . opposed the Frying Pan–Arkansas [since] it is similar to the Upper Colorado program." Aspinall did accept partial blame for the fact that both the Irrigation Subcommittee and the full Interior Committee had given the Fry-Ark legislation only a limited hearing. "I feel that the full Committee was hasty in its action but I have not considered that what to me was an ill-advised procedure, was sufficient to call for an adverse position on my part." Aspinall conceded that this explanation might not be satisfactory, but said that he had made his decision based on what "appeared to be just and equitable for all concerned."[13]

Aspinall's explanation did indeed turn out to be unsatisfactory to voters in Aspen. The depth of their disagreement with his position became apparent in the September 1954 primary election when Aspinall, who had no official opponent in the race, "lost" in Pitkin County to a write-in candidate. The "victor" in Pitkin County was John Saylor, a Republican congressman from Pennsylvania who also was a member of the Interior Committee and a vocal critic of the Fryingpan-Arkansas Project. Pitkin County voters again expressed their dissatisfaction with the congressman in the November election when they gave the Republican candidate, Charles Wilson, 550 votes and Aspinall 149. One of the votes for Aspinall's opponent came from the Democratic County Chairman, who had publicly endorsed Wilson. Aspinall's political relationship with Aspen never recovered. Over the next eighteen years he only managed to win Pitkin County two times, including an eleven-vote victory in 1960 and a wider victory margin in the Lyndon Johnson landslide of 1964.[14]

In later years Aspinall spoke of Aspen with the same contempt he reserved for environmentalists (and increasingly the two groups overlapped). Yet in the battle over the Fryingpan-Arkansas Project the conservation movement was conspicuously absent. Conservationists in Colorado who spoke out against the Echo Park Dam also had expressed concerns about the Fry-Ark Project. National conservation leaders, however, seemed more puzzled than provoked by the proposal. David Brower, partly in jest, asked, "Why must the people from southern Colorado covet Western Slope precipitation when they are capable of such superb snow jobs right in their own back yard?" The Sierra Club did consider opposing the Fry-Ark, but Brower warned that doing so might "harm" the club's efforts to block the Echo Park Dam by making it appear that conservationists were opposed to any reclamation projects.[15]

The campaign for approval of the Fryingpan-Arkansas Project started again with the beginning of the Eighty-fourth Congress in 1955. The bill progressed slowly as the House Subcommittee on Irrigation and Reclamation, now chaired by Aspinall, held hearings on the project over several months. While the Fry-Ark hearings lacked the contentiousness of the hearings over the Echo Park Dam, Aspinall repeatedly focused his questions on a series of topics: (1) how much water would be diverted; (2) if this diversion would affect existing prior appropriations of this water; (3) whether the project would be hindered if the Colorado River Storage Project was not constructed; and (4) if the Fry-Ark was simply a starting point for the larger Gunnison-Arkansas Project. Seemingly satisfied by the assurances offered by project supporters, Aspinall became a quiet supporter of the bill, which the subcommittee sent to the full Interior committee with a favorable recommendation.[16]

In January 1956, the Interior Committee passed the Fryingpan-Arkansas bill and sent it on to the House Rules Committee. There the bill languished for seven months until the Rules Committee finally scheduled it for consideration by the full House. Aspinall, however, had doubts about the viability of the measure, reportedly having said in May that unless the Republicans delivered more than a hundred votes the bill did not have enough Democratic support to pass. Before the House could vote on the merits of the Fry-Ark bill it first had to decide whether or not to even consider the measure. In the brief debate before the House voted on this question, Colorado's three other congressmen spoke on behalf of the project. Aspinall did not make a formal statement supporting the bill, but he did participate in the floor discussion, and he voted in favor of it. The final vote, however, was 179 in favor of further considering the bill, and 194 against. The House had killed the Fryingpan-Arkansas Project again.[17]

In the aftermath of the bill's defeat, Aspinall was quick to blame Republicans for the failure. In a lengthy letter to a friend back in Colorado, the congressman listed several mistakes that supporters had made, including: bringing the bill before the full House too late in the session; Colorado Congressman J. Edgar Chenoweth's public spat with House Speaker Sam Rayburn; and "the failure of certain Republicans" to support reclamation projects in areas other than their own districts. The greatest mistake, according to Aspinall, was that Republicans had refused to support a Democratic proposal to build several dams at Hell's Canyon in Idaho, thus angering the Speaker of the House, who was a Democrat.[18]

Others, however, felt Aspinall was to blame for the defeat of the Fryingpan-Arkansas legislation. Harold Christy, who had lobbied on behalf of the project, complained that the congressman originally promised to give active support to the Fry-Ark once the Western Slope and the Arkansas Valley reached an agreement on the project. However, when both sides did finally agree to the operating principles for the Fry-Ark, Aspinall then withheld his support, claiming that Congress needed to approve the Colorado River Storage Project first. This contradicted the official position of the state of Colorado, which had endorsed making the Fryingpan-Arkansas Project the first priority. Christy reported that following the passage of the CRSP in 1956 Aspinall had said that the Fry-Ark was his next priority. Yet at the start of the congressional session in 1957, Aspinall reportedly only gave the project his "silent consent."[19]

Rep. Chenoweth reintroduced a Fryingpan-Arkansas bill at the start of Congress in 1957, and once again the Subcommittee on Irrigation and Reclamation held hearings. Aspinall, still serving as chair of the subcommittee, presided over the hearings but largely abstained from the debate. He did, however, state for the record his belief that the Western Slope, in general, had a legitimate reason to be concerned about water transfers to the Front Range. Despite these hearings, however, the Fry-Ark legislation never received serious consideration during the Eighty-fifth Congress, and it died when the session ended.[20]

When Congress adjourned in August 1958, one observer, Felix Sparks, had a harsh assessment of Colorado's failed efforts to get the bill passed. Sparks, who had recently become Director of Colorado's State Water Conservation Board, remarked that "this legislation has not been well handled by the official agencies of Colorado, including our congressional delegation. [We] must accept a major share of the responsibility for the unfavorable treatment of the project legislation in Congress to this date." To help jump-start the process again, Sparks traveled to Washington to meet with Aspinall. The two were old political acquaintances, having first met during the 1948 election when Sparks was a successful Democratic candidate for district attorney in western Colorado. Given his Western Slope background, Sparks recognized that Aspinall was in a difficult position. The director also realized that the only way to secure House approval of the project was to gain the congressman's support.[21]

In examining the two previous failed attempts, in 1954 and 1956, to pass the Fryingpan-Arkansas legislation in the House, Sparks concluded that it had been Aspinall's own inaction that had doomed the bills. Although Aspinall's subcommittee and the full Interior Committee had approved the legislation each time, Aspinall's failure to endorse the project had undermined attempts to have the bills brought up for consideration by the full House. The congressman, in effect, had a veto over the Fry-Ark legislation. When Sparks and Aspinall met, the director charged the congressman with sabotaging the Fry-Ark, but the congressman just laughed. Aspinall did tell Sparks what had to be done in order to get the bill passed in the House. If the director got the various water agencies in Colorado to agree to a unified plan, then the congressman would push the measure through the House. Aspinall also told Sparks not to bother him again until that happened.[22]

Negotiations between the various state water groups dragged on for a year. The key breakthrough came when all sides agreed to a revised plan for the compensatory reservoir on the Western Slope. The original plan had called for a 28,000 acre-foot reservoir near Aspen. The water power brokers on the Western Slope had complained that the reservoir was too small, while the residents of Aspen had complained about having any reservoir above the town, regardless of its size. The revised plan proposed a new reservoir located on the Fryingpan River. This reservoir would be more than three times larger and in a remote location, thus eliminating both of the problems with the Aspen Reservoir. The size (100,000 acre-feet) was of particular advantage since it would more than offset the annual diversion for the Fryingpan-Arkansas Project (70,000 acre-feet), thus providing the Western Slope with "bonus" water. This water had not been claimed and used in the past because there were no facilities for capturing it, something the project would rectify. As a result, on April 30, 1959, all the parties in the dispute signed a formal intrastate water pact. With this agreement in place, Aspinall publicly announced he could now fully support the Fryingpan-Arkansas Project.[23]

The year 1959 had a great deal of political significance for Aspinall, for at the start of the Eighty-sixth Congress he became chair of the full House Interior and Insular Affairs Committee. His elevation capped a remarkably fast rise (due to deaths, defeats, and retirements by other members) through the ranks of the committee. Aspinall had gone from being fourteenth (the second to last position) in seniority to first in only ten years. He would continue to serve as chair until his failed bid for re-election in 1972, one of the longest tenures ever for a chairman for the Interior Committee. Aspinall became only the second congressman from Colorado to chair a full House Committee (Ed Taylor had served as head of the Appropriations Committee), and it would be another twenty-eight years after Aspinall left Congress before a member from Colorado would again serve as a committee chair.[24]

The new chairman quickly imposed his own style on the workings of the Interior Committee. His tenure was noted for punctual meetings, tight discipline, and large volumes of legislation. In 1973, political scientist Richard Fenno published a study of congressional committees that contained a lengthy discussion of the House Interior Committee during the

Aspinall years. One of the hallmarks of Aspinall's tenure, according to Fenno, was the chairman's fierce independence not only from the executive branch, but from the Senate as well. The congressman dominated his committee more than most chairs, and the reactions by committee members to his style ranged from "very fair" to "dictatorial."[25]

Aspinall controlled the Interior Committee by acting "as the funnel through which all legislation must pass." The chairman determined if and when the committee would consider a piece of legislation. As one observer noted while Aspinall was still in Congress, "he fixes priorities, fixes subcommittee agendas, and decides when a bill shall move from the hearings phase into the decision phase." The congressman was particularly active in controlling the subcommittees associated with the Interior Committee. Most committee chairs rarely attend subcommittee meetings, but Aspinall almost never missed one and frequently ran them even though he was not the presiding officer. As one representative observed, "You can't get the subcommittee chairmen to do anything, they won't budge without his say-so." The chairman also closely scrutinized the wording of legislation, leading one committee member to despair, "we sit there and nit-pick for hours on something when most of us don't give a God damn about the outcome."[26]

While Aspinall's tight rein on the Interior Committee helped to ensure its legislative productivity, Aspinall himself also benefited from serving as chair during an era when the power of committee chairs was nearly unlimited. Aspinall's power also grew because of the national prominence that environmental issues gained during the 1960s. The election of John Kennedy as president brought an end to the limited federal initiatives that had frustrated Aspinall during the Eisenhower administration and ushered in an eight-year period in which the federal government played an active and expansive role in such issues as reclamation and national parks. These environmental concerns, however, would eventually go too far in the congressman's opinion. By the time Republicans returned to the White House in 1969 the attitudes most Americans had about the environment had radically changed to favor preservation rather than development, and Aspinall was in the twilight of his congressional career.

Aspinall had known John Kennedy since 1949, when their House offices were across the hall from each other, and the two remained in contact after Kennedy was elected to the Senate in 1952. Following Kennedy's election in November 1960, speculation arose that Aspinall might be appointed Secretary of the Interior. (It is unclear if the president-elect and his staff ever seriously considered this idea, or if it was merely an idle rumor.) Eventually, however, Rep. Stewart Udall of Arizona, who had actively campaigned both for Kennedy and for the cabinet post, received the job.[27]

Whatever interest he might have had in the Interior position (and it is not clear that he had any), Aspinall did not let the issue interfere with his fairly cordial working relationship with the new administration. In contrast to the Eisenhower presidency, Aspinall had regular contact with Kennedy officials, such as Secretary Udall, who seemed to share the congressman's enthusiasm for federally funded reclamation projects like the Fryingpan-Arkansas. One issue, however, on which the administration and the chairman did not agree was the proposed Wilderness Bill.[28]

The idea of federal legislation that would permanently protect wild portions of the federal land reserve (wilderness being defined as a place without permanent human presence or sign thereof) had originally developed in the late 1950s but had languished in Congress until President Kennedy endorsed the idea. Rep. Aspinall, perhaps not surprisingly given his pro-development point of view, did not favor the concept, describing wilderness areas as "mausoleum-like museums in which people can go to see resources that cannot be utilized."[29]

In a prescient letter in 1958, Aspinall told a resident of his district that, while he believed in multiple use for public lands, he would base his stance on the Wilderness Bill on his constituents' wishes. "However, I think that the people, especially the users of the public lands in the West, must realize that in the final analysis the political power in the United States is not with us. The people of the United States generally are the landlords of the public lands and if the problem presented by the Wilderness Bill is permitted to bloom into a controversy with the users of the West and the people generally, then the users of the West will be in the minority." Thus Aspinall recommended that western users "try to determine with what kind of bill they can live." "[A] satisfactory compromise . . . is much more to be preferred than to be run over by the steam roller of the majority." Aspinall's suggestion that his constituents might have to subordinate their wishes to those of other Americans is particularly interesting, since he rarely practiced this advice himself. Despite his call for a compromise, when the

President Kennedy signs legislation on May 28, 1963, establishing the Outdoor Recreation Bureau. From left to right are an unidentified man, John Carver, Jerry Verkler, Edward Crafts, Tom Morris, Ralph Rivers, Hubert Humphrey, Aspinall, Henry Jackson, Stewart Udall, Clinton Anderson, John Kyl, John Saylor, Laurence Rockefeller, and Joe Penfold. Almost all of these men played major roles in shaping water and environmental legislation during the 1960s. (Courtesy of the Archives, University of Colorado at Boulder Libraries)

Wilderness Bill finally came before Aspinall's committee in the early 1960s he ignored the public's wishes and fought a stubborn campaign to gut the bill.[30]

Although the Senate quickly passed a pro-wilderness version of the bill in 1961, Aspinall first blocked the House bill and then, in 1962, pushed legislation through his committee that allowed extensive development to continue in proposed wilderness areas. To protect his bill, Aspinall informed the Speaker of the House that he would only permit the bill to go to the floor for a vote if no amendments were allowed. When the Speaker refused, Aspinall adjourned the Interior Committee and went home to Colorado, killing any attempt to pass a wilderness bill for the session.[31]

The chairman's actions did not escape public notice, and he drew severe criticism in the national (and even local) press.[32] When Congress returned for a new session in the spring of 1963, Aspinall appeared willing to broker a deal. He would allow a bill to go to the floor of the House, where it could be amended, if it contained two provisions: an explicit statement that

Congress alone would decide whether a specific area was to be classified as wilderness, and a clause allowing mining exploration in wilderness areas for another twenty years. (Aspinall intended for the latter requirement to protect the extensive mining industry in his district from being locked out of any potential wilderness areas in Colorado.) In addition, Aspinall demanded the establishment of a national commission to review all federal laws applying to public lands and to report on any needed reforms.[33]

President Kennedy accepted the chairman's request for the public land commission as well as the wilderness mining clause, and, as a result, by the fall of 1963 the prospects for an agreement on the Wilderness Bill seemed "extremely bright." One remaining point of contention was the matter of whether the president or Congress would designate the land to be included in the wilderness system. Two days before he was assassinated, Kennedy spoke with Aspinall on the phone and agreed to congressional control of the selection process. In the aftermath of the president's death, Congress finally passed the Wilderness Bill in August 1964.[34]

One unexpected beneficiary of the fight over the Wilderness Bill was the Fryingpan-Arkansas Project. Although the Kennedy administration generally, and Secretary Udall in particular, supported reclamation projects (despite the president's own doubts about rampant dam building), the need to curry favor with Aspinall undoubtedly encouraged White House support for the project. The chairman, who became a fully converted supporter of the Fry-Ark following the 1959 compromise, began actively to smooth the way for congressional passage that same year. Despite his efforts, however, the new Fry-Ark legislation had made no real progress by the time Congress adjourned in 1960—a situation that frustrated Aspinall and which he largely blamed on the supporters of the project for not getting the technical reports finished on time.[35]

In May 1961 the Interior Department formally endorsed the revised plan, and Secretary Udall, reversing his earlier opposition, announced that the project was a "must" for the administration. In light of these favorable comments, Colorado water officials embarked on an all-out push to get the project passed. In January 1962 Aspinall, now convinced that the Western Slope would benefit from the project, publicly announced he would mount a "do or die" effort to pass the Fryingpan-Arkansas Project during the coming year. The bill had cleared Aspinall's committee in 1961 and now needed to be scheduled for a vote by the full House. In his push to get the legislation approved Aspinall rebuffed an attempt by Secretary

Udall to include the Fry-Ark in a larger reclamation bill with a variety of other water projects because the congressman feared that the president would veto the whole package. Aspinall also advised some of his own constituents to hold off on their plans to promote a new Western Slope reclamation project so that their effort would not distract from the focus on the Fry-Ark.[36]

The congressman's hard push for passage encountered a few setbacks. In February President Kennedy sent a message to Congress on the nation's agricultural crop surpluses. The message contained a prediction that less farmland, rather than more, would be needed in the coming decades. Although the president's message did not discuss reclamation projects, Aspinall, clearly overreacting, called Kennedy's remarks "the most damaging blow to the reclamation program in the last decade." The chairman, who now believed his political prestige was linked to the fate of the Fry-Ark bill, saw his worst fears materialize in April when the House Rules Committee voted not to release the bill to the full House. A week later, however, following heavy lobbying by Western congressmen (who saw a defeat for the Fry-Ark as a threat to their own reclamation projects), the Committee reversed itself and sent the bill to the floor of the House of Representatives for debate.[37]

In late May, the Colorado water lobby launched a massive blitz to win House approval of the Fryingpan-Arkansas Project. Felix Sparks, the director of the State Water Board, had been recalled to active military duty, but with the help of Rep. Aspinall Sparks arranged a two-week leave to conduct the campaign. The chairman had earlier told Sparks that he would make sure the bill made it through the Interior Committee and Rules Committee but would not allow it to come to a vote in the full House until the director could promise him that enough votes were lined up to guarantee passage. Aspinall, however, refused to lobby other representatives on behalf of the bill, instead insisting that Sparks do the lobbying himself.[38]

Although Aspinall's hands-off strategy irritated Sparks, the director quickly assembled a lobbying team. The project soon gained bipartisan backing and, apart from Aspinall, the active support of Colorado's congressional delegation. The chairman did, however, agree to write a "personal message" to his House colleagues urging their support for the bill. In the letter Aspinall pointed out that the project had been modified from earlier "failed" versions, "and, in my opinion, is only now ready for autho- rization. For the first time the project provides for development in both eastern and western Colorado and has the unqualified support of the entire State." After two weeks of lobbying, Sparks told Aspinall that he had lined up 300 votes for the project in the House. The chairman agreed to bring the bill up for a vote.[39]

On June 12, 1962, debate began in the House of Representatives. As- pinall gave a lengthy floor speech in support of the Fryingpan-Arkansas Project. He said that this project was important because "the most valuable resource that this Nation has outside of its people . . . is water without which this Nation can be expected to decline and waste away." The chair- man acknowledged that this was a complicated project, but he replied, "[t]oday we have run out of simple projects; however, we have not met the need for continued development."[40]

Aspinall then set out to rebut specifically the various arguments made against the Fry-Ark. He argued that the project could not be economically built as smaller components and claimed that this was a "rescue project" designed to stabilize the availability of water in the Arkansas Valley, since local water sources were quickly being over-tapped. The Fry-Ark would not contribute to crop surpluses since it would not bring new land into production but instead would provide additional water for existing land. Aspinall also tried to distinguish the "new and improved" Fryingpan- Arkansas Project from past failures by noting the unified state support for this plan. "The point I am making is that the Fryingpan-Arkansas Project we have before us today is physically different, economically and finan- cially improved and enjoys much greater support than the Fryingpan- Arkansas Project previously considered." Given Aspinall's own limited comments about the Fry-Ark during previous congressional debates, the "greater support" he was referring to also included his own.[41]

Aspinall's firm control of the bill on the House floor could be seen in the fact that of the five amendments offered by project opponents, the only two that the House accepted were ones the chairman publicly supported. Finally, on June 13, the House voted on the bill. When John Saylor, a harsh critic of the Fryingpan-Arkansas Project, tried to force a roll call vote in order to create a record of which House members had supported the bill, only twenty-eight other representatives backed his motion. Instead the bill was passed on a voice vote, which was the norm for any bill with an expensive price tag. The Senate passed the bill on August 7, and the president signed it a week later, shortly before travelling to Pueblo to attended groundbreaking ceremonies.[42]

After almost ten years of debate Congress had finally passed a Fryingpan-Arkansas bill, a version Rep. Aspinall could both accept and endorse. The long struggle over the bill revealed, in part, the chairman's determination to defend what he believed were the interests of his district and to make sure that his district received some sort of compensation in exchange for its water. While Aspinall spoke publicly in favor of national and state reclamation programs, he was not willing to support projects he perceived would be at the expense of the Western Slope's water interests. However, the struggle also showed that Aspinall recognized that there were valid reclamation claims beyond the needs of his district (and that he would ultimately need the support of other western politicians in order to pass his own projects); for if the congressman had been motivated solely by a desire to protect his district, he never would have accepted the compromise.

The final passage of the bill in the House was also a reflection on the growing influence Aspinall had with his fellow representatives on reclamation issues: the Fryingpan-Arkansas Project did not pass until Aspinall said it was ready to pass. The chairman was now in a position to exert significant influence on the terms for reclamation legislation, to set the agenda for House hearings on water projects, and to guarantee that the water interests in his district would not be plundered by other regions. Aspinall's influence and power would be on display again when the chairman became involved in the effort to pass another major reclamation bill: the Colorado River Basin Project of 1968.

5

The High-Water Mark

There is a river, whose streams shall make glad the city.
—Psalms 46:4

THE YEAR 1963 BROUGHT a watershed event for western reclamation. In June the U.S. Supreme Court issued its long-awaited decision in the case of *Arizona v. California,* which dealt with the apportionment of water between the two states in the lower basin of the Colorado River. The case aimed to resolve this dispute once and for all, but the Court's decision complicated matters as much as it clarified them. As a result Rep. Aspinall would spend the next five years trying to secure passage of legislation that would help resolve the problems that arose from the Court's decision. His effort on this front would resemble two of his earlier major reclamation efforts, because this new legislation, like the Colorado River Storage Project before it, would again contain massive regional projects. The chairman would also support some parts of the legislation and oppose other parts, just as he had with the Fryingpan-Arkansas Project. In the end the legislation would be passed, but only when Aspinall found the terms acceptable.

The conflict between Arizona and California over Colorado River water originated in disputes that, by the time the Supreme Court issued its ruling in 1963, had spanned more than a half century. The two states had argued about the river before the Court in the past, and at one point had very nearly fought a border war over the matter. Arizona was the only river basin state that refused to sign the Colorado River Compact in 1922. Arguing that the agreement was too favorable to California, Arizona held out for twenty-two years before finally signing in 1944. California, in the meantime, obtained congressional approval of the Boulder Canyon Project Act (Hoover Dam) in 1928, which unilaterally declared that California would receive 4.4 million acre-feet (maf) of Colorado River water each year, Arizona would receive 2.8 maf, and Nevada .3 maf. When Arizona finally signed the compact in 1944, the Secretary of the Interior also signed an agreement pledging to build a project that would allow Arizona to use its share of the water. However, attempts by the state's congressional delegation during the late 1940s to obtain approval for a Central Arizona Project (CAP) were unsuccessful. California, in particular, raised serious objections to the plan, which potentially would curb its use of the river's water.[1]

Arizona's members of Congress tried again in the early 1950s to pass a Central Arizona Project bill. Their leader in this effort was Sen. Carl Hayden, who had first been elected to Congress in 1912 when Arizona became a state, and who had served in the Senate since 1927. Given Hayden's seniority, the Senate easily approved a CAP bill in both 1950 and 1951. Both times, however, the bill died in the House of Representatives. The 1951 defeat of the CAP bill was a particularly serious setback for Arizona. Not only did the House Interior Committee, at the behest of Democratic Rep. Clair Engle of California, vote down the CAP bill, but it also approved a resolution, introduced by Republican Rep. John Saylor of Pennsylvania, to bar further congressional consideration of any Colorado River reclamation program for Arizona until the lower basin states of California, Nevada, and Arizona had reached a formal agreement among themselves on the distribution of their share of the Colorado River's water. (Arizona had never officially accepted the terms of the Boulder Canyon Project Act.) Rep. Aspinall, who feared that the ban might delay upper basin projects as well, attempted to pass a motion simply delaying further hearings, but he was unsuccessful.[2]

Rather than negotiate an agreement with California, Arizona filed suit in 1952 before the Supreme Court over the water matter. The case would drag on for twelve years (the longest in the Court's history), involve 50 lawyers, 340 witnesses, 4,000 exhibits, result in 25,000 pages of testimony, cost $5 million, and offer perhaps the clearest example of how seriously states viewed water issues in the West. When the Court agreed to hear the case it appointed a Special Master to evaluate the evidence and make a recommendation. The recommendation was submitted in 1961 and the Court then reviewed the matter for two years before issuing its initial opinion on June 3, 1963, and a final decree in March 1964.[3]

Both the press and Arizona officials hailed the Court's 5–3 decision as a victory for the state. It upheld Arizona's claim to 2.8 maf of Colorado River water per year, a claim which California had argued Arizona had forfeited when it initially refused to ratify the Colorado River Compact and later challenged the constitutionality of the Boulder Canyon Project Act. The Court also ruled that when there were surpluses or shortages of water in the Colorado River it would be up to the Secretary of the Interior to apportion the amounts not only among the different states, but also among users within the states. Since California had routinely been using all the surplus water in the river, this ruling represented a serious threat to that state, and it would become a point of contention during the subsequent congressional debate over plans to develop new reclamation projects on the Colorado.[4]

Even before the Court's verdict, Aspinall began investigating possible reclamation scenarios for both the lower and upper basins of the Colorado River. In a November 27, 1962, letter to Secretary of the Interior Stewart Udall, Aspinall inquired how the Department planned to respond when the Supreme Court finally issued a ruling. The chairman placed particular emphasis on the question of whether or not there was an adequate amount of water in the Colorado River to sustain any further reclamation projects, such as the Central Arizona Project. "[I]t is becoming increasingly apparent that the available water supply in the southwest . . . is inadequate to sustain the area's economy on a long-term basis," Aspinall said. "[F]urther lower Colorado River water resource development must be related to an effective, comprehensive and coordinated plan."[5]

In August 1963, Stewart Udall formally responded to Aspinall's query with the Pacific Southwest Water Plan (PSWP), an ambitious, multistate reclamation project. The Plan called for the construction of seventeen different water projects—among them the Central Arizona Project, an expanded California State aqueduct, and two major dams, one located upstream and one downstream from the Grand Canyon. The strategy behind Udall's plan was to secure approval of the CAP by offering potential opponents their own projects as well. Southern California, which stood to lose Colorado River water if the CAP was constructed, would benefit under the Plan by receiving an increased amount of water from northern California. The two Grand Canyon dams would serve as "cash registers" through the sale of hydroelectricity, which would help pay for the costs of these various projects. Like most plans designed to please everyone, the PSWP ended up pleasing no one and never received serious consideration by Congress.[6]

A month after the secretary unveiled the Pacific Southwest Water Plan, Chairman Aspinall publicly outlined his views of what needed to be done to pass a reclamation project for Arizona and the lower basin in general. The occasion was a speech he gave before the Arizona State Reclamation Association. In his talk Aspinall endorsed the PSWP but warned that Arizona and California must first resolve their disputes over the Colorado River before the Plan could receive congressional approval. "My committee and the Congress have been following a policy of not deciding differences within a state and hesitate to consider a basin water development program where there is a serious controversy between or among the states involved." Aspinall also counseled patience, noting that "Arizona should not expect the Congress to lay aside all the other projects and water policy matters it has been working on and studying over the last several years in order to give immediate attention to Arizona's desires." Aspinall also stated the two key elements that any Southwest water plan would have to contain in order to be successful: (1) "an area-wide approach," which does not "benefit one area to the detriment of another," and (2) "better water management and . . . new water supplies." These last two elements explain why Aspinall was willing to even consider a project for Arizona, because Colorado potentially could benefit as well.[7]

Supporters of the Central Arizona Project recognized that Aspinall's support would be crucial if the Project was to receive congressional approval. As an *Arizona Republic* reporter bluntly put it, "The lives and fortunes of generations of Arizonans yet unborn may hinge on the judgments of Wayne N. Aspinall of Colorado." Most Arizonans believed that, given Aspinall's general support for reclamation, he would support their project as well. The basis of this optimism was the belief that because Arizona had supported the passage of Aspinall's Colorado River Storage Project in 1956, he now would return the favor by backing the CAP. At the time Congress passed the CRSP, Stewart Udall even remarked that "fair play" would demand that an Arizona Project be approved. Sen. Hayden also recognized the control Aspinall would have over the CAP bill and quickly tried to reach an agreement with the chairman over the Project's fate.[8]

While both Udall and Hayden knew there would be opposition to the CAP, neither seemed to have foreseen serious difficulties with Aspinall (and he did not initially indicate that there would be). Thus when the congressman later began to actively hinder passage of the project, Arizonans viewed his actions as a bitter betrayal. Arizona Rep. John Rhodes later complained that he and Udall had supported the CRSP in expectation that Aspinall and other upper basin politicians would then support the CAP. "We should have had it in writing because not only did they not reciprocate, they fought us every inch of the way." For his part, Aspinall dismissed the notion that there was any CRSP debt to be paid back. In a letter to a friend in Colorado Aspinall remarked that Arizona's "representatives in Congress have supported the Upper Colorado Basin in their ambitions," but "[Arizona] has never been too cooperative as far as the overall problem of division of waters of the Colorado River."[9]

In 1964, however, the open rift between proponents of the Central Arizona Project and Chairman Aspinall had not yet developed, and various officials in the Interior Department continued to count the congressman as one of the Project's key supporters, even though he had only endorsed the PSWP in general and not the specific CAP plans. The Secretary of the Interior instead spent the year trying to appease the CAP's California critics. One of the major demands state officials made was that any project had to include a plan to somehow increase the amount of water in the Colorado River, a demand that would raise new problems and create new opponents for the Central Arizona Project. The idea of augmenting the flow of the Colorado River grew out of the emerging realization among water officials in both the upper and lower basins that the river was at risk of being over-allocated. Although the question of how much water flows through the Colorado River system would seem to be fairly straightforward, the answer can be quite complicated and has frequently depended on whether or not the person asking supports or opposes a particular reclamation project.[10]

The river was at risk of being over-allocated because of a flaw in the Colorado River Compact of 1922, which assigned specific allotments to the upper and lower basin based on the scientific estimate that the Colorado River had an annual flow of 16 maf or more each year. In later years scientists decreased their estimates to 13 maf, but the basin states continued to use the original erroneous figure as the basis for requesting new reclamation projects. By the 1960s, as the various basin states promoted an increasing number of reclamation projects, the realization dawned that there might not be enough water to allow all these projects to be built. Rather than acknowledging that the Colorado River had a finite capacity that had already been developed to the fullest extent possible, reclamation promoters concluded that the solution to this problem would be simply to import more water into the river basin. This new water would flow to the rescue, allowing reclamation development to continue.[11]

The size, scope, and diversity of the proposed importation schemes varied from conventional to epic. Secretary Udall's PSWP called for indirectly addressing the problem by diverting water from the Trinity and other rivers in northern California for use in Southern California. This diversion would help the water situation in the Colorado River by decreasing California's dependence on the river. Another plan, which would actually increase the water in the Colorado River, called for diverting 2.4 maf a year from the Snake River in Idaho by building an aqueduct across Nevada and dumping the water into Lake Mead. This plan paled, however, when compared to scenarios for importing water from the Columbia River, which could augment the Colorado River by up to 15 maf of water each year.[12]

Colorado River reclamation proponents viewed the Columbia as the solution to all their problems. The Columbia River had a water volume ten times greater than the total annual flow of the Colorado. Given the Pacific Northwest's natural abundance of moisture, state reclamation officials in the arid Southwest believed they had strong justification for seeking to divert the Columbia's water. They decried the "waste" of allowing millions of acre-feet of water to flow into the sea unused. Not surprisingly, the residents of the Pacific Northwest reacted with alarm to this threat to their water. Despite promises by the Bureau of Reclamation that water diversion canals would only be built at the mouth of the Columbia River, where there could be "no conceivable future use" for it, active local opposition to the plan quickly developed. The leader of this opposition was Sen. Henry Jackson of Washington, who, in his capacity as chair of the Senate Interior Committee, had veto power over any reclamation legislation. While Jackson initially supported the Central Arizona Project, he quickly indicated his dissatisfaction with the proposed Columbia River diversion plan.[13]

If these massive schemes to augment the water in the Colorado River were not controversial enough in and of themselves, one of the proposed ways to pay for them triggered a major public backlash. The Pacific Southwest Water Plan called for the construction of two hydroelectric dams bracketing the Grand Canyon. The proposed Marble Canyon Dam would be located just upstream from the national park, while the proposed

Bridge Canyon Dam was to be built nearly one hundred miles downstream, but would back water up through the full forty-mile length of Grand Canyon National Monument, and thirteen miles into Grand Canyon National Park.[14]

These two dams would provide no irrigation reclamation benefit; the cost of pumping water directly out of the canyon precluded that. Their sole purpose would be to produce electricity and serve as "cash registers." Part of the hydroelectricity would be used to power the pumps farther down river that would divert water from the Colorado into the Central Arizona Project. The surplus electricity would be sold to southern California and the revenues from these sales would initially be used to pay for the CAP. Once the CAP was paid for, the "surplus" revenue would go into a Colorado River Basin Fund, which would help pay for other reclamation projects, including the massive water diversion from the Pacific Northwest. Instead of generating electricity, however, the proposed dams ended up generating the largest environmental protest since the Echo Park Dam dispute.[15]

In early 1965, however, these storms of protest over the different aspects of the Central Arizona Project and related reclamation plans had yet to appear. In January, several members of Congress introduced legislation to authorize a scaled-back version of the Pacific Southwest Water Plan, called the Lower Colorado River Basin Project (LCRBP). Unlike the PSWP, the LCRBP omitted any internal California water diversion plans, since officials in that state had objected to the idea. The LCRBP did contain two new provisions: one guaranteed that the CAP would have to bear the burden of any water shortages in the Colorado River during times of drought, and another committed the Secretary of the Interior to investigate augmenting the natural flow of the Colorado River from other sources, such as the Columbia.[16]

Central Arizona Project supporters made these changes to the original Pacific Southwest Water Plan in order to address California's concerns. However, CAP proponents also realized that they needed to retain the support of Rep. Aspinall as well. In February, one of Stewart Udall's assistants suggested that the secretary arrange to have Floyd Dominy, the Commissioner of Reclamation and a friend of Aspinall, brief the chairman on the latest plan, and see what Aspinall's reaction was to the revisions. Udall, who viewed Aspinall as a master tactician, pointed to the congressman's handling of the passage of the Colorado River Storage

Aspinall and Floyd Dominy, the commissioner of the Bureau of Reclamation, stand atop Glen Canyon Dam on November 8, 1964, during a tour of Lake Powell sponsored by the Bureau of Reclamation. (Courtesy of the U.S. Department of the Interior, Bureau of Reclamation)

Project in 1956 as a model that Arizona's lobby should follow. During the first few months of 1965 CAP lobbyists continued to express optimism that, based on his past statements, Aspinall would support their project.[17]

In reality, however, Aspinall was beginning to have serious doubts about the advisability of Congress approving the Lower Colorado River Basin Project legislation. The chief source of his concern was the question of how much unused water remained in the Colorado River. Aspinall worried that if the total amount of water in the river was less than the Interior Department figures in the PSWP had suggested, and the Central Arizona Project was built, then Colorado might never have the chance to develop the majority of its own share of the river's water since the river would be over-allocated. In May Aspinall wrote the president of a water conservancy district in southwestern Colorado that "[b]oth the Upper and Lower Basins are in trouble as far as the availability of water is concerned."[18]

The chairman had indirectly expressed his concerns in a March 2 letter to the Secretary of the Interior, in which he had asked Udall to provide projections on how much revenue the Colorado River Storage Project would earn from future hydroelectric sales, based on different water levels in the river. The secretary replied with a lengthy letter that focused on the question of what historical baseline to use for predicting water levels in the river. Aspinall had suggested using the period from 1930 to 1964, which had been fairly dry, as the baseline. Udall replied that the Interior Department preferred using the period from 1914 to 1945 instead, which had experienced much higher levels of precipitation. It was not surprising that the two men would disagree on which set of numbers to use, since each was choosing the data that favored his position.[19]

Aspinall raised the issue of water scarcity more explicitly on May 21. He sent a letter to each of the seven state governors in the Colorado River Basin, asking them to supply his committee with their best estimates of the water in the Colorado River. The chairman also stated that he would not schedule congressional hearings on the Lower Colorado River Basin Project until he received a response from each of them. The members of Arizona's congressional delegation viewed Aspinall's action as an attempt to stall the LCRBP bill rather than to kill it outright, but they were concerned that Aspinall might restrict the focus of any congressional hearings on the LCRBP to the question of the Colorado River's water supply.[20]

On June 9, Morris Udall and John Rhodes, the two Interior Committee members from Arizona, wrote a letter to Aspinall responding to the chairman's questions about water levels in the Colorado River. The two wrote, "It is our hope that neither the Interior Committee nor the Congress, nor the 7 Basin states, will be caught up in a numbers game involving the waters of the Colorado. Certainly no living man can predict with *complete accuracy* the flow of the Colorado for the next 10, 25, or 50 years. Different results can be, and have been, attained by hydrologists and engineers depending on the assumptions which are made and the years which are selected for river history." Udall and Rhodes's comment on how unreliable numbers are suggests that the Arizona delegation was afraid that they would not win a "numbers game."[21]

To demonstrate how different time periods produced different results, the two congressmen included a table showing that between 1906 and 1959 the average amount of water in the river was 15.3 maf, while between 1930 and 1962 the average was only 13 maf. Udall and Rhodes then noted that the higher 1906–1959 figure had been used to justify upper basin projects, which "would be marginal or unfeasible if 1930–1963 hydrology were used." Ultimately, the two congressmen maintained that it was pointless to argue over how much water was in the Colorado River since everyone agreed that "[i]mportation of water will inevitably come" and that the LCRBP was the first step in that process. In a response two days later, Aspinall agreed that a "numbers game" would not be productive, but he again stressed the importance of a water importation scheme, noting that "there are certain problems pertaining to the development of the remaining water resources that require solution now, while there is incentive and opportunity." What these "certain problems" were became more apparent when a group of California and Arizona congressmen met with the chairman in mid-June and he again refused to schedule hearings on the LCRBP. Instead Aspinall insisted that the Colorado River Basin states first had to reach an agreement to protect the interests of the upper basin states, although he did not specify what assurances he believed were needed.[22]

While Arizona's congressmen were trying to talk Aspinall into dropping his emerging public opposition to the Lower Colorado River Basin Project, their colleague in the Senate, Carl Hayden, opted for a more confrontational approach. The eighty-eight-year-old senator had been trying for twenty years to obtain congressional approval of a Central Arizona Project, and he saw any attempt to interfere with his intended political legacy as a personal affront. In a June 10 letter to Floyd Dominy, Hayden noted that Aspinall had questioned whether there was sufficient water in the Colorado River to support new reclamation projects. If Aspinall's fears were accurate, Hayden continued, then this suggested that "the financial feasibility of the Colorado River Storage Project and its participating projects will be adversely affected [by the lack of sufficient water]. The sáme will be true of the Frying Pan–Arkansas Project." Hayden then asked Dominy to submit a list of suggestions on how federal spending for these projects could be curtailed. Dominy managed to prevent a clash between the senator and the congressman by claiming that there was enough water for new projects, such as the Central Arizona Project, but that it would be necessary to augment the Colorado River to allow for anticipated future regional growth. Hayden clearly intended to send a warning to Aspinall that if the congressman tried to claim that there was not enough water in the Colorado for the CAP, then Hayden would retaliate by claiming there was not enough water to allow the CRSP and the Fry-Ark to be built and would cut off funding to both projects.[23]

Water importation schemes for the Colorado River suffered a sharp setback when Sen. Jackson amended the National Water Resources Planning Act of 1965 to prevent the government from doing research into the topic without first obtaining congressional permission. When Rep. John Rhodes pressed Aspinall about why he had accepted the anti-importation amendment during the House-Senate conference negotiations over the final bill, the chairman replied that in conference, "[t]here is always some give and take. *I didn't want to do it* [his emphasis]. However, it was insisted upon by Senators Anderson, Jackson, Allott, and some others."[24]

By late July the members of the Arizona congressional delegation had become concerned over the lack of action on the Lower Colorado River Basin Project bill in the Interior Committee. In a memo to other CAP supporters, Rep. John Rhodes analyzed the situation, noting that Aspinall had "showed very little desire to move on the . . . bill." Rhodes suggested that the chairman had probably sought out the opinions of the seven Colorado Basin governors for three reasons: (1) "to determine the attitude of the various states as to the availability of water," (2) "to reassert the concept of the [Colorado River] Compact concerning the supremacy of the states [over the river rather than federal control]," and (3) "to pursue some kind of action other than holding hearings on a bill." Rhodes believed that Aspinall was trying to gather evidence before holding hearings in order to demonstrate that the CAP would violate the Colorado River Compact by over-tapping the river.[25]

At the end of July, Aspinall wrote his own assessment of the situation in a personal letter to former Colorado Governor Ed Johnson. The chairman stated that, although he had not publicly said so, he planned to hold congressional hearings on the Lower Colorado River Basin Project at the end of August. Aspinall predicted that, given Arizona's eagerness to have the CAP approved, the state's delegation would "be in a more favorable frame of mind to confer and possibly agree with us" than they had been in the past or might be in the future. In assessing his own role in the legislation Aspinall wrote, "I think I can say in all modesty that the Central Arizona Project legislation cannot pass the House without my support." The congressman promised, however, not to be simply an obstructionist. "To resist for a purpose is one thing, but to resist for the sake of resistance itself is something else. This does not mean that I am about to give away any of Colorado's rights but it does mean that I am hoping for and expecting some affirmative action [to benefit the Upper Basin]." Aspinall closed by noting that "I think that perhaps the most dangerous problem we have before us is the matter of making it absolutely clear that the Upper Basin is to distribute its own water and to have control of the releases of the water [to the Lower Basin]."[26]

Although Aspinall had decided to hold hearings at the end of August, he continued to withhold this information from the Arizona delegation in an apparent attempt to get them to compromise—a strategy that only further irritated them. Aspinall meanwhile expressed displeasure over the slow response rate from the Colorado River Basin governors. When Aspinall ran into Arizona Rep. Morris Udall in early August, "he shook his finger in Udall's face and said, 'You've let me down. I don't have your Governor's statement on water supply.'"[27]

When the House Subcommittee on Irrigation and Reclamation finally convened hearings on August 23 for the Lower Colorado River Basin Project, Aspinall's tone was still contentious. Rep. Walter Rogers of Texas normally chaired the subcommittee, but Aspinall opted to run several of the sessions himself. The chairman tried to focus as much of the testimony as possible on the question of how much water was available in the Colorado River. He frequently interrupted witnesses to interject this question, even grilling friendly witnesses for their insight on the matter. At one point, Aspinall badgered Commissioner Dominy, forcing him to admit that any new lower basin projects would have to rely on upper basin water unless water was imported into the Colorado River.

> MR. ASPINALL: [The LCRBP] depends upon . . . water that cannot be used in the upper basin in order to assure the feasibility of this project.
>
> MR. DOMINY: That is very correct. But . . . that has been taken into account in the justification of the project. . . . But at no time have we figured we would be using water that is entitled to be used in the upper basin after the time the upper basin is capable of using it.
> [Omission]
>
> MR. ASPINALL: But the fact is without that water which the upper basin is not using this project could not be here before the Congress.
>
> MR. DOMINY: I agree.[28]

What Aspinall hoped to establish was a clear record in the witnesses' testimony that, based on the existing amount of water in the Colorado River, any new water projects in the lower basin would be reliant upon the upper basin's allocation. This in turn would strengthen the case for importing water into the river.

The exchange between the chairman and the commissioner was friendly compared with the later exchange that took place between Aspinall and Sam Goddard, the governor of Arizona. Goddard got off to a bad start when he repeatedly tried to dodge a question Aspinall asked him about what benefits the lower basin states receive from the Colorado River Compact. When the governor failed to answer the question, Aspinall took the opportunity to talk about the benefits to the upper basin, stressing that the chief benefit "was the stoppage of the operation of the laws of prior appropriation with respect to the waters of the Colorado River." Aspinall's reason for discussing the Compact and the doctrine of prior appropriation was his belief that if the lower basin states were allowed to use upper basin water, this might undermine the Compact's intent and enable the lower basin to establish a permanent legal claim to the water.[29]

The chairman then asked Goddard several more questions about lower basin water development, which the governor continued to avoid answering. Goddard instead said that the witness representing California could provide the congressman with the information he had requested. In response, Aspinall snapped, "you cannot answer my question by stating that [the California witness] is going to testify [on your behalf]." Later in the hearing the chairman asked the governor point blank whether or not the LCRBP would be dependent upon upper basin water, but before Goddard had a chance to respond, Aspinall attempted to cut him off. As if Goddard's testimony had not been enough of a disaster, he also referred to Aspinall as "Aspinwall," a mistake the congressman quickly corrected.[30]

The chairman was equally intolerant of the testimony from Upper Basin state representatives. When Steve Reynolds, the state engineer for New Mexico, appeared before the Committee and suggested a more moderate position than Aspinall's on water usage in the Colorado River, the chairman quickly attacked his statement:

MR. ASPINALL: [W]here is there anything in your statement, where is there anything in what you have said . . . that would lead me to believe that you are still interested in the welfare of the upper basin in connection with this unused water?

MR. REYNOLDS: Well, we are, of course, very much interested in our upper basin problems. We have upper basin interests.

MR. ASPINALL: But, Mr. Reynolds, you already have authorization for the projects which will use all of the water to which you are entitled under the Colorado River compact, as far as the upper basin is concerned, and under the upper Colorado River compact.

MR. REYNOLDS: Well, Mr. Chairman, if I may, I think that what you have just said is substantially correct. Perhaps I should add just a bit of detail to make this clear.

MR. ASPINALL: I want you to align yourselves with your sister States in the upper basin States or completely divorce yourselves. That is what I am trying to get you to do.[31]

Aspinall's badgering of Reynolds was due to the chairman's fear that, because New Mexico had already developed most of its river allocation, the state might be tempted to break ranks with the rest of the upper basin states and support the Central Arizona Project without any guarantees for the water rights of those states.

Although Rep. Aspinall's chief concern was the amount of water available in the Colorado River, and many of the hearings focused on that question, another issue soon emerged that threatened to undermine the chairman's goal: the proposed Grand Canyon dams. The public outcry by conservationists opposed to the dams in Bridge Canyon and Marble Canyon raised many of the same issues that had been debated during the controversy over the Echo Park Dam a decade earlier. While conservation leaders had expressed opposition to the Grand Canyon dams almost as soon as the federal government proposed them, Central Arizona Project supporters remained optimistic that both dams, or at least one, would be approved.

Even Aspinall, who had reservations about parts of the LCRBP, strongly supported the two dams because of the revenue they would generate for the Colorado River Basin states. In a February 1964 letter, he speculated that the Marble Canyon Dam, which was upstream from the Grand Canyon, would "be the one that can go through the earliest, provided the people of Arizona will go for such a program." A few months later, after inspecting the two dam sites by air, Aspinall wrote that although a "high" (or tall) Bridge Canyon Dam "would cause only a minimum amount of harm to the Grand Canyon, I am not convinced that we need that particular dam." The chairman instead endorsed a "low" Bridge Canyon Dam which "would not inundate any part of the National Park." In subsequent months Aspinall shifted his stance slightly on the high Bridge Canyon Dam and began arguing that because the resulting flooding "will be only a few feet deep in the bottom of a very deep canyon, and because there will be little fluctuation in the water surface, I doubt whether there will be any appreciable damage to the park." The chairman did, however, promise that his committee would thoroughly investigate the matter and would not approve any project that would cause damage, although it would be up to the committee to define what damage meant.[32]

By the summer of 1965 the Interior Department had announced plans to delay any Bridge Canyon Dam (but not the Marble Canyon Dam) "pending further study," in an apparent attempt to avoid having a conservation controversy sidetrack the rest of the LCRBP bill. This strategic withdrawal did little to mitigate criticism of the two dams during the August hearings. Government witnesses and committee members largely ignored the dams during the hearings, but it was the chief topic discussed by the public witnesses. More than twenty-five different individuals spoke in opposition to the dams. Most of them acknowledged the need for water development in the Southwest but argued that including the dams in the plan was a mistake.[33]

David Brower, the executive director of the Sierra Club, suggested in his testimony that the dams were not necessary for the financial viability of the plan. Brower instead argued that the energy and revenue demands of the project could be met just as effectively with a coal or nuclear power plant. (Aspinall was dismissive of this nontechnical testimony, noting that "this matter has to be left to the engineers.") Other conservation representatives echoed this position as well, some of them with a great deal of passion. Anthony Wayne Smith, president of the National Parks Association, fired questions back at the Committee members until Aspinall ordered him to stop, noting, "[W]e have got to have a little dignity to the procedure of the committee." The chairman indicated his irritation by further commenting that "maybe sometime we will sit before Mr. Smith's body and he will ask us questions."[34]

Although he was exasperated by the conservation witnesses, Aspinall's chief concern centered on preserving Colorado's allotment of upper basin water. As a result, the chairman faced a quandary in the fall of 1965. Congressional hearings had done nothing to ease his concern that the Central Arizona Project could only function by using part of the upper basin's water, a condition that was unacceptable to Aspinall. The chairman did support the importation of water into the Colorado as a way to solve this problem, but any effort to import water would face stiff opposition from the Pacific Northwest. Yet if Aspinall scuttled the Lower Colorado River Basin Project, he would likely never be able to secure enough votes to win approval for future reclamation projects in his own state. Aspinall decided the solution to this dilemma was simply to combine the two objectives. The chairman would demand the inclusion of upper basin reclamation projects in the Lower Colorado River Basin Project bill.[35]

Aspinall unilaterally added five projects to the legislation, which now dropped the term "Lower" and became the Colorado River Basin Project (CRBP). Despite his professed belief in upper basin solidarity, all five projects were located in the congressman's district. The projects included the Animas–La Plata, near Durango; the Dolores Project, northwest of Durango; the San Miguel Project, farther to the north; the Dallas Creek Project, near Montrose; and the West Divide Project, near Glenwood Springs. None of these projects were new when Aspinall added them to the CRBP bill, and in fact he had been promoting them, individually and collectively, for several years without success. The chief reason for the delay in formal approval of these projects was that the administrative agencies with oversight on reclamation projects, such as the Interior Department and Budget Bureau, had not yet completed their final reports. Despite the lack of progress, the congressman remained both publicly and privately committed to supporting the projects. As the chairman remarked to a reporter, "I am not about to give away any of the water to which the Upper Colorado River Basin is entitled." To Aspinall's way of thinking, the best interests of the upper basin and the Western Slope were interchangeable.[36]

While Aspinall justified his decision to add the five projects to the Colorado River Basin Project bill as an attempt to protect Colorado's upper basin water rights, the contemporary perception of his action by the media and reclamation advocates was that Aspinall had committed a blatant act of extortion, demanding "his pound of flesh" in return for not killing the Central Arizona Project in his committee. A June 17, 1966, article published in *Science* magazine espoused this interpretation when it stated that "[t]he five Upper Basin reclamation projects . . . have been included in [the CRBP bill] as part of the price Representative [Morris] Udall [of Arizona] has had to pay for the state of Colorado's support for

CAP. Colorado can speak softly on such matters and still be heard. One of her citizens, Representative Wayne N. Aspinall, is chairman of the House Interior Committee." This "extortion" theory has continued to gain support in the years since the passage of the Colorado River Basin Project. In a recent interview former Secretary of the Interior Stewart Udall maintained that the five projects were, indeed, a type of "blackmail."[37]

Blackmail may well have been the only way that Aspinall could ever have gotten the five projects approved by Congress, since all of them have questionable financial profiles. Normally, for the Bureau of Reclamation to recommend a project, the cost-benefit analysis has to show that the project will generate more revenue than the government will have to invest. While critics often claim that the Bureau's economic analyses of projects tend to be too optimistic, even Reclamation officials could not finesse the numbers on the five projects Aspinall wanted. Bureau officials projected that four out of the five projects (Animas–La Plata, Dallas Creek, Dolores, and West Divide) would barely break even, while the fifth (San Miguel) would actually lose money. Reclamation supporters, even in Colorado, expressed reservations about the financial feasibility of the five projects and worried that a public backlash against these projects might erode support for reclamation in general.[38]

Even Floyd Dominy, the commissioner of Reclamation, tried to talk Aspinall out of the projects, or at least the irrigation portions of them. Since Dominy knew that the real reason Aspinall was pursuing these projects was to preserve Colorado's allotment of river water, he suggested simply building big storage reservoirs to hold the water and dropping the irrigation aspects of the projects, which were the reason the projects could not pass financial muster. From the narrow point of view of physically protecting the Western Slope's water rights, Dominy's idea made sense. Aspinall, however, quickly rejected the suggestion. "The Reclamation program knows no such thing as a project without beneficiaries. The answer is no."[39]

If the financial numbers did not add up on the five projects, the way Aspinall selected the projects for inclusion in the Colorado River Basin Project inspired even less confidence. Bill Cleary, the congressman's chief administrative assistant, later recalled that Aspinall told Bureau of Reclamation engineers to "get me some projects that will put Colorado's entitlements to use, and I don't care how far along they are [in the review process], but get me those that look the best." Cleary stated that Aspinall believed this was the last chance to secure a massive expansion in the federal reclamation program for Colorado. He also said that the congressman did not care if the numbers for the individual projects were "iffy" as long as collectively they were okay. Aspinall all but admitted this in a 1980 letter to then U.S. Senator Gary Hart.

> I am not so much interested in the so-called benefit-cost ratio of single projects in Western Colorado. In the Colorado River Basin Project we considered all five of the projects as a single project unit, and that is the way that we took care of the economic benefit feasibility test. Personally, I think that such an approach is logical.
>
> My ambition has been to secure all of the reservoir capacity in Western Colorado to take care of the share of the Colorado River Waters to which Colorado is entitled. To me this is a single undertaking, as far as our welfare is concerned. . . . As long as we are tied to the construction of the single project philosophy we run the greater risk of losing our share of the water to users in the Lower Basin.[40]

This philosophy guided Aspinall throughout his congressional career. To the chairman the only way to protect Colorado's water interests was physically to impound the water, and the real value of the various projects he sponsored was not their individual, and often questionable, reclamation purpose but how they contributed to this longstanding goal.

One apparently hidden selection criterion Aspinall used was to avoid choosing projects that might lend themselves to transmontane water diversions to the Front Range. Felix Sparks, the director of the Colorado Water Conservation Board and a former resident of the Western Slope, helped Aspinall select the five projects. Sparks later said that he and Aspinall "didn't want to let the cities and industry have the water. We picked those projects on the basis that it would be impossible, physically impossible, for Denver to get its hands on that water."[41]

By the end of 1965 one CAP supporter noted that, with the addition of the five Colorado projects, Aspinall had now dropped his opposition to passage of the Central Arizona Project. If the congressman believed that the addition of the five projects for western Colorado would alleviate his concerns about lower basin reclamation projects, he had apparently not anticipated the difficulties he would encounter getting the Interior Department and the Budget Bureau to endorse these projects. Over the next several months Aspinall and other upper basin water officials worked to coerce various federal agencies into approving the five projects, and the chairman eventually ended up holding the prospect of further congressional hearings hostage until these agencies accepted the projects.[42]

The first sign of difficulty came on February 11, 1966, when the Budget Bureau (the predecessor of today's Office of Management and Budget) issued a report criticizing the proposed Animas–La Plata Project as financially unacceptable. In particular, the Bureau pointed to three factors as the basis for its rejection. First, the bulk of the cost of the Project would be paid for out of the Upper Colorado River Basin Fund, and only a small percentage would be paid for by the actual users. Second, the per-acre cost to bring new farmland into production as part of the Project was extremely high. Third, only a small percentage of the Project's water would go toward municipal or industrial use, which would offer a better financial return for the project.[43]

The Budget Bureau's rejection of the Animas–La Plata presented a serious problem for supporters of the Central Arizona Project. Chairman Aspinall had previously announced that no hearings on the Colorado River Basin Project bill would be held until favorable reports on all five Colorado projects had been released by the Interior Department and Budget Bureau. In a March 9 meeting with Arizona Congressmen Morris Udall and John Rhodes, Aspinall further stated that Colorado could not support a CAP bill that did not include the five projects. It was this inflexible stance that led Orren Beaty, Stewart Udall's assistant, to write a memo that same day to the secretary in which he described Aspinall's actions as "Operation Blackmail." Beaty in particular was outraged that the Bureau of Reclamation had determined that two of the projects would have an average development cost per acre of $1,500, well above the Bureau's normal $1,000-per-acre limit. Beaty also reported that Rep. Udall had informed him that "favorable reports by the Department [are] imperative if there are to be hearings this year in the House."[44]

Secretary Udall, recognizing Aspinall's power in this situation, ordered the Bureau of Reclamation to work overtime to complete the reports for the five projects, even though all but one "were either months or years away from being ready under ordinary timing." In the case of the Animas–La Plata Project, reclamation officials from all over the country met in Denver to adjust its economic profile in order to secure approval by the Budget Bureau. In order to accomplish this goal some marginal irrigation land was dropped, and the Bureau of Reclamation persuaded the city of Farmington, New Mexico, to become part of the project, thus increasing revenues by guaranteeing more municipal water sales. At the end of March, officials from several different federal agencies met to review the status of the project reports. Dan Dreyfuss, from the Bureau of Reclamation, announced that all the reports (from the Departments of Commerce; Labor; Agriculture; and Health, Education, and Welfare; as well as the Federal Power Administration and Army Corps of Engineers) were favorable, except for the report from the Rural Electric Administration, which had objected to the San Miguel project. Colorado Rural Electric Administration officials, however, had already convinced their supervisors in Washington to reverse that report.[45]

The one person who did not seem to be actively lobbying for the five projects was Aspinall himself. In his March 9, 1966, meeting with Rhodes and Udall, the two Arizona congressmen had pressed him to write a letter to the Budget Bureau to expedite its review of the project reports. The chairman, however, expressed reluctance to do so, suggesting that even if he did write the Bureau it might respond to the pressure by not sending the reports, or might issue unfavorable findings. Rhodes and Udall then warned Aspinall that if the CAP project did not receive congressional approval during this session it was possible that the state of Arizona would seek to build the project on its own (which would, implicitly, end the regional support for the five Colorado projects). As a result of this pleading and pressure, Aspinall agreed to go ahead and write the letter.[46]

In his March 14 letter to the director of the Budget Bureau, Aspinall stated that a consensus had been reached among the Colorado River states concerning the development of the water in the basin, but that Colorado's support of this agreement depended upon the approval of the five projects.

[U]ntil we have the final Bureau of the Budget clearance of the five projects proposed for authorization in Colorado, I personally do not feel that there actually is a consensus among the States upon which Congress can make its decision.

I realize that the Bureau of the Budget may have some questions with respect to the benefits attributable to one or two of the Colorado projects. However, in my opinion, there can be no question as to the engineering feasibility or the financial feasibility of these projects, nor can there be any final decision other than a decision that they should be authorized and constructed.[47]

Aspinall's letter clearly indicated that if the projects were rejected he would kill the CRBP bill and blame the Budget Bureau for his action. His claim about the viability of the projects was undoubtedly part of this strategy, since, if the projects received unfavorable reports, it would allow him to attack the Bureau's decision as being politically rather than economically motivated.

All the pressure brought to bear on the Interior Department and Budget Bureau produced rapid results. On March 16, the Bureau of Reclamation issued its revised reports on the Dallas Creek, San Miguel, and West Divide Projects. On April 6 the Interior Department sent the final reports to the Budget Bureau, which had approved the Dolores project on March 4. The Interior Department also sent a revised Animas–La Plata report to the Budget Bureau on April 13, which said it would issue its final reports as quickly as possible to meet the deadline Aspinall had set in order to begin congressional hearings.[48]

If securing a favorable review was Aspinall's intent, he only achieved a partial victory. On April 30 the Budget Bureau released its final report, in which it stated that four out of the five projects met the benefit-cost ratio criterion (San Miguel did not), but that all of the projects would have high costs per acre. As a result, the Budget Bureau recommended deferring three of the projects (Dallas Creek, San Miguel, and West Divide) until Congress established a National Water Commission that would help create a reclamation development strategy. Although the unfavorable report from the Budget Bureau did not mean that the projects were dead, it did make it more difficult for supporters to justify them to Congress.[49]

Aspinall was understandably disappointed by the Budget Bureau's report, although he realized that it could have been more critical. In a May 10 letter to a friend back home, the chairman remarked, "The Bureau of the Budget representatives of course sit back here, and, although many of them are knowledgeable of, and friendly to, the West, nevertheless, they do not see these values as we do. On the other hand, I am sure that using the formula that they did, they could have written a much more difficult report for us than the one we received." Publicly, Aspinall continued to put a positive spin on the five projects and to gloss over the Budget Bureau's opposition. In the May 13 edition of his weekly column in the Grand Junction newspaper, the congressman argued that the five projects "would provide additional storage area for water which belongs to the state, but which now flows down stream because of a lack of storage area. The water is greatly needed to pick up sagging economies in some parts of the state, to stabilize agriculture in the established areas, and to allow the expansion of agriculture in new areas. It is needed for growing [Western Slope] cities and industries and the reservoirs will provide recreational opportunities." Aspinall acknowledged the Budget Bureau's recommendation to defer three of the projects, noting the Bureau's belief that these projects cost too much, but to this assertion he replied that "[t]he water people from Colorado, however, have pointed out that the cost will be borne by Colorado's share of the upper basin fund, and they assert it should be the state's decision as to how the funds are used." In this way Aspinall tried to reframe the debate over the five projects as a state's rights issue.[50]

Finally, on May 9, congressional hearings began on the revised Colorado River Basin Project bill. Originally Aspinall had planned to hold only a brief set of hearings lasting three or four days, with the testimony restricted to the five Colorado projects; his reasoning was that all the relevant testimony for the Central Arizona Project had already been heard. However, the ongoing controversy over the Grand Canyon dams and the water augmentation plans for the Colorado River forced the chairman to hold a six-day hearing on a variety of aspects of the Colorado River Basin Project. Aspinall attempted to expedite the hearings by imposing a five-minute limit on each of the seventy-six witnesses' testimony before the committee—half the time presenters had been allocated the previous year.[51]

In addition to time limits, Aspinall thought the hearings would go more smoothly for the CRBP bill if as many friendly witnesses as possible were included. In late April Rep. Udall reported to another CAP supporter that

This morning at the [Interior] Committee hearing, Wayne Aspinall called me over to urge that I have an Indian, preferably the Chief, from the Hualapai Tribe, present at the hearings to testify for three or four minutes in support of the bill. He remarked that he wants to put those who oppose Bridge Canyon Dam [which bordered the tribe's reservation] in the position of being anti-Indian and suggested that we might have Indians do some lobbying along the line that this project will end their poverty problems and assure the success of this reservation.

Aspinall's cynical hope was to combat the emotional appeal of the conservationists' arguments against the dam by making it appear that this opposition was selfish and would injure Native Americans. (The chairman of the Hualapai Tribe did, in fact, testify during the hearings in support of the dam.)[52]

The agenda of the hearings ended up being broader than Aspinall had originally hoped, but the chairman tried to focus as much attention as possible on his five Colorado projects. The testimony of Jack Vinger, president of the Dolores Water Conservation District, was typical. He was accompanied by two local residents who supported the Dolores Project. Each of them submitted brief written statements and numerous letters from local residents and organizations expressing support for the Project. After their five-minute presentations, Aspinall asked the witnesses to again state for the record that "this project is supported by the people and the various interests of the area." When they answered in the affirmative, he yielded the floor to another committee member.[53]

Although most Irrigation and Reclamation Subcommittee members refrained from questioning witnesses supporting the five projects, one member who did ask questions was Rep. John Saylor of Pennsylvania, the ranking minority member of the full Interior Committee and a staunch environmental critic of the reclamation program. One witness in particular Rep. Saylor grilled was Colorado Governor John Love, who testified that the five Western Slope Projects were necessary for the state to endorse the larger CRBP bill. Whereas Aspinall had asked Love a series of easy questions, Saylor immediately went on the attack, greeting the governor with the acid remark (and veiled reference to Aspinall), "First, let me say that you folks from Colorado are pretty good bargainers. I always like to find a man who places $360 million as a price tag for support. I congratulate you, Governor. The people of your State are shrewd bargainers." Saylor also challenged other project witnesses, such as Jack Vinger. The Pennsylvania Republican seemed particularly interested in forcing the Dolores Project supporter to admit that the upper basin would lack sufficient water to allow this project to be built unless the river was augmented.[54]

Assistant Interior Secretary Kenneth Holum also expressed reservations about the five projects. In his comments the assistant secretary only endorsed the two projects, the Dolores and the Animas–La Plata, that the Budget Bureau had recommended. Aspinall quickly brought up this limited endorsement during the question period, presenting the five projects as an issue of states' rights.

> MR. ASPINALL: Do you think the State of Colorado has the ability and authority to determine how to use its water . . . ?
>
> MR. HOLUM: I would hope . . . that the State of Colorado would welcome the opportunity to receive advice from . . . an eminent and distinguished group of water experts who are looking at these problems on a national basis.
>
> MR. ASPINALL: If I have learned anything from the hearings this morning, I learned that it is almost an impossibility, if you get this matter on too large a focus, to get anything out of it.[55]

Aspinall's quick dismissal of the idea of national water planning grew out of his belief that the idea was just a stalling tactic by opponents of the five Colorado projects, as well as an indirect way for Sen. Henry Jackson, who was sponsoring legislation to establish a National Water Commission, to block any diversion of water from the Pacific Northwest.

The chairman and the assistant secretary also clashed over the proposed Grand Canyon dams. The Interior Department continued to support the upstream Marble Canyon Dam, but it now recommended deferring the Bridge Canyon Dam. Aspinall, who still favored both dams, challenged Holum's claim that the dam at Marble Canyon could produce by itself all the power and revenue necessary for the Central Arizona Project, and he even got Floyd Dominy, who was testifying at the same time, to contradict Holum's statement.[56]

The chairman, however, reserved his strongest contempt for the testimony of the conservationists who were opposed to both dams, especially David Brower, the executive director of the Sierra Club. Before Brower could begin his presentation, Aspinall angrily denounced allegations that he had stacked the hearings in favor of dam proponents and that government witnesses opposed to the Grand Canyon dams were being intimidated by their superiors into not testifying. While Aspinall did not mention Brower by name during this outburst and claimed that he had not yet examined all the materials the Sierra Club leader had submitted, the fact that Brower's supporting materials did raise the suppression allegation suggests that the chairman was using this occasion to make a public rebuttal.[57]

In the three years since Congress had begun actively debating the Central Arizona Project, Aspinall had expressed plenty of criticisms regarding the project—much to the surprise and disappointment of the Arizona delegation. However, although the congressman may have had his own reservations about the CAP in general, he firmly believed that the financial key to any further development of the Colorado River depended on building one or both of the Grand Canyon dams. Thus the chairman saw the criticisms expressed by conservationists as a direct threat to water development, not just in the lower basin but in Colorado as well.

Part of Aspinall's frustration and anger in dealing with Brower arose from the fact that each represented a different source of political power. The chairman's position of strength derived from the institutional power of the House of Representatives, where members deferred to those with more seniority and everyone was expected to negotiate mutually acceptable compromises. By comparison, Brower and other conservationists represented an outside power base, similar to the civil rights or student protest movements, that viewed its demands as nonnegotiable and compromise as failure. The anger and contempt Aspinall had for Brower in May, though, was nothing compared to the anger the congressman would have for him during the coming months when the Sierra Club leader launched a national advertising blitz to rally opposition to any dams in the Grand Canyon.

6

Flooding the Sistine Chapel

I have always believed that the Creator placed natural resources to be used as well as viewed, and to be used by
people generally.—Wayne Aspinall[1]

THE CONCLUSION OF THE House hearings in May 1966 did nothing to
change Aspinall's stance on the Colorado River Basin Project bill.
He was willing to support a Central Arizona Project as long as he received the five reclamation projects in his district in return. The chairman also wanted a commitment to explore ways to import water into
the Colorado River, and he believed that the only long-term way to
finance such imports would be to build at least one of the Grand Canyon dams.

Aspinall outlined his position on the Grand Canyon dams controversy
in a June 20, 1966, letter to a constituent, in which he maintained that the
dams would have little effect on the Grand Canyon except that "some of
the rough water, especially in the upper end of the canyon, would be
smoothed out by the Marble Canyon Reservoir." Then Aspinall outlined
what he "would personally like to see done to the Colorado River."

> I would like to see the Bridge Canyon Dam built. This is at the lower
> end of the canyon where river running is not engaged in too much;
> in fact, very little. Then, I would like to see the north side of the
> canyon where the Grand Canyon National Monument is present and
> 13 miles of the Grand Canyon National Park taken out of the Na-
> tional Park category for two miles on each side of the river so that the
> reservoir would not upset people who feel that there is an invasion [of
> the park], although I don't think this personally. Then I would like to
> see the Grand Canyon National Park extended up river to Lee's Ferry
> with at least two miles on each side of the Rim incorporated within
> the Park. This would tie up once and for all the best part of the free
> flowing water in the Colorado River and would keep the Grand

Canyon in a National Park category from Lee's Ferry clear down to the head waters to the Bridge Canyon Reservoir.

Aspinall seemed to believe that the real problem conservationists had with the dams was that they would affect a national park. Thus, he reasoned that if the dam sites were removed from the park system it would resolve the problem. The chairman maintained that he had received some support from conservationists for his ideas, but "I doubt that the Sierra Club group or those who give blind support to them will go for anything except the extreme position."[2]

Aspinall gave further reasons for his support of the Grand Canyon dams in another letter to a constituent, written in August 1966. He claimed that any reservoir water in the National Park would not adversely affect the tourist experience since "there are no roads, trails, or lookouts from which any of the dam or lake could be sighted in the park." In addition, the dams would create "the possibility of a boat trip up into the lower reaches of the Grand Canyon so that thousands of tourists who could not make the arduous climb down into the canyon could then see its beauty from the Floor."[3]

The congressman also mentioned some of the other potential benefits from the Colorado River Basin Project bill. "[T]he bill provides for water for the Hualapai Indians in Arizona who have been in poverty and without [the] water they needed for many years." Aspinall also noted the dire shortages the bill would address. "Farm after farm has been forced to close down, and its occupants to leave their homes in Arizona because the water table is dropping fast and their wells have gone dry. The stories of these many good Americans is sad to contemplate." He then briefly discussed his own conservation philosophy.

> I have always considered myself to be conservation minded—for many years I have lived on the Western Slope of the Rocky Mountains in Colorado, and there, if anywhere, a person learns to love the beauty of the wonderful world God has given us.
>
> My definition of "Conservation" is "wise use". And that is what we are striving for with the Colorado River Basin bill.[4]

Aspinall's attitude toward the environment was clearly human-centric. God had given nature to humans to use as they saw best, and for the congressman the best use was economic development.

Aspinall's definition of conservation stood in sharp contrast to the definition David Brower embraced. In a May interview in *Life* magazine focusing on the Grand Canyon controversy, Brower attacked the sort of "wise use" approach Aspinall espoused.

I dislike the word conservation. It's sort of dull and sounds a bit self-righteous. But it's the best we have. And it's strange that with a word as poor as that, so many people fight to use it as a defense of what they are doing. You go to meetings of almost any group that is using up resources and somewhere along the line they will say, "We're conservationists too." Usually they would like to conserve other things—not what they are exploiting.

If the Grand Canyon dams really had to be built to insure the nation's survival, or even a region's, then there'd be something to argue about. But they are absolutely not necessary. Their being proposed is one of the saddest examples of obsolete engineering thinking.

Some of our most beautiful scenery is sacrificed to "progress." I don't accept the notion that more growth is automatically good for any of us.[5]

The sharp dichotomy between Aspinall's and Brower's points of view in part reflects the economic realities of where each one lived. Aspinall represented a rural district with little industry and believed that the development of natural resources was the best way to strengthen the local economy. Brower, in contrast, came from the San Francisco Bay Area, a region that by the 1960s was already trying to mitigate the problems that overdevelopment had caused.

Brower's interview was part of a larger publicity campaign by the Sierra Club to rally public opposition to the Grand Canyon dams. The big breakthrough for the Sierra Club's campaign came on June 9, 1966. That day the Club took out full-page advertisements in the *New York Times, Washington Post, Los Angeles Times,* and *San Francisco Chronicle.* The professionally designed advertisements bore a headline reading "NOW ONLY YOU CAN SAVE THE GRAND CANYON FROM BEING FLOODED . . . FOR PROFIT." The advertisements featured preprinted coupons addressed to the president, Secretary Udall, and Rep. Aspinall, among others. The advertisements were a huge success, and they triggered an avalanche of public reaction. Hundreds of thousands of coupons, letters, and telegrams flooded into the Capitol and other Washington offices protesting the proposed dams. One senator claimed it was the biggest letter-writing campaign he had ever seen.[6]

The campaign, however, did garner the Sierra Club some unwanted attention. At 4 P.M. the day after the newspaper advertisements ran, a "small faceless man in a dark blue suit" arrived at the Sierra Club's headquarters in San Francisco to hand-deliver a letter from the Internal Revenue Service. The letter notified the Sierra Club that its tax-deductible status was under review. (The Club did eventually lose its status following the review.) The timing of the IRS's action struck Sierra Club officials as suspicious and led them to conclude that someone in the government who supported the dams had asked for the investigation.[7]

If Central Arizona Project supporters had hoped that the IRS action against the Sierra Club would help to mute the public's opposition to the Grand Canyon dams, they were sadly mistaken. The government's heavy-handed decision actually inspired an even larger backlash against the dams and transformed the issue from a battle over conservation into a challenge to free speech. New memberships in the Sierra Club soared when national newspapers as politically diverse as the *New York Times* and the *Wall Street Journal* published editorials denouncing the IRS's decision. Commenting later about the sudden surge in support for the Sierra Club, Brower remarked, "People who didn't know whether or not they loved the Grand Canyon knew whether or not they loved the IRS." With nothing left to lose, the Sierra Club on July 25 published another series of advertisements in national newspapers. This time the advertisements were designed to mock one of the arguments dam proponents had made: that the proposed Grand Canyon reservoir would allow more people to see the beauty of the Canyon up close. The headline for the new advertisement read, "SHOULD WE ALSO FLOOD THE SISTINE CHAPEL SO TOURISTS CAN GET NEARER THE CEILING?"[8]

Aspinall's response to the Sierra Club's ad campaign was extremely hostile. In his correspondence that summer the chairman remarked that he lay the responsibility for the public's misunderstanding of the Grand Canyon situation "squarely on the shoulders of the extremists in the conservation movement who have approached this matter from an emotional standpoint and have not bothered to let facts stand in their way." Aspinall's chief complaint was that the conservationists were (successfully) making their public case against the dams on largely aesthetic, rather than economic, grounds. The chairman also indicated how personally he took these attacks on the dams when he warned that "I am not too hot about the Marble Canyon Dam, but if the Sierra Club leaders keep carrying on their campaign as they are, they may drive me into the absolute and unlimited support of both dams."[9]

Aspinall's harshest comments about the Sierra Club's tactics, however, were also his most public. In a July 6 front-page article in the *Grand Junction Daily Sentinel,* he denounced the Club for its "nasty, indecent and ignorant attack. . . . The Sierra Club has transgressed far beyond the limits of propriety in lobbying against [the dams], and they should be made to pay for such transgressions." While Aspinall stated that he had nothing to do with the IRS's action against the Club, he thought the action was warranted. The Sierra Club quickly responded to the chairman's attacks. Jeff Ingram, the Club's southwest representative, wrote a letter two days later expressing dismay over Aspinall's comments. In closing his letter Ingram wrote:

> I do hope that your remarks . . . do not represent the tenor at which this momentous issue will be decided. I do not question that this is a bitterly emotional issue, that it may be a turning point in our history, that it may even determine the place in history—as hero or villain— of such men as yourself. Nevertheless, I do not see how the implication that we are "nasty, indecent, and ignorant" can contribute to a decision based on the public interest, a concept which I know you have always kept to the fore in your decisions.[10]

For both sides of this dispute the debate had moved beyond a simple difference of opinion over regional economic development and had become an intensely personal conflict. Although both sides pretended to be polite to each other, the degree of hostility raised the prospect that compromise was no longer possible.

The chairman was not just angry with the Sierra Club, he was growing increasingly impatient with all the critics of the proposed dams. During the summer of 1966 Aspinall engaged in a back-and-forth exchange over the issue with Richard Lamm. The correspondence sheds a clear light on the "environmental gap" developing not just between wilderness and development advocates, but also between different generations and different branches within the Democratic Party—a gap that six years later would spell the end of Aspinall's political career and usher in a remarkable realignment in Colorado's politics.

The correspondence began in late June when Lamm, in his capacity as vice president of the Young Democrats of Colorado, sent Aspinall a routine letter reporting that the state convention of the Young Democrats had voted unanimously to oppose the Grand Canyon dams. The letter stated that the Young Democrats "are proud of you as our Congressman of greatest influence; yet we seriously question whether you fully appreciate the ever increasing threat to our scenic resources, the ever increasing need to preserve some of America in its natural state, to save some from those who plow, pollute, and pave under (as well as dam up) our major scenic resources." The letter closed with a plea to defeat the two dams.[11]

In response to the letter, Aspinall wrote four days later to Frank Plaut, the president of the Colorado Young Democrats, complaining about the fact that no one had signed the letter and that it was missing a signature line. Plaut apologized in his response, explained that Lamm had written and sent the letter, and welcomed the congressman's reactions to its content. Aspinall responded a week later and noted that, while he appreciated working with the "younger members" of the Party, he had

> never been able to understand people who wish to take an extreme position on any issue, especially one that has to do with the conservation and development of our natural resource values.
>
> I was born in a beautiful part of Ohio and have lived for sixty-two years in one of the most beautiful areas of the western part of the United States.
>
> I have always believed that the Creator placed natural resources to be used as well as viewed, and to be used by the people generally.
>
> In building Curencanti and Glen Canyon, we spoiled a great deal, but what we received in return is just as beautiful and will be used by thousands, where formerly it was viewed, and [in] some instances, used by only a few.
>
> The [Grand Canyon] dams . . . will not spoil the beauty of the Canyon and will not destroy any of the real scientific values. They will make available recreational uses, as well as energy uses, that will be needed by the people of this country for centuries to come.
>
> I wish I had the opportunity to show you [pictures which would prove that] the only thing that will be destroyed will be some wild

water, used by only a few people each year. This will be replaced by beautiful blue water, not the muddy water we see so often in the Canyon now.[12]

Once again Aspinall had set forth his belief that the primary purpose for nature was human use. While beautiful places were to be admired (and to be as widely accessible as possible), that beauty should not preclude these places from being used, and, in any case, that humans had the capability to create beauty to replace whatever was lost. To Aspinall, nature in its natural state had little real value.

Plaut then passed Aspinall's letter along to Lamm, who responded in a letter dated August 1. Lamm's tone was far more critical than it had been in his June letter:

> Please do not make the mistake of assuming that when a group feels strongly about something, that they are "extremists." My experience with the philosophy that resources are to "use" is beyond question; my father is the president of the biggest strip mine company in your district, (Pittsburg and Midway) and I realize that resources are to "use"; what my generation doesn't appreciate is "waste" and that is what you propose to do by putting "cash registers" in the world's only Grand Canyon.
>
> I believe that what makes a politician "great" is not his ability to rule iron-handed over a committee; but his ability to understand the changing times. This you have failed to do: to understand that we no longer have the scenic resources left that we can spend them on "cash registers." You fail to understand the changing needs of people in a world which will double in population in the next 40 years, and their needs for some untrampled part of our natural heritage.
>
> The Colorado State Convention passed a resolution [opposed to the dams]. You have ignored this and proposed instead to placate Colorado with five dams. Whatever the merits of these dams, there can be no justification short of a national emergency which could justify molesting the Grand Canyon.
>
> I am very sorry to have to disagree with a Colorado Democrat; but I feel that putting "cash registers" in so important a part of our national heritage is "extreme," and I never could understand extremists.[13]

Lamm's response, which clearly was designed to insult rather than persuade, represented a complete rejection of Aspinall's view of the natural world. Nature, rather than having a value based solely on human consumption, instead provides a refuge from an increasingly overcrowded world (a perennial Lamm topic). Lamm's shot at the five Colorado dams is interesting in light of the fact that a dozen years later, as governor of Colorado, Lamm would vehemently object to federal attempts to drop the projects.

Aspinall wrote a brief, quiet reply on August 4, in which he remarked in part that "It's good that we live in a country where people of even the same party can disagree, as apparently you and I do on matters of natural resource values." After a brief rebuttal to Lamm's strip-mining remark, Aspinall closed: "I understand your position and respect you for your stand. I do not believe it is necessary to call names or question sincerity in these matters." In his August 12 response, Lamm also sheathed his rhetorical sword, thanking Aspinall for "your measured and fair reply," adding that he "certainly did not mean to reduce our argument to name calling." Lamm closed his letter by stating that while the Young Democrats might disagree with Aspinall about the Grand Canyon, "we are also very proud that a Colorado Democrat is in the position you are in."[14]

Although Lamm's comment was most likely not intended to be ironic, the position that Aspinall found himself in during the summer of 1966 was an almost impossible one. The congressman's efforts to secure passage for the Colorado River Basin Project were foundering because the various members of the coalition supporting the CRBP had conflicting legislative agendas. In addition, now the bill was under constant fire from conservationists. Following the House hearings on the bill in May, the Subcommittee on Irrigation and Reclamation met to determine the final wording for the legislation. During the often contentious "mark-up" sessions, Aspinall indicated that the bill would have "top priority before the Committee and will be scheduled again and again [on the daily agenda] until action is completed." He also privately told Morris Udall that he was satisfied that there were enough votes in the Committee to assure its approval. Aspinall did warn, however, that if subcommittee members removed the provision to study augmentation of the Colorado River from the bill, he would "oppose it with all of his ability." After a week of negotiations the subcommittee approved the bill on June 9 and forwarded it to the full Interior Committee, which in turn, on July 29, voted 22 to 10 to endorse the CRBP bill and send it to the House Rules Committee.[15]

In early August Aspinall used his weekly newspaper column to tout the merits of the Colorado River Basin Project bill and put the best public face on its patchwork nature. Behind the scenes, however, he had lost his earlier optimism about the passage of the bill in the full House of Representatives in light of ongoing public controversy over the various parts of the legislation, particularly the Grand Canyon dams. In an August 29 letter, Aspinall wrote that the "question at the moment is whether the legislation has enough votes to get it out of the Rules Committee and through the House. On this, there seems to be a great deal of doubt and the outlook is not promising."[16]

At the end of August Reps. Rhodes and Udall met with Aspinall to review the status of the CRBP legislation. The chairman used the occasion to outline his current position on the bill and the attempts to revise it. Aspinall stated that he "would be extremely displeased . . . to abandon [the bill] in favor" of the one endorsed by John Saylor (which stripped everything out except the Central Arizona Project and a coal power plant in place of the Grand Canyon dams). The chairman further stated that "there was no time left in this session to take necessary steps for passage of whichever legislation was finally agreed upon." Aspinall also told the two Arizonans that even though Congress was not going to adjourn for another month, he was leaving Washington for the year at the end of the week but would be willing to return if some sort of breakthrough occurred on the bill.[17]

Although CAP supporters continued to try to come up with a compromise bill, by early September the chairman considered the bill dead for the session. When Congress finally adjourned in October without passing the Colorado River Basin Project bill, the Central Arizona Project officially died, meaning that the legislative process would have to start all over again the following year. Some supporters of the CRBP blamed Aspinall for its failure and claimed that he had deliberately let the bill die in the House Rules Committee. Aspinall later admitted that while he had not necessarily killed the bill in the Rules Committee, he had deliberately neglected it there. The congressman maintained that he had done this because he feared that if the bill made it to the House floor opponents of the CRBP would have stripped it of everything except the Central Arizona Project, and the five Colorado projects would have been lost.[18]

With Congress finally adjourned for the year, Aspinall returned to Colorado to begin campaigning for re-election. Some of his speeches, however, were not aimed solely at the local audience. Instead, the congressman used several of these public occasions to discuss his reactions to the recently failed Colorado River Basin Project and to list his demands for any revived bill—demands that he correctly anticipated would be covered by the press. On September 24, Aspinall gave a speech in Vail. While most of his talk focused on the various national park proposals his committee had passed, the chairman also talked briefly about the Grand Canyon dams controversy. First, however, Aspinall outlined his attitude toward using natural resources.

Nobody knows the full extent of our future resources; consequently no one can honestly say when our environment will reach its saturation point. That is the basic reason why one of our most important national policies has been aimed toward the multiple use of the resources available to us.

The Scriptures tell us that upon the event of the Creation, God commanded: "Be fruitful, and multiply, and replenish the earth and subdue it." This we—and our fathers and our father's fathers—have diligently pursued.[19]

Here again Aspinall set forth his belief that God intended humans to use nature to the fullest extent possible. While he acknowledged that it might be possible to over-use the environment, such a possibility seemed too remote to concern Aspinall.

After noting that "recreational demand is probably proportionally outstripping the other demands on our environment," and discussing Congress's efforts to address this problem, Aspinall discussed the Grand Canyon controversy.

Notwithstanding the great demand for outdoor recreation resources, the Committee recognizes that other important human needs also demand attention and which may be in direct conflict. This was the situation with regard to the "Colorado River Development Plan." In spite of the fact that this undertaking would make available to the public-at-large a massive new recreation potential, critics claimed that the program would, to use their words, "destroy" the Grand Canyon. Whereas the intention of the Committee was to make possible the wisest and fullest use of the Colorado River to meet a basic human need for water in the arid West, it did not seek—nor did it provide for anything in the legislation that would—hinder the public enjoyment of the Grand Canyon. Quite the contrary, we viewed the development of the river as the only reasonable, practicable, safe and logical way for millions of Americans and visitors to enjoy the canyon bottom which to date so few have had an opportunity to visit or view.[20]

Aspinall clearly believed that the best recreational opportunities were the ones that served the most people. Throughout the congressman's career, he repeatedly denounced conservationists for "locking up" areas and limiting access to them. Instead, Aspinall claimed that beautiful places should be opened up to the maximum number of visitors, and he had no hesitation about altering natural areas to accommodate the public.

Ten days later Aspinall gave a speech to the Colorado State Grange in which he outlined his vision for a new Colorado River Basin Project bill. The congressman began by discussing why the state of Colorado had a stake in legislation primarily designed to help Arizona, noting that "our rights to water of the Colorado River are in terms of 'beneficial consumptive use.' We firm up our rights only if we put the water to use. If we don't put it to use we will eventually lose it." Thus Colorado's involvement in the CRBP bill "was simply a matter, first, of protecting the water supplies that are rightfully ours and, second, looking to our future water needs."[21]

Aspinall then summarized why water was so important to Colorado's future. "The future economic development of our State depends upon protecting and holding our water from encroachment of use by others during the years before it is put to final use. I am fearful that, if it is temporarily put to use elsewhere, it will be permanently lost." Aspinall firmly believed that if the more populous states of the lower basin received permission to start using upper basin water, they would never relinquish it, and they would have the political clout to block any efforts by the upper basin to reclaim it.[22]

The chairman went on to outline the three provisions a Colorado River Basin Project bill should include: (1) criteria for operating the reservoirs (chiefly Lake Powell) on the Colorado River; (2) studies to augment the Colorado River; and (3) authorization for the five Colorado projects. Aspinall also used this occasion to blame the bill's failure to pass on various groups and events, including the Johnson Administration, the Sierra Club, opponents in the Pacific Northwest, the "early disintegration of the seven [river basin] state agreement," and "the economy bloc" in the House.[23]

Aspinall explained why he had not tried to force the Colorado River Basin Project bill through the House on his own:

> One of the dangers of bringing it up was the possibility that a substitute bill . . . would be adopted. The substitute would have stripped from the bill all of the major features which made the legislation acceptable to Colorado. In these circumstances, it seemed to me that a lingering death in the Rules Committee was preferable to bringing the bill to the Floor where we would not only run the risk of defeat but face the possibility of having a bill passed which would be completely unacceptable to Colorado and the other upper basin states.

Aspinall's comments suggest that he realized how limited the support was for his five Colorado projects.[24]

The chairman closed his speech by answering the question "where do we go from here?" He predicted that the Colorado River Basin states would spend the next few months reevaluating their positions on the CRBP bill, but that Colorado's role should continue to be one of cooperation "as long as Colorado's water rights and water supplies are not placed in jeopardy." He also predicted that, at a minimum, both the Animas–La Plata and the Dolores projects should be approved as part of the CRBP bill the following year, and hopefully the other three projects as well. In closing Aspinall pledged himself to "take all necessary actions on behalf of water development in Colorado and the future economic well-being of our state."[25]

Following his re-election to a tenth term in Congress, Aspinall had another opportunity to talk about his position on the Colorado River Basin Project, this time at the meeting of the National Reclamation Association. In his speech to the Albuquerque conference, the chairman used the occasion to express his scorn for the Sierra Club and other opponents of the Grand Canyon dams. In a hypocritical remark, he commented:

> We have found from experience that some groups don't want to recognize the meaning of the word [negotiation]. To some, "compromise" means "do it our way."

Had there been a willingness on the part of the spokesmen for those opposing the dams to negotiate in an atmosphere of good faith, I believe there could have been an agreement reached.

Referring to his proposal to shift the boundaries of the park, Aspinall continued:

I felt that in the interest of reaching agreement without jeopardizing project feasibility we might have both water development and additional park preservation by giving up Marble Canyon and perhaps expanding the park to include the Marble Gorge. It was a great disappointment to me that, during the hearings, it was not possible to work out a compromise agreement along these lines. However, this was not possible because the essential elements for compromise— good faith and flexibility—were missing on the other side. The spokesmen for the Sierra Club, which was leading the fight against the dams, maintained an extreme and inflexible position.

Aspinall then sought to drive a wedge between the different conservation groups opposed to the dams.

I believe that most of the leaders of organizations interested in our national parks . . . are beginning to realize that the massive and misleading campaign of the Sierra Club against the two dams was not in the best interests of their cause. They know that the tactics used were distasteful to many true friends and supporters of their programs.

Thus, I look for a more conciliatory attitude from these organizations and I believe that, given time to negotiate in good faith, we can reach an agreement which will serve both causes—water development and park preservation.[26]

Aspinall's remarks clearly were not designed to open a dialogue with conservationists, who remained solidly unified despite the chairman's claims. Instead they were designed to convince the public at large that he was a reasonable man who was willing to compromise.

In his speech the chairman was far more sympathetic in discussing the fears of the Pacific Northwest over the possible diversion of water from the Columbia River.

They were not satisfied with the assurances—given verbally and by language in the legislation—that their future water needs would not be jeopardized. We were not able to convince representatives of the Northwest that the study provisions were intended to cover all possible means of augmentation and that no considerations would be given to importing water from any area unless it was proved to be surplus to any possible future need. Personally, I believe that the fears of the Columbia Basin States were unwarranted but, being from a state whose future also depends upon its water resources, I certainly understand and respect their position. The important point is that the states of the Northwest are not opposed to a westwide water resources study or to water planning on a westwide basis. The differences are on method of accomplishment.[27]

Unlike the conservationists, who had nothing to offer Aspinall, the chairman's restrained comments about the Pacific Northwest clearly were designed to win the trust of the region's representatives and to encourage a compromise with them.

Aspinall made further remarks later at a strategy session involving the Colorado delegation attending the conference. He informed the group that he favored the Colorado River Basin Project compromise that Felix Sparks, of the Colorado Water Conservation Board, had suggested. That plan called for dropping the Marble Canyon Dam and adding the area to the Grand Canyon National Park, building a lower Bridge Canyon Dam that would not back water into the National Park, and conducting a limited study on the possibility of importing water from the Pacific Northwest. Both Sparks and Aspinall warned the Colorado delegates that such importations might never be feasible given the potential program costs and political difficulties. In the absence of any importation the five Colorado projects would then be even more important as a way to partially guarantee the state's allotment of Colorado River water. Aspinall further warned the group that "if Colorado does not get its upper Colorado River projects while it has the [Interior] committee chairmanship it may be 20 years before these projects are authorized. . . . Colorado has a chance now—we may never have it again."[28]

While Aspinall's speech and comments at the conference received substantial press coverage, the chairman's visit was partially overshadowed by David Brower's decision to attend the meeting. The Sierra Club executive director had been invited to participate on a panel discussing the Grand Canyon dams, and to the surprise of the conference organizers he accepted the invitation. Brower struck a diplomatic tone in his remarks, saying that "[t]here will always be two sides to the conservation coin, one concerned with intelligent management of renewable or substitutable resources—the other concerned with intelligent preservation of irreplaceable resources. No matter how thin the coin wears, it will still have two sides, both inevitable, both essential, each to be concerned with the other as long as civilization lasts." In contrast to Aspinall's harsh comments, Brower sounded far more conciliatory, although the fact that he was addressing a hostile audience undoubtedly affected his remarks.[29]

Brower's most memorable moment at the conference, however, occurred when he and Aspinall ran into each other in a hallway between conference sessions. A quick-thinking photographer asked the two men to stand next to each other so he could take a picture. The chairman instead blew up, yelling "No picture of mine is being taken with that liar! He's been filling the newspapers with a bunch of damn lies!" before storming away. The "essential elements for compromise" Aspinall had referred to in his speech seemed also to be lacking in his own response.[30]

When Congress reconvened in late January 1967, numerous different versions of a Colorado River Basin Project bill were introduced in both the House and the Senate. In early February Secretary Udall released a revised plan that he hoped would end the controversy surrounding the CRBP. Udall's plan called for eliminating both Grand Canyon dams and instead building a coal-powered plant to provide the electricity necessary for the Central Arizona Project. Udall also proposed dropping the annual guarantee to California of 4.4 maf of river water, the five Colorado projects, and the Pacific Northwest water import study.[31]

In response to the Interior Department's CRBP bill, Aspinall introduced his own measure in Congress. H.R. 3300 called for building the five Colorado projects as well as the Bridge Canyon Dam (which Aspinall viewed as the "cash register" needed to finance the whole CRBP), extending the boundary of Grand Canyon National Park sixty miles upstream to the east to include the Marble Canyon Dam site (Aspinall had given up trying to get this dam approved), adding 80,000 acres to the western side of the National Park, and—the most controversial element—eliminating the Grand Canyon National Monument (located adjacent to, and downstream from, the National Park) and transferring oversight of the area to the Lake Mead National Recreation Area. Aspinall's dubious rationale for this last provision was that, since conservationists had opposed the Bridge Canyon Dam because it would flood a national monument, the easiest solution would be simply to eliminate the monument, and thus eliminate the objections.[32]

When the House Interior Subcommittee on Irrigation and Reclamation opened formal hearings in March 1967, Aspinall's bill rather than the secretary's plan was the focus of the discussion. On March 14, the second day of the hearings, Stewart Udall sent President Johnson a memo updating Johnson on the situation concerning the Colorado River Basin Project bill, predicting that a version similar to the administration's plan "will pass in this session." Udall noted that "Aspinall appears to be wavering. I am confident that he will not risk going to the House floor with a controversial [Bridge Canyon] dam in the bill."[33]

Udall's optimism seemed unfounded given the verbal thrashing he had taken at the chairman's hands during the hearings. Although Aspinall remarked just before Udall's testimony that "there will be no bloodletting this morning," he forgot that promise as soon as the questioning began. While the chairman expressed reservations about the legality of the federal reclamation program running a coal-powered plant, he quickly focused his questions on his favorite topic: the amount of water in the Colorado River. When the secretary stated that he was "trying to stay out of controversy," the chairman replied, "We thrive on it in this committee."[34]

Aspinall repeatedly asked Udall where the water would come from for the Central Arizona Project; would it be dependent on the upper basin's allotment? Udall professed to be confused by the question and stated that the water "moves down the river by gravity." Reclamation Commissioner Floyd Dominy, who had accompanied Udall to the hearing to provide technical information, finally intervened and admitted that the project "in the early years" would utilize part of the upper basin's allotment. The chairman, who clearly had grown frustrated with this roundabout way of getting answers to his questions, remarked to Udall and Dominy, "I have told you already that I was in favor of this project, but I am not about to permit the entitlement of the upper basin to be jeopardized by this project."[35]

In an interview with the *Denver Post* after the hearings concluded, Aspinall further denounced Secretary Udall's comments and his department's shift in position on the Colorado River Basin Project. Aspinall also stated his disappointment that Commissioner Dominy had not been "permitted to express his own evaluation of some of the questions asked department witnesses." Aspinall, however, remained optimistic that he could secure passage of his CRBP bill in the House, and he said he expected to be able to resolve any differences with the Senate version, which was closer to Udall's plan.[36]

Efforts to pass a Colorado River Basin Project bill, however, soon foundered. Aspinall continued to insist publicly that any bill had to include both the Bridge Canyon Dam and an augmentation study for the Colorado River. A number of politicians, however, had privately indicated that these demands were not acceptable, given the environmental opposition to Bridge Canyon and Pacific Northwest opposition to any augmentation study. As a result, by late June efforts to pass the bill had ground to a halt. In a June 28 letter Aspinall confessed, "I have gone from one who was optimistic until two weeks ago to one who is now more or less pessimistic. I am still of the opinion that the [CRBP] legislation has a possibility of being enacted in this Congress, but apparently not in the first session."[37]

The chairman blamed the breakdown on an "attempt of the people of Arizona to push their legislation through Congress regardless of whether or not it hurts people of other areas in the Colorado River Basin." Aspinall warned that if a CAP-only bill was passed it would leave "folks in the Upper Basin . . . entirely at the mercy of the Federal Government and . . . without any practical possibility of our own projects being constructed in the future." The chairman also complained that he had no success in trying to gain some cooperation from the Pacific Northwest. He closed by saying, "As far as I am concerned, I think we are better off in Colorado, even though we are interested in our projects, to sit tight for awhile."[38]

Aspinall continued his litany of complaints in two July letters. In a July 17 letter to a constituent, the chairman continued his long-running argument that augmentation was necessary, pointing out that with current water levels in the river the CAP could only function if Arizona relied on water to which it had no legal claim.

> It is a known fact that there is not sufficient water in the River for the Central Arizona Project, unless it uses water to which the Upper Basin is entitled under the provisions of the Colorado River Compact. This means that the success of the Central Arizona Project is not

assured, unless there is augmentation of a water supply over and above the natural flow in the Colorado River.

What all this boils down to is the hard fact that unless additional water is placed in the Colorado River Basin, the future development, both in the Upper and Lower Basins is in trouble.

Then in a July 27 letter to former Colorado governor Ed Johnson, Aspinall further complained that "[i]n the beginning I did my best to cooperate with the Department of Interior in its desire to get an over-all program." "Since then the secretary has changed his position three times and the Administration . . . with the president of the United States involved indirectly at least, has capitulated to the wishes of Senator Jackson." In light of these actions, Aspinall wrote,

> My position has been . . . that if Senator Jackson, and others in the Northwest, can be provincial enough to protect their interests . . . and the representatives of the states of California and Arizona . . . can present a completely selfish position in trying to take care of their needs at the expense of the Upper Basin, then Wayne Aspinall . . . certainly has the right and duty of protecting the needs of the Upper Basin and their entitlements. . . . This I intend to do . . . if the representatives of the state of Colorado will stand with me.

The chairman's criticism of the other representatives seems hypocritical considering that Aspinall closed his letter by demanding, "I want the five Upper Basin projects. . . . This I have determined to stand upon."[39]

In order to force Central Arizona Project supporters to meet his demands, Aspinall decided to employ a tactic he had used successfully during the debate over the Wilderness Bill in 1962. In early August he announced his intention to adjourn the Interior Committee and go home for the remainder of the congressional session, which was scheduled to continue until mid-October. Aspinall's decision was in response to the fact that the Senate Interior Committee had passed a Colorado River Basin Project bill in July that did not include either the Bridge Canyon Dam or the water import study (but did include the five Colorado projects). When the bill cleared the Senate committee, Aspinall said that it was "the death knell for any Colorado River legislation this year." Even with the five Colorado projects, the chairman still would not accept a bill that did not include augmentation of the Colorado River or the Bridge Canyon Dam. By adjourning the Interior Committee, Aspinall would make it impossible for the House to consider the Senate bill, since the committee would not be able to review it.[40]

In response to Aspinall's maneuver, Arizona's congressional delegation tried to have the leadership of the House pressure the chairman into proceeding with the bill during 1967. On August 11, Rep. Morris Udall wrote a letter on behalf of the Arizona representatives to the Speaker of the House, John McCormack. In it Udall stressed that Aspinall's Interior Committee had, for the past four years, held extensive hearings on the matter and that the bill was now ready for a vote. Udall stated that even though "Chairman Aspinall has announced that the bill is 'dead' for this year . . . I am hopeful that we can change his mind." While Udall acknowledged that McCormack "cannot control Chairman Aspinall," the Arizonan hoped that the speaker could "inquire of [Aspinall] the status of this legislation, mention its importance to us, and our request to you for help."[41]

McCormack did, in fact, contact Aspinall. In an August 18 letter the chairman responded and outlined his position on the issue. After giving a summary of the history of Colorado River water legislation, which emphasized that there was not enough water in the river for both the Central Arizona Project and future upper basin projects, Aspinall stressed that the main point of contention was the lack of agreement among the seven Colorado River Basin states over a plan to augment the water in the river. To resolve this issue, the chairman wrote, "[w]hat I am asking for at present is 'time' for the purpose of trying to get this agreement." He closed by complaining about the selfish actions of lower basin representatives, who forced Aspinall into "a position where I must defend the values belonging to the people of my area."[42]

The people in Aspinall's constituency, however, did not completely agree with his decision to stall on the Colorado River Basin Project bill. The *Durango Herald* published an editorial on August 9 criticizing the chairman's actions as threatening the fate of the nearby Animas–La Plata and Dolores projects. This criticism prompted Aspinall to respond in an August 14 letter to the publisher. The congressman wrote that while he had "pledged my support to do everything that I could to get to the construction of the two projects," he also wanted "to see to it that the remaining water to which the Upper Basin is entitled is put to use . . . especially in Colorado."[43]

Aspinall then explained that he supported five Colorado projects instead of just these two because "I think that I can promise you . . . that with the exclusive authorization of the Arizona Project and the Animas–La Plata and Dolores Projects . . . there will be no further authorization leading to construction of any additional projects in Western Colorado unless Colorado goes it alone. I am afraid that the latter approach is not open to a state which has no greater economic foundation than ours." In two other letters to southwestern Colorado residents, Aspinall attempted to blunt the criticism directed toward him by presenting himself as simply a passive servant of the state government's wishes. The chairman correctly insisted that his current stance on the CRBP bill reflected the official water policy of the state water board, and that "I do my best to follow [water] policy established by duly constituted political agencies of Colorado."[44]

Despite his professed devotion to the state government's position, Aspinall did ultimately change his stance. In late August, just a few days before he adjourned the Interior Committee, Aspinall dropped his demand that a Bridge Canyon Dam be included in any Colorado River Basin Project bill. The chairman announced his shift in a newspaper interview, but he also stressed that any bill would have to include a guarantee to the upper basin states that "they will get the water they are entitled to . . . together with a guarantee that they will get the necessary authorization and funds to build their projects in the future." This compromise offer, however, was partly undermined by the fact that in his off-the-record remarks, which Central Arizona Project supporters quickly discovered, Aspinall indicated that he was still inclined to "just 'sit' on his [CRBP] bill as far as present action is concerned." Tired and frustrated, the chairman, who had talked about retiring in the next few years, even went so far as to suggest that maybe he would leave the whole matter to his successor, or that the problem would simply "go away" if Arizona went ahead and built the project by itself.[45]

Aspinall's "compromise" prompted a flurry of action in late August. While members of the Colorado Water Conservation Board, which had endorsed the Bridge Canyon Dam, expressed concern over this break in their ranks, Arizona officials tried to see if the chairman's shift could lead to a renewed consideration of the CRBP bill. Aspinall initially suggested he might allow this to occur if a compromise was reached, but he indicated that a compromise would only be possible if Arizonans "will quit trying to bull their way through." The chairman's conciliatory attitude, however, was fleeting. In a September 6 speech to the National Conference of State and Federal Water Officials, Aspinall again lashed out. Promising to "speak very frankly," the congressman attacked Secretary Udall and blamed the whole legislative breakdown over the CRBP bill on the Interior Department's shift in position in February. Before then, Aspinall argued, all the parties involved in the negotiations had nearly reached an agreement. Then the department had made decisions "to appease two groups not directly involved [environmentalists and the Pacific Northwest]," and the whole effort had collapsed. The chairman insisted that "[t]he only answer to the Southwest water situation is to develop new sources of water from outside the Basin."[46]

Aspinall announced an even more unyielding position during a September 8 meeting of the Colorado Water Conservation Board, stating that the Central Arizona Project would remain in his committee "until Arizona takes a more reasonable approach to Colorado River use" by reversing their support for the Senate bill. In a speech given that same day at the dedication of the Rifle Gap Reservoir near Glenwood Springs, the congressman stated that he was "willing to talk about ways and means to get the Colorado River legislation back on track." However, Aspinall then added an additional demand that if and when Congress approved the CAP, "the [five] Colorado projects will not only be authorized but will be built concurrently with the Central Arizona Project." Aspinall worried that even if the five Colorado projects received authorization along with the CAP, the Central Arizona Project would be built first. The chairman reasoned that once the CAP was built, Colorado would have no political leverage to force the construction of its own projects.[47]

The harshness of the congressman's stance was clearly in response to the political threats he was receiving from other members of Congress who objected to his continued efforts to block passage of the Central Arizona Project. He confidently predicted on September 8 that "[t]here isn't going to be any blasting out of my Committee of [the CRBP] bill" and that "all of these threats are not going to come to fruition at all." But Aspinall was, in fact, about to be drawn into a serious political brawl over the legislation. Sen. Carl Hayden of Arizona, angry with Aspinall's stalling on the Central Arizona Project, initiated more drastic measures and launched a two-pronged "power play" to punish the chairman and to take away his control

Gamesmanship

The *Denver Post* published this cartoon by Pat Oliphant on September 24, 1967, in the midst of the Hayden-Aspinall feud. (Oliphant © Universal Press Syndicate; reprinted with permission, all rights reserved)

of the CAP bill. Hayden took his first step in mid-September when he threatened to cut funding for the Fryingpan-Arkansas Project. As chairman of the Senate Appropriations Committee, the senator was in an excellent position to carry out his threat.[48]

Hayden next launched an attempt to make a procedural end run around the House Interior Committee to take the CAP bill directly to the floor of the House of Representatives. The senator announced that he intended to attach the Central Arizona Project legislation to a public works bill. If the Senate approved the bill, upon arrival in the House it would bypass the Interior Committee and instead go to the House Public Works Committee. Hayden justified his unusual, but not unprecedented, action by claiming that Aspinall had blocked action on the CAP bill and had "refused to indicate when, if ever, a bill would be reported to the House."[49]

The strategy of making an end run around Aspinall had been suggested to Hayden a year earlier in a confidential letter from Floyd Dominy. The commissioner of Reclamation suggested that Hayden "force the issue by working it into the Public Works Appropriations Act." "I think you could make [a legislative move] that any reasonable Member of Congress could recognize as being a legitimate mechanism for getting an expression of the Congress and dispose of it in this manner." At the time Hayden declined the suggestion, but by September 1967 he was willing, as Dominy put it, "to proceed in a manner that is not in accord with the normal procedures of the Congress."[50]

In order for Hayden's maneuver to work, the Arizona delegation had to line up support in both the Senate and the House. After a series of private meetings, Hayden gained the backing of the chair of the House Public Works Committee, and Secretary Udall secured a promise from Speaker John McCormack to expedite consideration of the bill once it reached the House. Arizona Rep. John Rhodes later recalled that when word of the plan was deliberately leaked just before Hayden put it into action, Aspinall "started making phone calls to everybody he could think of and found that everybody he talked to had already agreed to support the CAP—they were committed to us."[51]

As a result, Aspinall flew back to Washington to try to salvage the situation as best he could. The chairman clearly remained in full command of his committee when he called it back into executive session on October 10, and the members voted to make the Central Arizona Project legislation the first item to be considered when Congress reconvened in early January. Afterward, Aspinall insisted that this had been his plan all along. Although this offer would not result in the CAP bill's being passed during 1967, Sen. Hayden was satisfied, and he dropped his plans to attach the CAP to the Public Works bill.[52]

In the aftermath of his very public clash with the senator and of the negative press coverage it had triggered, Aspinall tried to repair some of the damage to his political reputation. On October 11, he wrote a letter to Governor Love of Colorado, outlining his version of what had happened. The chairman insisted that his committee had agreed in January to adjourn as soon as possible after July 1 and, in fact, had stayed in session until August 30. In early August, the chairman continued, he and Rep. John Saylor had agreed to defer final consideration on four pieces of major legislation until the next session of Congress so that there would be enough time to examine the bills more thoroughly.[53]

Aspinall further stated that in July he told Sen. Hayden and Rep. Udall that "if the [CAP] bill came over to the House . . . from the . . . Senate without the [Bridge Canyon Dam] or some equally desirable cash register project . . . then there was no possibility of the House . . . considering further legislation having to do with the Colorado River during this session of Congress." The chairman then claimed that the reason he had returned to Washington in early October was to support two pieces of legislation unrelated to Interior matters, and that while he was there he had decided to hold a scheduling meeting for the Interior Committee.

> I did not return solely for the purpose of the entanglement involving Arizona vs. the rest of the Colorado River Basin States. However, when I got to Washington I conferred with Mr. Saylor and we decided it would be in the best interests of the Members of the Committee . . . to have a Committee meeting in order to advise the Committee as to what had taken place and what was planned in the way of future Committee operations.

Aspinall then complained that

> As you know, several statements have been made during the last three months about the position of the senior Member of Congress from Colorado [Aspinall] that are not factual and not in the keeping with ordinary courtesies that should be prevailing between interests and people engaged in trying to solve a very difficult problem.

Interestingly, the chairman's explanation of the events received a partial boost when John Saylor said that both he and Aspinall had agreed to adjourn the Interior Committee early, although Saylor added that it was Aspinall's idea. Saylor claimed that both of them had felt that the CRBP bill needed further consideration by the Interior Committee before it could be scheduled for a vote.[54]

Although he had clearly backed down in his clash with Sen. Hayden, Aspinall continued to be publicly defiant about whether or not his committee would approve the Central Arizona Project legislation. At a town meeting in Craig, Colorado, Aspinall stated that the news from Washington claiming he had promised to release the bill from his committee was false. "I'm going to oppose the Central Arizona Project and I'm not going to report the Bill out of Committee." His subsequent actions, however, suggest that this comment was intended more as face-saving rhetoric than as a prediction of continued legislative gridlock.[55]

Behind the scenes negotiations resumed in early December when Aspinall wrote Secretary Udall a letter stating that the chairman no longer believed that either of the Grand Canyon dams could be approved by

Congress. Aspinall then returned to the question he had focused on for the past three years: whether or not the Central Arizona Project would be dependent on the upper basin's allocation of Colorado River water. The chairman asked the secretary to submit a full report on the matter during House subcommittee hearings in late January.[56]

On January 2, 1968, Aspinall met with Rep. Morris Udall to negotiate an internal Interior Committee compromise before hearings began and committee members started working on the final wording for the legislation. In his meeting, the chairman indicated that, public comments aside, he recognized that a CAP bill would be voted on by the full House during the coming session. Aspinall seemed worried, however, that Rep. Saylor might successfully try to have the Committee vote in favor of the Senate version of the CAP bill, which omitted any study of augmenting the Colorado River. This concern helped prompt the chairman's willingness to negotiate with the Arizona lobby. In a memo reporting on the meeting, Udall wrote that Aspinall's comments indicated a willingness to accept the best House bill possible and an openness to compromise.[57]

When the House Subcommittee on Irrigation and Reclamation opened hearings on January 30, Secretary Udall and his assistants were the only witnesses. (With the Grand Canyon dams no longer under consideration, conservationists dropped their active opposition to the CRBP.) Aspinall stated that his goal for these hearings was to get "a resolution of the problem that is bothering us and bring peace along the River for a generation or two." The focus of the hearings was on the question that the chairman had raised in his December letter to the secretary: whether or not the Central Arizona Project was a threat to the future development of the upper basin's water allotment (which implicitly raised the question of whether augmentation would be necessary). Udall, not surprisingly, argued that the CAP was not a threat, and Commissioner Dominy insisted that given the rate of development in the upper basin, it was unlikely that the region would suddenly need its full allotment during the next two decades.[58]

Aspinall, who dominated the questioning during the hearings, disagreed with this analysis and pointed out that Arizona was threatening to build the Central Arizona Project itself if Congress did not approve the plan. This, the chairman warned, could lead other states to build their own projects and, as a result, undermine the water allocations outlined in the Colorado River Compact. In addition to raising questions about water use in the river, Aspinall also inquired as to how viable the coal-powered electrical plant would be as a source of power for the CAP, and whether or not the Project could pay for itself. The chairman complained to the secretary about the cost of the CAP and the fact that this project would be competing for funds with other authorized reclamation projects. He also entered into the record a lengthy statement in which he cited numerous studies indicating that the Colorado River was at risk of being over-allocated. Aspinall's strategy appeared to be to build a case in the hearing transcripts showing that augmentation would eventually be necessary.[59]

After the hearings concluded, the Subcommittee met to begin marking up the final version of the bill for consideration by the full Interior Com-mittee. At the start of this process, Aspinall announced that "he was now through taking advice from his people in Colorado and was acting upon his own responsibility as a Congressman." The chairman apparently hoped that other subcommittee members would make the same pledge, thus limiting the negotiations to just the people in the room and excluding the various water officials and lobbyists. Aspinall's hope was to reach a com-promise more quickly by limiting the number of people involved. (The chairman's request was largely observed, and only two participants, Reps. John Saylor and Harold Johnson, were willing to discuss the negotiations with reporters.)[60]

The mark-up session lasted until March 1, and, despite numerous at-tempts by Saylor to amend it, the bill that emerged was basically the revised version that Aspinall had introduced in January. Following a seventeen-to-five vote, the bill was sent to the full Interior Committee. Central Arizona Project lobbyists praised the bill and Aspinall's role in shaping it. "What made this mark-up so smooth and the vote so great was due in large part to the fact Chairman Aspinall was working from his bill and assuming leader-ship of the proceedings." The public praise for Aspinall's efforts marked a complete reversal by Arizona's CAP contingent.[61]

On May 15 debate finally began in the House of Representatives on the Colorado River Basin Project bill. Under a standard House agree-ment, debate was limited to four hours (spread over two days): two under the control of Chairman Aspinall, and two under the control of ranking minority committee member John Saylor. The chairman spoke first for fifteen minutes, reviewing the history of development in the Colorado River Basin, discussing the various features of the bill, and explaining why certain elements had been included.[62]

Aspinall closed his remarks by saying that timing was of the essence for this bill. Despite objections to the bill's cost, particularly during the Vietnam war, the chairman warned that "[t]he understandings that are embodied in this legislation and the procedures that will be set in motion by its enactment are so very important that this legislation must not be held up for economic reasons." Although CAP supporters had worried that Rep. Saylor might try to mount one last effort to add crippling amendments to the bill, by the second day of the debate it was clear that no serious challenges were forthcoming. The bill was not even put to a roll call—it ended up being passed by an overwhelming voice vote.[63]

Following the vote in the House, supporters and even opponents congratulated each other on bringing to an end the long and difficult struggle to pass the measure. Morris Udall wrote Aspinall a letter in which he thanked the chairman "for the great leadership you have provided on the water problems of the Colorado River. . . . Your generalship on [the bill] was superb and I was proud that you would let me play a role in the Committee and in the debate." Udall closed his letter with the promise that during the negotiations with the Senate, "You will be my leader, as always." Rep. John Rhodes also wrote a letter to the chairman in which he too commented on "the great leadership on [Aspinall's] part which has made this possible. All the way through, you have quarterbacked the whole team, and have made your moves with the skill and sense of timing which we have all come to expect and appreciate."[64]

In his reply to Rhodes, Aspinall commented that passage of the bill had "appeared to help restore some confidences that had been somewhat badly strained. It made me appreciate once more the values that can be secured in a real team effort." Aspinall stressed in his closing, however, that not all team members were equal. He noted that "I intend to use my position as chairman to control the decisions in [the House-Senate] conference as far as the House is concerned. This does not mean, however, that I shall be arbitrary. I think you know me well enough to understand what I mean."[65]

Despite all the praise, final passage of the Colorado River Basin Project bill would not take place for several more months. In the meantime, behind-the-scenes negotiations went on between the House and the Senate, primarily between Rep. Aspinall and Sen. Henry Jackson, to resolve their differences over the water importation issue. On July 15 a formal House-Senate Conference was established to work out the differences between the House and Senate versions of the CRBP bill, with each chamber represented by seven members. After two weeks of meetings, the conference committee voted thirteen to one to approve a compromise bill, with pro-conservationist Rep. John Saylor casting the only negative vote. Congress then recessed for the rest of August.[66]

During the recess Aspinall went home to campaign for the fall election. In a newspaper interview he expressed general satisfaction with the compromise bill, especially the requirement that Colorado's five projects be constructed at the same time as the Central Arizona Project. The only feature he criticized, but accepted, was a provision Sen. Jackson had insisted on that formally barred the federal government for ten years from even investigating the possibility of importing water into the Colorado River. Aspinall, however, was philosophical about the ban. "[T]he time will pass quickly and meanwhile we can continue studies of augmenting the river through [other means]." On September 5, the chairman once again appeared before the House of Representatives to introduce and endorse the conference committee's version of the Colorado River Basin Project bill. Following a brief debate the bill passed on a voice vote.[67]

Almost as soon as President Johnson signed the Colorado River Basin Project bill into law on September 30, 1968, the coalition that had secured passage for the measure began to fall apart. Chairman Aspinall's warnings that the CRBP bill could well be the last chance for Colorado to secure new reclamation projects for itself turned out to be prophetic. In the thirty years since Congress approved the CRBP no new major reclamation projects have been authorized by the federal government. In some ways it was already too late in 1968 for Colorado's five newly authorized reclamation projects. Despite the chairman's best efforts to link construction of these five projects with the construction of the Central Arizona Project, the Colorado projects quickly lagged behind the CAP when subsequent Congresses simply ignored the requirement that they be developed simultaneously. Eventually only two of the five projects, the Dolores and the Dallas Creek, would be built; a third, the Animas–La Plata, remains in developmental limbo.[68]

The passage of the Colorado River Basin Project was the logical culmination of Aspinall's legislative career. Throughout his political life, Aspinall had always been vigilant about protecting Colorado's water allotment. In this instance, however, Aspinall may have been too vigilant. His position as chairman gave the congressman a *de facto* veto over reclamation projects and ensured that water legislation would have to meet his demands, in this case the inclusion of the five Colorado projects. The ultimate failure of these projects and the collapse of the larger CAP coalition was due in part to anger over Aspinall's use and abuse of his influential position.

Whereas representatives from Arizona thought that Aspinall would automatically support the Central Arizona Project since they had supported the earlier Colorado River Storage Project, the chairman felt no obligation to return past favors and instead exploited the situation to further benefit his district. Although Aspinall believed he was protecting the future interests of the upper basin, other members of Congress resented what they saw as the chairman's heavy-handed exploitation of his position for personal political gain. Although the battle over the CRBP demonstrated the considerable power Aspinall had acquired in water issues, the political tide was rapidly turning against him. In 1970 he would face the first primary election challenge of his congressional career, and two years later he would be swept from office.

All the King's Men

> Too often, it seems [Aspinall] serves the Western Slope that
> elected him the first time more than two decades ago . . . not
> the Western Slope that exists today.
> —Ian M. Thompson, *Durango Herald*[1]

B Y THE EARLY 1970S Wayne Aspinall had developed a national reputation as a politically powerful member of Congress and one of the most
influential legislators on natural resources issues. This position of prominence was reflected in the articles about the chairman, bearing laudatory
headlines, published in national newspapers. The *New York Times* published a profile of Aspinall entitled "Persuasive Land Use Counselor," and
the *Washington Post* called the congressman "Boss of the West," while the
Wall Street Journal gave him the most exalted description, "Ruler of the
Land." These articles shared a common theme: Aspinall, "more than any
other man, has been responsible in the last dozen years for shaping use of
land and water in America." Even GOP officials acknowledged the chairman's influence. At the 1968 Republican National Convention, Rep.
Rogers Morton, a Republican from Maryland, waxed so laudatory about
Aspinall while speaking to the Colorado delegation that he neglected to
mention any GOP officeholders from the state.[2]

Even as the chairman basked in this national visibility, various factors
were eroding his influence and power. Among these elements were his
advancing age, the growing environmental movement, changing presidential administrations in Washington, new and emerging voter demographics back home, and shifting congressional district boundaries. Aspinall also came under attack from prominent people who viewed him as a
symbol of the corrupt, seniority-based, pork-barrel system in Congress.
All these factors combined to raise doubts about whether Aspinall could,
or should, continue to dominate natural resource decisions to the degree
that he had in the past. Aspinall did make some effort to understand and
adapt to these changing political realities, but his efforts ultimately proved
unsuccessful.[3]

The most obvious challenge to Aspinall's continued political prominence was his advancing age. The chairman turned seventy-four in 1970, well past the age when most people have given up an active career. While old age does not automatically preclude one's seeking political office (particularly in Washington, D.C.), it can undermine a politician's clout if the public comes to believe that he or she will soon be leaving office. In fact, rumors of Aspinall's imminent retirement had been circulating for more than a decade, often at the congressman's own instigation. Aspinall's retirement, however, always remained four to six years away. The constant recession of this event seems to have been partly due to the chairman's preoccupation with seeing all the reclamation projects he had authorized reach the construction stage. He also seemed concerned that there were no other Colorado politicians of equal stature who would be able to defend the state's interests in Washington once he retired.[4]

There was a certain irony in the congressman's occasional talk about retiring, for he was quick to quell the discussion whenever anybody else raised the topic. When a rumor circulated in 1969 that he would step down, the chairman sent a letter to the editor of the *Durango Herald* dismissing the notion and observing, "I am carrying one of the heaviest loads on the Hill and enjoying it. When I no longer can put out more than the average Member . . . I'll bow out of the picture." In a separate letter to a constituent Aspinall insisted that he would not cling to the office, noting that "I have seen people stay too long and I don't intend to do that."[5]

Although the decision on whether or not to retire voluntarily was always his alone to make, one thing Aspinall could not control was the redistricting efforts of the Colorado Legislature. In 1964, as a result of a series of U.S. Supreme Court rulings on the "one man–one vote" doctrine, the state of Colorado was forced to redraw the boundaries of its congressional districts for the first time since 1921. Aspinall's Fourth District was particularly vulnerable, since it contained only 195,000 voters compared with the Second District's 654,000.[6]

After several months of debate, the Republican-controlled state legislature finally approved a plan that kept all of the Western Slope in the Fourth District. To increase the district's population base, the legislature added the Democratic stronghold of the San Luis Valley in south central Colorado, and the northern tier of Republican counties in the northeast corner of the state. Aspinall's newly configured district was geographically one of the largest in the country, covering 64,000 square miles and extending all

The Fourth Congressional District, 1964–1972. (Map by Stephen Cox and Alexander Smith Design)

the way from the border with Nebraska to the tip of Arizona. This new district presented significant political challenges for Aspinall, since it simultaneously gave him a more liberal Democratic Party membership with which to contend (thanks in large part to the addition of two college towns, Fort Collins and Greeley) and made the general voter profile for the district more conservative owing to the new Republican areas.[7]

The results of the 1964 election, however, suggested that Aspinall would have no trouble with his new district. Riding the coattails of President Johnson's 1964 election landslide, the congressman won every county in his district and received more than 100,000 votes—the highest vote tally of his career. Despite the success of his campaign, Aspinall remained cynical about the new additions to his district, later noting that as long as he continued to win his old district he only needed 10,000 votes from the Front Range to win, but he was quick to add that "I would like [the new voters] to be on my side, too."[8]

Even though the congressman did not worry much about the votes in the new parts of his district, he did look after the interests of the voters living there. Given his support for reclamation, it is not surprising that Aspinall quickly became a major proponent for a water project in the newly added part of his district. The Narrows Dam and reservoir, designed to regulate the flow of the South Platte River near Fort Morgan, had been under consideration for nearly sixty years by the time Aspinall inherited the region. The chairman worked with the Bureau of Reclamation to promote the project and even obtained a congressional reauthorization of the Narrows in 1970 (the project was originally approved in 1944). Ultimately, though, after Aspinall left office, the effort was abandoned when local farmers, the supposed beneficiaries of the project, expressed opposition to it and questions arose about the project's financial viability.[9]

In the early 1970s Aspinall also continued to lobby for construction funds for the various unfinished projects on the Western Slope. He was particularly active on behalf of the five Colorado projects for which he had obtained approval as part of the Colorado River Basin Project in 1968. The chairman was becoming increasingly impatient with the slow pace at which these projects were proceeding. With a Republican president in office, the congressman found his influence with the White House and the Interior Department sharply curtailed, and with no new major reclamation projects pending in the West, Aspinall had fewer options for political horse-trading. Facing these political realities, Aspinall tried to use his prominent position as a bully pulpit to build public support for reclamation and to warn water project supporters about the dangers of inertia.[10]

If Aspinall thought it was acceptable to criticize the Nixon Administration and its policies, other people thought it was the chairman who deserved criticism. The chairman's two most prominent critics in the late 1960s and early 1970s were the journalist Jack Anderson and the consumer advocate Ralph Nader. The two, however, criticized different aspects of the congressman's public life: Anderson attacked Aspinall's practices, while Nader attacked his policies.

In his weekly newspaper column, Jack Anderson published several articles sharply criticizing Aspinall for engaging in activities that, according to Anderson, showed the chairman to be a corrupt mouthpiece for the extractive industries. In a December 1969 column, Anderson reported on a private retreat that Aspinall hosted at a West Virginia resort for top Interior Department officials and lobbyists from the oil industry. Three months later, Anderson complained about a gathering sponsored by the cattle lobby that took place at the Rayburn House Office Building. Although lobbying events were not normally held in the building, the columnist noted that the person who arranged to have the reception there was also the guest of honor at the event: Chairman Aspinall. In October 1971 Anderson reported that Aspinall, in his capacity as chair of the Public Land Law Review Commission, had hired a lawyer, at taxpayers' expense, to devise a plan showing that oil and coal production did not damage the environment. Aspinall, for his part, dismissed Anderson as having "a questionable reputation for . . . use of half-truths and innuendoes and . . . outright lies."[11]

While the chairman largely ignored Anderson's accusations, he reacted far more angrily to Ralph Nader's criticisms. In November 1971, Nader's Study Group released a report that attacked the federal reclamation program in general and Aspinall in particular. Nader's group reported that the reclamation program had harmed the environment and wasted millions of dollars on cost overruns. The report was particularly critical of Chairman Aspinall and the role he played in adding the five Colorado projects to the Central Arizona Project bill. The report concluded that the whole reclamation program was suffering from "Aspinall Syndrome": the justification of public spending based on questionable economics and special-interest politics.[12]

The congressman quickly dismissed Nader's report. In a press release two days later, the chairman stated that the attack was "so unrealistic and unsupported by facts that it does not deserve serious consideration by knowledgeable individuals." In a letter to a constituent several days later, Aspinall continued to be dismissive of the report but conceded that he had not read it and was basing his opinion on what had been published in the newspapers. Aspinall ignored Ralph Nader in subsequent years when the consumer advocate, as part of a larger investigation of Congress, published a report that called attention to the fact that the chairman received most of his political contributions from natural resource development industries. Nader also published a report that criticized Aspinall's heavy hand in chairing the House Interior Committee.[13]

Aspinall could, to a certain extent, ignore criticisms from the press and public advocates, but it was more difficult for him to ignore complaints from his own committee members. By the early 1970s Aspinall faced a serious challenge to his iron-handed control of the Interior Committee. The leader of "the Crazies," as the committee rebels were called by other committee members, was Democratic Rep. Phil Burton. A tall, loud ultraliberal, Burton was the complete antithesis of the short, taciturn, conservative chairman. Rep. Burton joined the Interior Committee in 1964 and quickly set his sights on breaking the chairman's power. He bragged about this goal at the time to Sierra Club leader Edgar Wayburn, who thought Burton's idea was absurd.[14]

The California congressman later explained the reason he clashed with the chairman. According to Burton, the committee was "[l]ike a kindergarten. You [had] to raise your hand to ask to go to the bathroom." Even with permission, a member left a committee meeting at his own risk. Burton recalled that one time he offered an amendment to a bill and then went to the restroom. "My amendment was deleted while I was in the can. . . . That was the trigger mechanism [for my rebellion]." Aspinall responded that "Burton's trouble was that he didn't want to go to kindergarten. He came in as a freshman congressman, but he wanted to run before he could crawl."[15]

Perhaps a more apt description would have characterized Burton as a rebellious teenager determined to "show the old man." In a direct challenge to Aspinall's authority, Burton deliberately arrived late one day to a committee hearing, stopping to talk with spectators in the room, blowing his nose loudly once he sat down at the committee table, and interrupting Aspinall when he was asking questions. Apart from such sophomoric conduct, Burton also began organizing a more serious challenge to the chairman's power. The California congressman began to recruit other liberal politicians to join him on the Interior Committee. Along with this bloc of "Crazies," Burton cultivated the support of more restrained committee members, such as Morris Udall and Tom Foley (who later would become Speaker of the House), who agreed to support his push for organizational reform. He even gained support from Republican members of the committee who objected not only to Aspinall's rigid reign but also to the heavy-handed control of their own ranking minority member, John Saylor.[16]

Before the rebels could act, Aspinall lost part of his power as a result of a reform bill passed by the House in 1970. Under the new rules, the majority party caucus gained a veto power over committee chairs's selection of subcommittee chairs, thus partially curbing the cronyism that pervaded the selection process. A more important change affecting the Interior Committee was that subcommittee chairs gained the right to set their own meeting agendas, a power Aspinall had always jealously guarded. In an apparent response to this development, Aspinall created a new Subcommittee on the Environment with the right to consider any legislation assigned to the full Interior Committee. Aspinall then appointed himself chair of this subcommittee.[17]

These changes, however, did not go far enough for the "Crazies," who pushed for further internal committee reforms the following year. When the Interior Committee met to organize itself formally for the new Congress, Burton submitted a list of rule changes, all of which were direct challenges to Aspinall's power, and all of which passed. One change was to allow subcommittee chairs to hire their own staffs (Aspinall had done all the hiring in the past). Another change, which garnered the support of Republican committee members, stipulated that there would be one minority staff member for every two majority staff members. Prior to this, the Republican members had all shared one staff person. One GOP representative later recalled, "This improbable alignment of bitter philosophical enemies had so much fun spanking the chairman, they kept it up for another full day and changed a whole series of rules." Among the other changes, the committee gained the right to vote on the selection of all subcommittee chairs and stripped Aspinall and Saylor of the right to appoint members to serve on House-Senate conference committees. Aspinall, who did not participate in the debate, accepted the rule changes when he realized he did not have the votes to stop them. Later, though, he complained that it was like "having the sergeants making decisions for the captain" and that he was resigned to letting the world "go to hell in a straight jacket."[18]

While the chairman had contempt for the open rebellion in his committee, a more worrisome, and less public, threat to his political power was also occurring—his personal friends were beginning to lose respect for him. By the early 1970s, supporters from Colorado who had known and worked with Aspinall for decades were beginning to feel that he had lost touch with the district and local people, was no longer accessible to constituents, and instead had become caught up in the power and prestige of his office.[19]

Charles Traylor, Aspinall's campaign manager from 1950 to 1970, later pointed to the chairman's frequent world traveling on congressional junkets as evidence that "power had gone to his head." Tommy Neal, a former staff member, said that Aspinall's public image as a "crusty old curmudgeon raping the environment and ramming his bill through" further undermined the congressman's political reputation at home, where voters were growing increasingly sympathetic to the environmental movement. Felix Sparks, the director of the Colorado Water Conservation Board in the 1960s and 1970s, claims that Aspinall started thinking he was too important to do the small tasks that helped maintain good relations with the people back in the district. Sparks in particular remembers two instances when he and other people from Aspinall's district arrived for previously arranged appointments with the congressman, only to have Aspinall blow up at them for bothering him. Aspinall did admit to having a temper, but he later claimed he was only "short with people who won't do their homework."[20]

Whether because of his temperament, his reputation, or his political point of view, Aspinall's grasp on his district was slipping. Although he had won a decisive victory in 1964, he had actually won a higher percentage of the vote four years earlier (71 percent in 1960 versus 63 percent in 1964), and his margin of victory steadily eroded as the 1960s progressed. The 44,000-vote margin he enjoyed in 1964 dwindled to 24,000 in 1966; by 1968 it had shrunk to 16,000. By 1970, Aspinall appeared vulnerable to a challenge not only from a Republican candidate, but from a Democratic one as well.[21]

In early 1970 rumors again circulated that Aspinall planned to retire. However, at the end of March, the congressman held a press conference at which he unofficially announced he would run again. Aspinall claimed that he had talked to various Democratic Party officials within his district and "I'm in a position to say that it appears to be the unanimous opinion . . . they'd like to have me run again." This blanket endorsement, in fact, caught his supporters by surprise, since many of them thought he should retire.[22]

The congressman had successfully dodged the threat of a primary race four years earlier, and in the spring of 1970 Aspinall gave no suggestion in his correspondence that he was expecting one this time around. He did indicate, however, that he anticipated increased political opposition from Larimer and Weld counties, and particularly from the faculty and student bodies at Colorado State University and the University of Northern Colorado. The congressman expressed puzzlement over this apparent political rift between himself and these college communities. "I cannot understand why it is that I have such difficulty getting support out of [college] personnel, but I do. Maybe I don't work hard enough at it." Aspinall did not seem concerned that he would be attacked by the college faculty and students for his environmental record; instead he feared that he would be criticized for his support of the war in Vietnam.[23]

Aspinall's political insight proved to be correct when a candidate did emerge to challenge the chairman for the Democratic Party's nomination. The congressman's first Democratic opponent since 1948 turned out to be the mayor of Greeley, Richard Perchlik, a political science professor at the University of Northern Colorado, who announced he would run on a peace platform. At a press conference Perchlik criticized Aspinall's age and the congressman's voting record on "human issues." He also criticized Aspinall's environmental record and said that congressional representation "means more to a nation than just water projects." However, even Perchlik readily admitted that he was "a long shot" to beat the congressman.[24]

Despite initial press hoopla over his candidacy, Perchlik ran a very simple (or, as one observer described it, poor) campaign, which was hindered by the fact that he spent only two weeks actively touring the district. In public statements, Perchlik did not focus his criticisms on Aspinall's environmental record, and in one newspaper interview he even expressed support for transmontane water diversions to the Front Range, a statement that did nothing to enhance his already poor political stature on the Western Slope. Perchlik instead focused his political criticism on Aspinall's past support for the Vietnam War, an attack weakened in part by the congressman's announcement that he now favored withdrawing from Vietnam as soon as possible.[25]

Aspinall also conducted a fairly limited campaign, and in fact insisted that he was not even actively campaigning (which would have forced him to publicly acknowledge he had a primary opponent), but merely touring the district. In a September letter, Aspinall explained his philosophy of campaigning, which had remained largely unchanged over the past forty years. "I think that continual handshaking, stating one's qualities, making as little reference as possible to one's opponent and just comradeship with the voters are the most important things. . . . Where there is a policy question . . . then we have to get out on a limb occasionally, which is perfectly all right." Given Aspinall's outspoken nature on most issues, this statement on campaign strategy was remarkably demure.[26]

Aspinall's modest approach to electioneering helped hide the fact that, behind the scenes, the congressman's campaign was receiving reports suggesting his support was soft. Charles Traylor, Aspinall's campaign manager, passed along a report that some party leaders were complaining that the congressman "paid more attention to the Republicans [voters] than the Democrats," and that Aspinall "no longer cared about the little problems of the Democrats," which one party leader attributed more to Aspinall's "ego than age." Perhaps the unkindest cut was that, despite all the congressman's efforts to obtain federal projects for his district, some constituents actually complained, "Well, what has our Congressman really ever done for this area?" Party leaders attributed this comment more to political amnesia than to a direct rejection of Aspinall's achievements.[27]

Despite all the grumbling, Democratic voters in the Fourth District eventually decided that they preferred the old over the new. Aspinall crushed Perchlik in the September primary, winning approximately 19,000 votes to Perchlik's 7,500, and taking most counties by a five-to-one margin. Perchlik won only two counties, Larimer and Pitkin, and even lost in his home county of Weld. Perchlik's primary challenge did, however, have a lingering effect on Aspinall. During the general election campaign the seventy-four-year-old congressman repeatedly stressed the fact that he was "relevant" and said he wanted to bring young people into the establishment in order to reach an "understanding between youth and their elders."[28]

Aspinall went on to beat his Republican opponent, Bill Gossard, in the November general election, but the results were closer than the congressman would have liked (55 percent to 45 percent). Aspinall claimed, however, that he did not worry much about election results. "I have always contended, and still do, that the people have been very good to me in their support and when they get ready to change their minds, I hope that I am man enough to accept the change of direction." Despite the congressman's professed relaxed attitude, this philosophy would be put to the test two years later.[29]

In response to the results from the 1970 census, the Republican-dominated Colorado legislature in 1972 again redrew the boundaries of the Fourth Congressional District. Early speculation suggested that the new district might be less favorable for Aspinall, but the congressman publicly expressed no fear. He even taunted Republicans in the fall of 1971 that they could "gerrymander this state anyway they want to, but I've been gerrymandered before." One of the congressman's staff members, Bill Cleary, indicated that "there really aren't too many ways that [the legislature] can hurt [Aspinall] with re-districting."[30]

This assessment soon proved too optimistic, as Republican legislators proposed a plan in the spring of 1972 that called for splitting the Western Slope between the Third and Fourth Districts. One GOP member even claimed that the legislature had specifically designed the proposal to target Aspinall, although most legislators seemed to believe that he could win again but would retire in the near future in any case. Aspinall was, not surprisingly, opposed to the division of the Western Slope and, despite claiming he did not wish to interfere with the Colorado legislature's decision, he wrote to legislators to let them know he opposed the measure. Aspinall's efforts were in vain, though, and the legislature approved the plan. Republican Governor John Love, a friend of Aspinall, announced that he was unhappy with the proposed split of the Western Slope, but that it would be "irresponsible" to veto the measure. Ultimately the governor allowed the bill to become law without his signature.[31]

By May Aspinall's earlier optimism that the legislature could do no harm had been replaced by the conviction that it could do no good. The congressman wrote, "I am of the opinion that its action was the worst possible action that could have been taken in the interest of Western Colorado and the relationship between Western Colorado and Eastern Colorado." Under the provisions of the new law, the nineteen counties in the southwest corner of Colorado were transferred from the Fourth District to the Third, while the northern portion of Aspinall's district was expanded to include four new counties. The biggest change to the Fourth district, however, was the addition of 90,000 Denver area voters in the northwest corner of Adams county.[32]

For the first time in his congressional career Aspinall would no longer be representing the entire Western Slope. Instead he would be representing a district in which 75 percent of his constituents lived east of the Continental Divide (360,000 on the east compared with 80,000 on the west), with a significant portion of them living in the suburbs of Denver. In addition to geographic changes, Aspinall also had to deal with a major demographic change. The lowering of the voting age to eighteen raised the potential for an influx of large numbers of new, often ecology-minded voters. It was predicted that the congressman's constituency would now include 66,000 young, first-time voters. In order to respond to these changes, Aspinall would have to attempt to reinvent himself politically.[33]

In light of the drastic changes in his district, rumors again circulated in early 1972 that Aspinall might opt to retire rather than adapt to a new

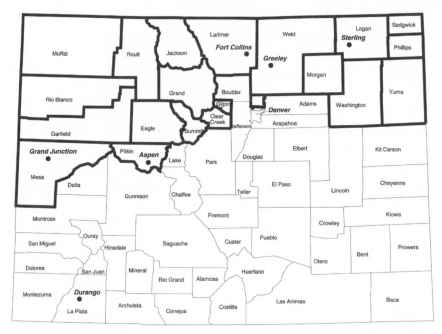

The Fourth Congressional District, 1972–1982. (Map by Stephen Cox and Alexander Smith Design)

constituency. These rumors gained momentum from the congressman's own ambivalent comments. In an April letter to a political supporter, Aspinall indicated that his decision to run would be based on the outcome of the legislature's redistricting debate. "If it is favorable, I am of the opinion that I shall make the race." The congressman then qualified his statement by adding, "I am not sure that I should, because I feel it is going to be a difficult one." A month later, when the legislature had approved an unfavorable redistricting plan, Aspinall changed his position on what would be the deciding factor on whether to run, now stating that while he thought he could serve another term, he "did not care for another primary." When another month had passed, and it became clear that he would indeed be facing a primary challenge, Aspinall wrote that "I have never shied away from a contest" but that his difficulty in reaching a decision was in "trying to figure out whether the people still want me." The congressman apparently felt a ground swell when several campaign supporters from throughout the district publicly called for him to enter the race. The next day he formally announced his candidacy. After launching his re-election bid, Aspinall insisted that the only reason he had decided to run was that there was no other viable candidate, either Democrat or Republican, to represent the Western Slope.[34]

Aspinall certainly did not think that either of his two Democratic primary challengers could handle the task. One challenger, Doug Phelps, was a twenty-four-year-old Harvard law student who maintained his legal residence in Fort Collins and described his politics as "radical populism." The second challenger was Alan Merson, a thirty-eight-year-old law professor at the University of Denver, who maintained a small law practice and residence in the town of Breckenridge. Merson attacked Aspinall on a number of issues: the war in Vietnam, the chairman's age, and the environment. On the latter issue, Merson accused the congressman of embracing "a 19th-century philosophy which holds that every damned square inch of public land must go to commercial use." This philosophy, Merson maintained, "helped win the West. But the West has been won. We are now losing it." Merson complained that Aspinall had lost touch with the people back home and instead now represented a "special constituency" of corporate lobbyists for the extractive industries.[35]

The Denver media largely dismissed the two challengers as political neophytes, and Aspinall privately spoke of them with a mixture of confusion, concern, and contempt. As late as April, Aspinall indicated puzzlement over who exactly "Mersin" was, and by early summer he was trying to find out information about the law professor. The congressman also made inquiries to local party officials about Phelps, and whether Phelps's candidacy would more seriously cut into Aspinall's support or Merson's. While he did acknowledge the possibility of defeat in the September primary, Aspinall seemed more inclined to dismiss his challengers. In a June letter to a constituent the congressman commented on the bearded Phelps and clean-shaven Merson, observing "I apparently have two opponents. One wears his hair long and over his face; the other apparently has worn his the same in days past."[36]

Initially the congressman had to worry only about the two opponents in the Democratic primary, but as the campaign got under way it became apparent that Aspinall faced an additional challenge—environmentalists were mounting a national campaign to defeat him. In June 1972 a group calling itself Environmental Action held a press conference in Washington, D.C., to announce that it had ranked Aspinall first on its list of Congress's "Dirty Dozen"—the top twelve "anti-environmental" congressmen the group would be targeting for defeat in the upcoming elections. The spokesman for Environmental Action issued a scathing critique of Aspinall, characterizing the chairman as "a devoted supporter of oil shale, lumber, and ranching interests" who had given away public land to oil companies and had tried to thwart attempts to establish Redwood National Park.[37]

The press conference received only passing coverage in the Colorado media, and the tone in most of the stories conveyed the message that Environmental Action was an insignificant group of environmental busybodies who had no real familiarity with Colorado issues and concerns. Politicians, however, were not as quick to dismiss the political effects of environmental labels. In September 1971, Sen. Gordon Allott sent a memo to the Nixon White House discussing potential election issues in Colorado for 1972. Allott identified the environment as one of the two most important statewide topics (the other was the economy), surpassing even the war in Vietnam. Rep. Pete McCloskey later recalled that congressmen learned to take the Environmental Action list seriously after seven of the twelve politicians on the first list were defeated in 1970 (one of whom was Denver Rep. Byron Rogers).[38]

Aspinall was publicly dismissive of the listing, viewing it as nothing more than rhetoric by extreme environmentalists. He professed no fear that it would have an effect on his re-election chances, although he also said that if he did lose as a result of such a tactic, "perhaps I'd be lucky to get out of Congress." In private, however, Aspinall requested an investigation of Environmental Action by the House Committee on Standards to determine if the organization had violated any tax laws. The congressman, however, soon had a more serious environmental problem to deal with when the League of Conservation Voters announced that it would contribute $15,000 to Merson's campaign—a sizable amount in 1972.[39]

Aspinall also had bad news from inside his campaign. For the first time in his career the congressman hired an advertising agency to help in the election. The agency prepared a lengthy paper examining Aspinall's current political status and focused on the redistricting challenge the congressman faced and the different groups targeting him for defeat. The report bluntly concluded "[r]e-electing Wayne Aspinall is a vastly difficult task and anyone involved in the campaign should start with the full realization that he is a definite underdog in the primary." The only way to win, according to the evaluation, was a hard-hitting campaign that actively targeted his opponent. One theme the agency suggested was that Aspinall, rather than the radical Left supporters of George McGovern, was the "real" Democrat. The report even discussed ways to deal with the "crotchetiness" issue.[40]

Advertising for the Aspinall campaign tried to follow the agency's recommondation of a proactive strategy designed to address potential attacks by the Merson campaign before the Merson campaign had a chance to make them. Among the themes the Aspinall campaign stressed was his seniority and influence in Washington, and the fact that the "interests" he represented affected everybody. The campaign also tried to discredit Merson for his stance on gun control and by linking him with student radicals.[41]

The first hurdle the campaign faced was the Democratic District Assembly in July that would determine the order in which party candidates were listed on the primary ballot. Aspinall indicated in letters to supporters that he assigned a great deal of importance to securing the first line on the ballot. "If I can get top line on the primary ballot, I think the primary will be hard-fought but it will be favorable to me." At the Assembly Doug Phelps failed to receive enough support to gain a place on the ballot, but Alan Merson scored an upset by beating Aspinall for the top spot. Despite this display of strength by Merson, Aspinall did not begin actively campaigning for re-election until late August, just a few weeks before the September 12 primary. At a press conference kicking off the campaign, Aspinall stressed that his seniority was a blessing for his district and for Colorado. The congressman also explained that he was running for re-election because of his involvement in three ongoing issues: land-use planning, surface coal mining, and a national energy policy.[42]

The day-to-day campaign Aspinall conducted was, he admitted at the time, not very different from his past campaigns. The chairman focused on personally visiting all the counties in his district to shake hands and talk with voters. This strategy, however, did not work very well in the new suburban parts of the congressman's district. In the past Aspinall had participated in sizable car caravan tours of the small communities on the Western Slope. With its loudspeakers and balloons, the caravan drew a lot of attention when it arrived, and people would turn out to hear the congressman speak when the caravan stopped in the town center. This caravan strategy was of little use in the suburban communities along the Front Range; often these communities did not even have a town center. Aspinall tried to adapt his techniques by visiting shopping malls, but, as the congressman's assistant, Bill Cleary, later reminisced, you could not even tell if the people you were talking with lived in your district or had driven there from somewhere else to go shopping. Once, after accompanying Aspinall on a campaign swing through Adams County, Cleary recalls, the congressman asked him whether he thought it had gone well. When Cleary replied that he could not tell, Aspinall confessed that he did not know either.[43]

Aspinall's reelection efforts suffered from strategic mistakes and bad publicity. Perhaps the most serious political mistake occurred when Rep. Aspinall failed to follow up on an endorsement offer from Floyd Marks, the district attorney for Adams County, who was active in local Democratic affairs. When Aspinall did not return Mark's phone call, the D.A., feeling his offer had been spurned, endorsed Alan Merson instead. Having bungled a potential endorsement, the Aspinall campaign then proceeded to invent one. In early August, Edgar Wayburn, a former Sierra Club president, sent Aspinall a routine letter thanking him for his vote in favor of legislation establishing the Golden Gate Recreation Area in San Francisco. The Aspinall campaign quickly issued a press release, which the local papers picked up, claiming that the Sierra Club had endorsed the congressman. The next day the Sierra Club issued a press release stating unequivocally that the organization had not endorsed Aspinall, and that Wayburn's letter was a personal communication and not an official club statement. Aspinall quickly called Wayburn to apologize and issued a formal retraction.[44]

In addition to self-inflicted political and public relations injuries, Aspinall contended with a rash of negative national coverage. In early September the *New York Times* criticized his environmental record and endorsed Merson in the primary. While the paper acknowledged that it was odd for it to take a stand on a congressional race in Colorado, "[b]ecause of the inordinate power that seniority carries with it on Capitol Hill, a local choice in the Colorado primary is clearly much more than a local concern." In response the Aspinall campaign issued a press release denouncing this "arrogant" and "insulting" intervention in Colorado's affairs.[45]

The *New York Times,* however, was not the only national publication to criticize the congressman. *Field & Stream* magazine also attacked Aspinall's environmental record. In a ranking of congressional candidates in its September issue the magazine listed the chairman as "in a class by himself. The man who absolutely must go." Harsh criticism also came from *Reader's Digest,* which in its September issue attacked Aspinall for allowing public lands to be taken captive by private interests and claimed that the congress-man was "180 degrees out of phase with today's environmental move-ment." When asked about these articles, Aspinall simply dismissed them as the rantings of "extreme environmentalists" who want "to 'lock up' vast areas of the West where they can 'play' and give no thought to the eco-nomic consequences."[46]

As the campaign drew to a close, no clear public consensus had emerged as to who would win, although the *Rocky Mountain News* wrote that Merson had "a solid chance to beat" the incumbent. On the day of the primary even Aspinall expressed uncertainty. In a letter to a friend that morning the congressman wrote, "This test today may be a little bit more difficult than some of my friends expect. It could be very, very close and again, I could win by a fairly good vote. We shall know later on this evening." In the end the election was close, and Merson won. The chal-lenger received 16,500 votes (53 percent) to the congressman's 14,900 (47 percent). Sixty-three percent of Merson's support came from the Front Range, with heavy support from Fort Collins and Greeley, but he also did better than expected on the Western Slope. Perhaps Merson's most lop-sided, and symbolic, victory came in Pitkin County, which chose him over the congressman, 1,158 to 99. While the county had long been hostile to Aspinall, the transformation of Aspen into a wealthy, liberal, pro-environmental town further reinforced the antipathy between the community and their congressman.[47]

The longtime chairman's defeat triggered an avalanche of press cover-age, much of it focusing on the question of whether Aspinall's loss was a good thing for Colorado and what the congressman's legacy would be. Most of the local newspapers expressed the opinion that "Wayne Served the West Well." The *Denver Post* titled its editorial "Aspinall's Achieve-ments Will Stand the Test of Time." Not all writers, however, were so laudatory. Tom Gavin wrote a column titled "They're Sorry Aspinall Lost," which contained a long list of all the extractive industries that had contributed money to the congressman's campaign. Perhaps the harshest commentary about Aspinall's loss came from Pat Oliphant, who drew a political cartoon showing a massive redwood tree that a man was in the process of chopping down when it fell over and crushed him to death. The caption read "The Old Politics."[48]

The most somber assessment came, perhaps not surprisingly, from the *Daily Sentinel,* which titled its editorial "Defeat for Slope." The newspaper

This cartoon by Pat Oliphant ran in the *Denver Post* six days after Aspinall's defeat in the September 12, 1972, Democratic primary. (Oliphant © Universal Press Syndicate; reprinted with permission, all rights reserved)

argued that Aspinall's loss showed "how a Republican redistricting plan has made the Western Slope the wagging tail of a Front Range shaggy dog." "Yes," the editorial agreed, "we felt Aspinall served his 'special interests,' but they were Western Colorado which he represented with understanding and dedication." The newspaper warned that with the congressman's defeat "we probably can kiss all [Western] Slope water projects farewell because neither [party's candidate] will have the clout and the political know-how to shepherd the projects to culmination—even if either happens to have the desire."[49]

The reaction among Aspinall's friends and supporters varied. Some supporters blamed the loss on a "McGovernite" takeover of the Democratic Party. One of them, Amos Allard, who had served as the Democratic Party's Fourth Congressional District chairman, even switched affiliation to the Republican Party. (This switch would have long-term political ramifications when Amos's son, Wayne, also changed party affiliation as a result of the election. Wayne Allard eventually would be elected to the U.S. House of Representatives, and, in 1996, the U.S. Senate.) Other supporters were more resigned to the loss. Howard Scott, a former staff member, wrote the congressman, "One is tempted to grumble about a new breed of carpetbaggers infesting a state or people who discover conservation and ecology only after peeling down whole mountainsides for ski runs. But our state is populated as it is and grumbling won't change it."[50]

In looking back at the primary, Aspinall identified four factors, two major and two minor, which he believed cost him the election. The two major factors were redistricting and the "McGovernite takeover" of the Democratic Party. The minor factors, according to Aspinall, were his age and environmental opposition. While there is merit in each of these factors, looking back thirty years later two factors stand out: redistricting and environmentalists. The shifting boundaries of the Fourth Congressional District clearly made Aspinall vulnerable to a challenge by eliminating much of his political and geographic base. However, given the fairly narrow margin by which he lost, and the fact that Alan Merson lost the general election by a narrow margin to Republican James Johnson, it seems quite possible that had Aspinall started earlier and run a more energetic and competent campaign, he might well have been re-elected.[51]

What ultimately seems to have made the crucial difference between victory and defeat for Aspinall was the role that environmentalists—or, more accurately, environmental money—played in the primary. Given Aspinall's antagonism toward environmentalists, it is perhaps not surprising that he would downplay any role they had in his defeat. Environmentalists raised half the money spent during Merson's primary campaign—money that was crucial to his ability to mount a serious challenge to the incumbent congressman. Merson's total budget for the primary campaign was $41,000, at the time considered extremely high for a congressional race in a largely rural district. Of that amount, $15,000 came from the League of Conservation Voters, a far higher amount than the League spent in other primary races that year and an amount that reflected their determination to remove Aspinall from office.[52]

Environmentalists also provided Merson's campaign with traditional types of election support, such as campaigning door to door and providing volunteer staff work. If Merson had not received this assistance—both monetary and voluntary—from environmental groups, it is questionable whether his challenge would have been any more successful than Richard Perchlik's effort two years earlier. Despite Merson's loss in the November election, environmentalists achieved their real victory by preventing Aspinall from serving another term as chair of the House Interior Committee.[53]

Aspinall's defeat was part of a larger political realignment that was taking place at both state and federal levels in the early 1970s. In Colorado Aspinall's loss was followed that November by the defeat of three-term Republican Sen. Gordon Allott. That same election saw Colorado voters choose Pat Schroeder for Congress and reject an offer to host the 1976 Winter Olympics on the grounds it would cost too much and harm the environment. The election of 1974 continued this trend when Gary Hart beat two-term Republican Sen. Peter Dominick and Tim Wirth beat five-term Rep. Don Brotzman.[54]

The common denominator for these successful challengers was that they were young, liberal reformers who had largely come to power outside the normal Democratic Party establishment. Perhaps the archetype of the New Democrats was "super environmentalist" Richard Lamm, who was elected governor in 1974, ushering in an era of Democratic control of the governorship that lasted nearly a quarter of a century. The statewide nature of this political realignment could be seen in the election results for Lamm. Not only did the young challenger win in the traditionally Democratic parts of the state, but he also carried Colorado Springs and the Republican-leaning rural portions of the state. Aspinall's own reaction to these changes was bewilderment over why voters would willingly give up "eighty-four years" of combined political experience for politically powerless newcomers.[55]

On the national level, Aspinall's loss marked what Rep. Morris Udall described as "the end of an era." The political leaders who had played a crucial role in shaping natural resource development in general, and reclamation policy in particular, during the previous fifteen years were quickly leaving power. The exodus began in 1969 when Secretary of the Interior Steward Udall left office at the end of the Johnson administration, followed a few months later by Commissioner of Reclamation Floyd Dominy (whether Dominy left of his own free will or was pushed out by the Nixon administration is a point of debate). Aspinall's defeat, coupled with Allott's, removed two major proponents of natural resource development from Congress. Environmentalists also suffered losses when Sen. Clinton Anderson retired, and Rep. John Saylor died in office in 1973. The departure of these four was part of a larger shakeup that was occurring in Congress. Younger challengers scored major upsets against entrenched incumbents during the 1970 and 1972 elections, and by 1973 nearly one third of all committee chairs in the House of Representatives had been voted out by their constituents.[56]

Even in the environmental movement's moment of apparent victory, some environmental leaders were able to remember the human element behind the ideological battles. Sierra Club leader Edgar Wayburn, a longtime opponent of Rep. Aspinall, later recalled his last visit with the chairman.

> After he was beaten, I went in one last time to see him. Whereas you always had to wait your turn, and there were other people waiting to see the chairman, and he would usually give me five minutes, that day there was no one in his anteroom. They ushered me right in, and I saw Aspinall sitting at his big desk, surrounded by his lost grandeur. And the first thing he said was, "Thank you for coming in. I know there is no reason. You have nothing to ask of me now." I said, "No, I haven't. I just wanted to pay my respects and say we've always been on opposite sides of the fence, but I respected you for what you were doing and for the fair treatment you gave us." He said, "Well, I have the same regard for you."

In the end, the congressman was able to display a degree of cordiality that had been all too often absent in the heat of legislative battles.[57]

Wayne Aspinall did not, however, retire from public life when he left public office. Despite his claim that "I do not care to be put in the position of trying to have any affect upon the general public," the former congressman quickly went to work as a consultant, lobbyist, and officer for a variety of extractive industries and pro-development organizations. This flurry of activities led one person to describe Aspinall in retirement as "a congressman in exile."[58]

Some of the former congressman's most active work grew out of his involvement with various regional and national groups that viewed themselves as counterbalances to the environmental movement. Aspinall teamed up with former Republican Colorado Governor Johnny Vanderhoof (who had lost his bid for reelection to Richard Lamm in 1974) to become the leaders of Club 20, a pro-business, Western Slope lobbying organization. Aspinall also later joined forces with Joseph Coors to help found the Mountain States Legal Foundation. This organization, headed by future Secretary of the Interior James Watt, was a public-advocacy law firm that challenged environmental regulations. (Gail Norton, another future Secretary of the Interior, worked as an attorney for the foundation.)

Aspinall also became involved in several business ventures designed to develop natural resources in Colorado. His most visible business connection was his job as a consultant/lobbyist for American Metals Climax (AMAX), which had a molybdenum mining operation near Crested Butte. For his services, Aspinall received a $1,750 monthly stipend.[59]

By 1976 Aspinall was feeling increasingly alienated from his own political party. The former congressman was extremely critical of the nomination of Jimmy Carter, whom Aspinall viewed as out of touch with the realities of the West and under the influence of "extreme environmentalists." Aspinall also worried that the Republican Party would not give its nomination to his good friend and former congressional colleague Gerald Ford. Two months later, Aspinall broke ranks with other Democrats and endorsed Ford for reelection. At a press conference Aspinall complained that Carter was not qualified to be president; he "knows nothing about western Colorado," and his advisers "want to lock up western Colorado for the interests and pleasure of a few people."[60]

Aspinall undoubtedly felt vindicated when, a month after Carter took office, his administration announced plans to eliminate a number of proposed but economically questionable reclamation projects, including five in Colorado. The former congressman harshly criticized the decision, which he described as the product of "ignorant provincialism" (a phrase that could have been used against some of his own past actions as well). He complained bitterly that the opponents of these projects "had their day in court. However, they never give up. They worm their way into places of responsibility where they can sell their 'wares' again new. It is too bad that uninformed and unknowledgeable public office holders (some in high places) become victims of the provincialism of extremists." Aspinall took Carter's decision personally: "I can tell you that it didn't set well with me to have an individual, even a President of the United States, come in and undo a great deal of the work which I had helped to accomplish over a period of two decades." "I think it is fair to say that a 'flat land cracker' has no idea what the West needs in the way of development."[61]

On March 21, 1977, Aspinall testified before a regional hearing held by the Department of Interior reviewing the status of various reclamation projects in western Colorado. In his rather bitter remarks, the former congressman reviewed the history of federal reclamation in Colorado and insisted that all previously authorized projects were sound. He then complained about the new project criteria that the Carter administration had set forth. In a burst of hyperbole, Aspinall concluded that "If this Administration proposes to balance its budget at the expense of wise natural resource development, then the future holds very little hope for the continuing strength and virility of our nation—of our civilization." Then in another complaint aimed at Carter, Aspinall commented, "We in the reclamation West have been wronged by a President who has listened only to the enemies of reclamation. If this be treason in this part of the country, then so be it." (The next day Aspinall publicly backtracked on the comment, saying he did not mean to accuse Carter of treason, only to suggest that if criticizing the president was treason then the former congressman was guilty of it.) Aspinall later complained that the hearing "was about the worst that I have ever experienced." Given Aspinall's harsh comments about the president, it is not surprising that when he wrote Carter a lengthy letter in April defending the projects he received only a brief *pro forma* response from a low-level assistant.[62]

The Carter administration eventually abandoned its campaign to eliminate questionable reclamation projects, but of the five projects they had targeted in Colorado, only two (Dolores and Dallas Creek) were ever built. Despite the shift in policy, Aspinall continued to complain about the Carter administration's reclamation policies. In the 1980 election the Democratic politician again endorsed the GOP presidential candidate, only this time in private and with less enthusiasm. In a May 1980 letter Aspinall wrote to a friend, "I too did not vote for Carter last election, and I am less pleased with him now than I was then. I am not pleased with the Republican choice for President, but to be honest I think perhaps it is time for a change."[63]

Even though Ronald Reagan ran as a candidate opposed to "big government," Aspinall and other water project supporters believed that his election would usher in a new era of federal reclamation spending. The key, Aspinall argued in a letter to Sen. William Armstrong, was "to convince President Reagan and his advisors that the monies spent in water resources development of any kind are monies being used for producing new wealth, and are not dollars spent for ultimate consumption, such as welfare and kindred activities." Initially it did appear that some long-delayed projects might finally be built, and Aspinall was particularly optimistic in light of the appointment in 1981 of James Watt, the former president of the Mountain States Legal Foundation, as Reagan's Secretary of the Interior. The former congressman even made the exaggerated claim that he was "now working closely with Secretary Watt."[64]

A year later, however, in a letter to Watt, Aspinall expressed alarm over the administration's proposal to require the states to pay, up front, 35 percent of the total costs (both construction and operating) of any new reclamation projects. Aspinall warned that if the proposed changes went into effect, "I can say this without fear of contradiction that there will be no more Federal water projects." Even though the Reagan administration did not impose the new cost structure, the administration did tighten the various financial requirements enough so that Aspinall's fear came true: no new projects were constructed. What Carter had tried and failed to do, Reagan achieved—the reclamation era was over.[65]

One of the reasons Aspinall was so preoccupied throughout his career with developing reclamation projects on the Western Slope was that water was vital to the development of the region's oil shale industry. Aspinall had played an active role in promoting oil shale development, both during his time in Congress and, particularly, after his forced retirement. The former congressman's professional involvement with oil shale dated back to the first oil shale boom of the 1920s, when he had served as the attorney for a developer who spent a million dollars, and eventually went broke, trying to extract oil from oil shale. The fate of Aspinall's client was not an unusual one, for oil shale refining in many ways resembles the curse of Tantalus: the wealth is so close, yet just out of reach. Unlike oil or gas, which naturally occur in underground pockets, shale oil is embedded in rock and can only be extracted through an expensive and inefficient distillation process, which takes a large amount of rock and water to extract a small amount of oil, and results in large quantities of spent shale rock and waste water.[66]

After Aspinall left Congress he became actively involved in the oil shale industry. He joined the board of directors for Paraho Oil Shale Demonstration, Inc., where his chief responsibility was to lobby former colleagues in Congress and the Colorado state government on oil shale issues. As a result of his efforts, Aspinall became known as a key player in the oil shale industry, which responded by making frequent financial contributions to regional organizations on his behalf. The former congressman's active support of oil shale, however, was not based on a desire for personal wealth. Although he was on Paraho's board of directors, Aspinall owned no stock in the company and only received a minor stipend. The former congressman's involvement in oil shale development came from his belief that oil shale was the key to the Western Slope's industrial expansion and would help strengthen the nation by decreasing its dependence on foreign oil. In a 1975 interview Aspinall predicted that "oil shale must make its contribution or otherwise we as a nation [will] suffer," and in a January 1982 presentation to the Western Mining Congress Aspinall again predicted "that [oil shale] will be developed when the national security of our nation demands such development."[67]

Aspinall told the Western Mining Congress that "the development of oil shale will not come about by the granting of large direct financial subsidies given by government at any level. [T]hrowing large sums of money . . . into the operation, will not . . . guarantee a viable oil shale industry." Given that the former congressman had spent most of his career trying to funnel federal money into his district, this seems like a rather odd, perhaps even hypocritical statement to make, particularly since the oil shale industry had always been heavily dependent on government funding. Aspinall, however, was concerned that over-reliance on funding from the government would lead to excessive control by the government.[68]

Although Aspinall worked actively on oil shale's behalf, he sometimes admitted to doubts about whether the industry would ever succeed. In a letter to the head of the Paraho Corporation, Aspinall, referring to his long involvement with oil shale, wrote, "I have seen so many starts and stops in relation to shale that sometimes I become quite pessimistic. On the other hand I want you to know that I continue to be the great booster." While Aspinall occasionally expressed doubts, the industry did not. By 1980, the future for oil shale looked so bright that Exxon spent $400 million to buy ARCO's oil shale project. In February 1982 the vice president of Paraho Corporation predicted that oil shale would produce 13 million barrels of oil per year during the 1980s, 160 million per year in the 1990s, and eventually level out at 2 to 2.5 billion barrels per year around the year 2010.[69]

Instead, on May 2, 1982, the oil shale industry collapsed in an event that came to be known as "Black Sunday." That day the Exxon Corporation unexpectedly announced its plans to shut down the $5 billion Colony Oil Shale Project located near Parachute, Colorado. This decision, which Exxon's board of directors had secretly made five days earlier, resulted in the immediate termination of 2,100 employees at the project, and left another 7,500 support workers facing an uncertain future. The impact of this decision was not merely limited to employees at the project site.

People living throughout the Western Slope quickly realized that the recent economic boom in their region had abruptly ended. Over the next three years, 20,000 people moved out of the area, unemployment climbed to 9.5 percent, and 14.2 percent of local homes became vacant. Approximately $85 million in annual payroll disappeared from the local economy, and the region lapsed into an economic depression.[70]

The key factor in Exxon's abrupt abandonment of oil shale after only two years of active development in the region was the same one that had undermined previous attempts to launch the industry: oil shale was not an economically viable product. Even the record high prices for oil during the late 1970s had not been enough to make oil shale profitable, and by 1982 prices were starting to edge downward, which prompted Exxon's pullout. Ironically, Aspinall in a 1975 interview had predicted that a drop in oil prices could "put a damper" on oil shale development, but he had also dismissed the possibility of prices actually dropping.[71]

The Exxon pullout tempered, but did not fully undermine, Aspinall's faith in oil shale. In an October 1982 letter to the Paraho Corporation Aspinall wrote, "I am worried about the future, of course. On the other hand, we may be sitting in just the right place. We shall hope so." By the following March the eighty-six-year-old former congressman, now suffering from terminal prostate cancer, seemed more pessimistic and now spoke in favor of government funding for oil shale. Writing to the president of Paraho, Aspinall expressed his hope that the federal government "will look upon Paraho's request [for a bailout] favorably, otherwise I see a rather hard go for us in the days ahead." Despite his hopes, the future offered no recovery for either Aspinall or the oil shale industry. Seven months later, the former congressman died.[72]

One of the core beliefs in Aspinall's life was that the future economic success of the Western Slope depended upon developing the region's natural resources. This belief caused Aspinall to become a major proponent of reclamation projects and an opponent of environmental protection, an opposition that led the environmental movement to target him for defeat in 1972. Even in "retirement" Aspinall continued to lobby on behalf of regional development projects such as reclamation and oil shale. After spending nearly forty years trying to obtain federally funded development of natural resources as a way to secure the economic growth of the Western Slope, it seems ironic that Aspinall's death occurred at a time when that very development had devastated the region rather than saved it.

8

With Every Drop We Drink

You can't take a drink of water in Colorado without
remembering [Wayne Aspinall].
—Richard Lamm[1]

ON OCTOBER 9, 1983, Wayne Aspinall died at his home on the
banks of the Colorado River in Palisade, Colorado (ironically, on
the same day that Interior Secretary James Watt resigned). The death of
the eighty-seven-year-old former congressman prompted a wave of commentary in the state newspapers noting his importance to the state and the
region. The *Denver Post* praised Aspinall as "the most powerful Western
voice on land-management questions of the post–World War II era," a
man whose "diligence and love of the West are inspiring legacies." The
Rocky Mountain News described Aspinall as having been, in his prime,
"Colorado's most influential national officeholder," who, with a small
group of Democratic congressmen, "virtually ran the House of Representatives and, in part, the country." Aspinall had not always been well-loved
in the past, but acclaim for the congressman seemed universal at the time
of his death and even transcended political partisanship. The governor of
Colorado at the time, Richard Lamm, a Democrat, said, "Any good Colorado history book will recount his contributions." Former Republican
Governor John Vanderhoof simply commented, "He was Mr. West."[2]

Four years after Aspinall's death, however, the former congressman's
longtime campaign manager, Charles Traylor, complained in an interview
that people had already forgotten who Aspinall was and what he had done
for the West. Not everyone, though, had forgotten Aspinall. Three years
after Traylor's comment, in 1990, when Democratic Rep. George Miller
became chair of the House Interior Committee, he ordered Aspinall's
portrait removed from the committee hearing room and relegated to the
basement of the Capitol.[3]

These three very different types of reactions to Aspinall's memory
(praise, indifference, and hostility) suggest that there is not yet a clear

consensus on what the congressman's legacy is to Colorado and the West, and whether that legacy was positive or negative. A year before he died, Aspinall lamented that the people who had served Colorado often received little recognition. However, he was quick to add that he was pleased to have lived long enough for people to recognize his contributions. During the latter years of his life Aspinall certainly received his share of adulation and recognition. Mesa State College in Grand Junction established a Wayne Aspinall Visiting Professorship, which each year brings a scholar or public official to campus for five weeks. Not to be outdone, Western State College in Gunnison built a Wayne Aspinall Conference Center. In 1978, in recognition of Aspinall's long service at both state and federal levels, a bust of the former congressman was placed in the state capitol. The plaque on the statue bears a lengthy list of the offices that Aspinall held. It also describes him as a "Fruit Grower–Educator–Lawyer–Statesman," and sums up his career by saying that Aspinall acted as an "Advocate for the People; Advocate for Wise Use of Our Natural Resources." Perhaps the most appropriate honor occurred in 1981 when the Curecanti Unit of the Colorado River Storage Project (consisting of the Blue Mesa, Morrow Point, and Crystal dams on the Gunnison River) was formally renamed the Wayne N. Aspinall Storage Unit.[4]

The former Congressman enjoyed all these honors, as he remarked in 1982 when he received an award from the Grand Junction Democrats. Aspinall, who had been in the hospital battling cancer, could barely speak as he accepted a plaque. "A politician never dies. He just fades away. I've been fading away for several years. It's rather unpleasant. This is a pleasant occasion." While Aspinall appreciated this recognition from others, he was not opposed to taking an active hand in promoting his own legacy. In a 1977 interview he claimed that the only inscription he wanted on his gravestone was "that people were good to me," but Aspinall ultimately selected something a bit longer. The seven-foot-long marble slab in Grand Junction's Orchard Mesa Cemetery reads in part:

"Mr. Chairman"
Educator—Attorney—Public Servant
Forty-eight Years of Elective Public Service
[List of various offices]
Chairman of Committee on Interior and Insular Affairs
1959–1973

Architect of:
Colorado River Storage Act
Colorado River Basin Act
Wilderness Act of 1964
Wild, Scenic and Recreation Rivers Act
Served with Five Presidents of The United States
[List of various fraternal organizations].

Aspinall's claim to be the architect of both the Wilderness Act and the Wild and Scenic Rivers Act would undoubtedly both amuse and horrify the environmentalists who fought for years to secure passage of these bills over his objections. The inclusion of these measures was the closest Aspinall ever came to acknowledging that, on some issues, the environmentalists were right.[5]

During his career, however, the congressman had sought to create a legacy that was more substantial than a mere gravestone. Despite his long interest in water issues, one of Aspinall's ultimate goals was to overhaul the way that the federal government administered the public lands and in the process prevent what he saw as an attempt by environmentalists to close the public domain to further development. In 1962, as Chairman of the Interior Committee, Aspinall had demanded the creation of a Public Land Law Review Commission (PLLRC) as the price for dropping his opposition to the proposed Wilderness Act, which he had to that point prevented from coming up for a vote before the full House of Representatives. The commission's mandate was to review all the federal regulations affecting the control and uses of the nation's public lands and to recommend any changes that would result in these areas being administered more efficiently.[6]

Aspinall served as the chair of the PLLRC, which met from 1965 to 1970. The commission comprised twelve members from the House and Senate Interior Committees, with six additional members appointed by the president, and a chair selected by the commission members. Observers noted that Aspinall dominated the PLLRC much as he did the Interior Committee (controlling the meeting agendas, selecting the committee staff), and environmentalists quickly gave up participating in the process. As a result, *Audubon* magazine reported that "[o]f the 62 persons who sought to advise the commission on how best to modify the laws that govern the use of public lands, 55 asked for the relaxation of the

The author at Aspinall's gravesite, located in the Orchard Mesa Cemetery in Grand Junction, Colorado. (Photograph by Stacy Sturgeon)

regulations or an outright giveaway of the federal lands to the state or existing users." Even the handful of pro-environmental commission members soon gave up. One observer commented that these members "knew that they could not match Aspinall and they simply did not come to many of the meetings. They knew that Wayne had the entire staff in the palm of his hand, and that the whole thing was rigged, so why get involved and risk being blamed?"[7]

In 1970 the commission issued its final report, titled *One-Third of the Nation's Land,* in a White House ceremony. As one political scientist described it, "given Aspinall's role as chairman, it came as no surprise that the report offered perhaps the best-articulated, most sophisticated defense of traditional [land-use practices] prepared during the twentieth century." Among the report's general conclusions were calls for Congress to take a more active role in administering the public lands, and thus limit the powers of executive-branch agencies (which Aspinall thought were not sufficiently responsive to local concerns). The report also recommended that states be given a greater say in the management of public lands. One surprise was that the report did not suggest the wholesale disposal of public lands, although it did recommend the sale of what it described as "single-use" property (such as timber stands, grazing ranges, and mines).[8]

Once the report had been issued, Aspinall moved quickly to secure passage of legislation implementing the commission's recommendations. His effort, however, had to compete with a bill that fellow commission member Sen. Henry Jackson had introduced. Aspinall's bill favored development of the public lands, while Jackson's bill stressed preservation. Environmentalists expressed opposition to Aspinall's legislation, and as his bill approached a vote during the summer of 1972, public opinion indicated opposition to the measure as well. The issue became moot, however, when Aspinall lost his re-election bid in the September primary. With the report's strongest advocate removed from Congress, neither bill ever came to a vote and public land administration quickly faded as a legislative issue—an outcome that Aspinall predicted following his defeat. Although he did later become a supporter of the "Sagebrush Rebellion," Aspinall's intended legacy of a wholesale reduction in the federal control of public lands never came to pass.[9]

While Aspinall did not leave behind the legacy he had hoped for, he did bequeath the state of Colorado a legacy that he could not have foreseen: a water project that continues to be funded but has never been built. The

Animas–La Plata Project (ALP) was one of the five Colorado projects that Aspinall inserted into the Colorado River Basin Project of 1968 in return for his support of the bill. The original plan for the Animas–La Plata Project was to divert water out of the Animas River south of Durango into the nearby La Plata River, where it would be used for irrigation.[10]

Like the other four Colorado projects in the CRBP bill, the Animas–La Plata had a questionable economic profile, and the Bureau of the Budget even initially rejected the project in 1966. To gain a positive review, the ALP was quickly revised to place a greater emphasis on the municipal water use by Durango and Farmington, New Mexico (which offered a better financial return), although the irrigation component was retained. Following passage of the CRBP, the Animas–La Plata languished for two decades without any progress toward actual construction. By the early 1980s it appeared that the ALP would join the San Miguel and the West Divide as congressionally authorized but never constructed reclamation projects. The chief reason for the delay, according to Western scholar Robert Gottlieb, was that the Animas–La Plata by the "1970s and 1980s [had come] to symbolize expensive [Bureau of Reclamation] projects with shifting objectives."[11]

One objective of the Animas–La Plata Project that distinguished it from other, abandoned projects, and perhaps the objective that kept the ALP alive, was the fact that it was partly designed to address Indian water rights. During the last three decades of the nineteenth century the Ute Indians of Colorado signed a series of treaties with the U.S. government that gradually restricted the tribes to two reservations in the extreme southwest corner of the state (the Ute Mountain Ute reservation and the Southern Ute reservation). In 1895, as part of one of these further relocations, the federal government promised to provide the two reservations with an irrigation system. During subsequent decades, although the courts continued to uphold the Utes' rights to an irrigation system, no action was taken to implement the promise.[12]

When Aspinall pushed for his five projects in the Colorado River Basin Project bill, he insisted that the Animas–La Plata Project be one of them. The chairman's insistence was not primarily motivated by a concern about the Utes' water rights, but he did consider Mountain Ute Chief Jack House to be a good personal friend and expressed his sympathy for the Utes' struggle to secure a source of water. "The Indians are worse off than any of the rest of us in Colorado because they used to own all the land and water and then the white man pushed them down to a southwest corner of the State where there isn't any water at all." It was Aspinall's active intervention that convinced the Utes to accept a revised version of the ALP in 1966 (which reduced the amount of reservation land to be irrigated) enabling the Bureau of the Budget to approve the project.[13]

In 1988 the two Ute tribes negotiated a formal agreement with the U.S. government in order to expedite construction of the ALP. Under the terms of the Ute Water Settlement Agreement, the two tribes received a guarantee that the project would be built, in exchange for which they waived their right to sue the government to enforce tribal water rights and agreed not to challenge existing water usage in the Animas and La Plata Rivers by non-tribal members.[14]

Despite the 1988 settlement, construction on the Animas–La Plata still did not start. The reasons for the continued delays reveal how much attitudes toward water projects have changed since the pro-reclamation era when Aspinall was in Congress. The biggest change over the past two decades has been in the legal strength of the environmental movement. The passage of the Endangered Species Act and the requirement for environmental impact statements on all federal construction projects has given environmental organizations, such as the Sierra Club, powerful tools with which to challenge reclamation projects such as the ALP. What environmentalists now fail to block in Congress, they can delay indefinitely in the courts. The Sierra Club and other environmental organizations have repeatedly, and often successfully, challenged different aspects of the ALP, thus further delaying the start of the project.[15]

Given the legal challenges and economic doubts surrounding the project, the only reason the Animas–La Plata is still under consideration is that it addresses Native American water claims, an assessment that the Bureau of Reclamation readily accepts. The justifications used during Aspinall's time to promote a reclamation project (regional economic growth, increased agricultural productivity) are no longer tenable today. Instead the chief factors that keep the ALP going are a sense of guilt over past injustices suffered by Native Americans, and the fear that the Ute tribes could successfully sue in court to strip the water rights away from their white neighbors. Perhaps it is not surprising that the project's biggest supporter, Sen. Ben Nighthorse Campbell, is the only Native American member of Congress.[16]

Continual delays in starting the Animas–La Plata have led to repeated revisions in the plan for the project—revisions that have steadily narrowed its scope and scale. The latest version of the project calls for the construction of a 120,000 acre-foot reservoir to store water for eventual use in settling Ute water claims, at an estimated cost of $343 million. One of the most notable features of this version of the ALP is what's missing. The current project has been stripped of all irrigation components. Thus one of the ostensible original reasons for building the project is no longer even under consideration. While Aspinall did not intend for the Animas–La Plata to be his official legacy, this reclamation project, with its fights among reclamation advocates, environmentalists, Native Americans, fiscal conservatives, and agricultural interests, is perhaps the most symbolically appropriate one.[17]

The debate over the Animas–La Plata project ultimately is not about Indian water rights, cost-benefit analysis, or environmental protection. It is about competing visions for the future of the American West, and it focuses on one question: how do we define progress? The philosopher William James confronted this dilemma during a visit to the mountains of North Carolina in the late nineteenth century. Passing through land where the timber had recently been removed, James observed, "The forest had been destroyed and what had 'improved' it out of existence was hideous, a sort of ulcer, without a single element of artificial grace to make up for the loss of Nature's beauty." Yet when James discussed the matter with his carriage driver, he discovered that the man viewed the same landscape as a symbol of progress and success.[18]

Aspinall would have understood the thinking of the carriage driver that James encountered during his trip. Although Aspinall always complained about "ignorant provincialism" and insisted that he served "country first, area second," his legislative record clearly indicates that the congressman made the economic development of the Western Slope his first priority. He also viewed the use of natural resources as a key element in that economic development, and in progress in general. As he remarked in an interview, "Colorado West cannot long survive economically and socially unless it is allowed to develop its Natural Resources base and secure for itself the new dollars therefrom. Otherwise the people of Colorado West will be solely dependent upon the economic strength of other areas. . . . [T]hen our economy is an artificial one—a parasitic one." In making this statement Aspinall clearly ignored the fact that utilizing natural resources can also be a parasitic activity, particularly when a corporation from outside the area controls the materials. Beyond the parasitic nature of this type of activity was the larger dilemma of how to create permanent economic growth while relying upon finite natural resources—a dilemma Aspinall never acknowledged. Instead he clung to a rosy, pioneer vision of the development of the West, claiming that the region "was settled by those who wished to establish new homes, make a living and make a profit for their efforts."[19]

The Fourth District congressman did not think that this progress and development benefited only a particular region; rather, he argued that it would benefit the nation as a whole. "[T]he initial aid given will be returned and beyond that new wealth will be spread throughout the nation. Such has always been the story of progress." Aspinall expressed frustration with those who did not understand this concept. "People who blatantly talk about so few people being served by a project, just don't know what reclamation is all about. A project serves not only the people whose lands happen to be under the project, but it also serves the entire community, and reaches even beyond the community lines to the national welfare." Aspinall's definition of progress and his model for western development should not be a surprise since they reflect the same philosophy that underlies the doctrine of prior appropriation for water. That doctrine holds that the best way for society to allocate natural resources is "first in use, first in right." Aspinall certainly was not the only, or most outspoken, advocate of this philosophy. During a public hearing in 1951 when ranchers protested that the proposed Curecanti project in Colorado would flood valuable grazing land, one project supporter replied, "If we are to progress someone must be hurt."[20]

In sharp contrast to Aspinall's views, David Brower, the executive director of the Sierra Club during the 1950s and 1960s, explicitly rejected the link between economic development and progress. "The menace is . . . the notion that growth and progress are the same, and that the gross national product is the measure of the good life," he said. "Some of our most beautiful scenery is sacrificed to 'progress.' I don't accept the notion that more growth is automatically good for any of us." While much of the public conflict between these two individuals was attributable to clashing, self-righteous egos, their respective efforts also reflected a genuine philosophical difference. Brower, and other environmentalists like him, represented a threat to Aspinall not just because environmentalists upset the old political, deal-making system, but also because their point of view was incompatible with Aspinall's. As one Sierra Club leader later explained, it is almost impossible to work with someone with whom you have no shared values.[21]

The fundamental philosophical difference between Aspinall and Brower can be seen most clearly in how each evaluated nature. Brower clearly viewed nature as having a value independent of human concerns, and therefore advocated preserving wilderness areas. By contrast Aspinall clearly had a more human-centric view of nature. Throughout his career Aspinall expressed a disdain for "locking up" remote areas that only a handful of people were ever going to see. The congressman at times seemed almost to be advocating a perverse Nielsen rating system for nature: the more people who went to see a particular place, the more worthy of preservation that place became.

During the debate over the Echo Park Dam, Aspinall readily agreed that Echo Park was a beautiful place. He also commented that nobody ever visited the place and with so many other equally beautiful places in Colorado, there was no real reason to save this one. Later, during the debate over the Grand Canyon Dams, Aspinall argued that flooding part of the canyon would allow more people to see the beauty of the area. Throughout his career Aspinall attacked environmentalists as aristocrats who locked up areas for their own use, excluding the rest of the public from using the same areas for different purposes. For Aspinall preservation was only acceptable when it allowed access by large numbers of people, a contradiction he never seemed fully to recognize. At times, the chairman's commitment to maximum access almost sounded like a form of outdoor populism. In 1963, when environmentalists were demanding that a small dam be constructed in Rainbow Bridge National Monument to prevent water in the newly created Lake Powell from encroaching underneath the Rainbow Bridge natural arch, Aspinall wrote a letter to the *Rocky Mountain News* in which he argued against building the dam because the influx of the water meant that "this wonderful and famous cultural monument will now be more readily accessible to the millions, rather than the hundreds, who have been privileged to enjoy its grandeur up to the present time."[22]

There is some merit to Aspinall's charge that environmental protection favors the few. Typically national environmental organizations are headquartered in cities far removed from those areas they seek to protect, and rarely do environmentalists stand to suffer financial loses from the limitations on land use that they advocate for others. Despite a flurry of interest by environmentalists in the 1950s concerning Dinosaur National Monument, only a small number of people visit the place today and most do not venture past the visitor's center. If the Echo Park Dam and resulting reservoir had been built, those numbers would undoubtedly be higher. Aspinall's attacks on environmentalists as elitists, however, were in many ways disingenuous, because his own policies also stood to benefit primarily a small number of people, chiefly the executives and shareholders in extractive industries harvesting resources from public lands.

In addition to his belief that nature should be accessible, Aspinall also believed that nature was "perfectible." This point of view held that nature in its natural state was wasteful and inefficient, and that these mistakes could and should be fixed. In other words, the world that God had created was merely a rough draft, and it was up to humans to perfect it. Aspinall repeatedly expressed the belief that nature was flawed. He supported timber operations in national forests rather than let them "become beetle infected, victims of fires, floods, and so forth." This intervention was necessary because "nature itself is not too good a housekeeper as we all know." The congressman also warned about problems with water, claiming that while the Colorado River did not "suffer from man-made pollution," it did suffer from "nature's pollutants such as silt and salinity." He even expressed satisfaction that the completion of Glen Canyon Dam put an end to Colorado River "water going unused into the Gulf of California."[23]

Today, instead of trying to perfect nature, government agencies like the Bureau of Reclamation are trying to imitate nature. An example of this change in philosophy came in March 1996, when Secretary of the Interior Bruce Babbitt ordered water released from Lake Powell to create artificial floods in the Grand Canyon in the hope of restoring some of the area's ecosystems. In the Pacific Northwest, the Army Corps of Engineers has begun to study, for the first time, safe ways to tear down dams on the Columbia River in an attempt to save the remaining salmon in the river. These changes have also had an impact in Colorado. The Denver Water Board, which in the past lobbied for permission to build dams on the South Platte River, instead announced in 1998 an ambitious plan to develop a unified recreation and wildlife corridor along the river.[24]

The most audacious and symbolic indication of the changing course in western reclamation, and the one to which Aspinall would most vehemently object, is the proposal by the Sierra Club to drain Lake Powell. In

1996 David Brower, by then a member of the board of directors for the Sierra Club, proposed that the organization formally endorse a resolution calling for draining the lake. Although initially dismissed as a crackpot notion, the resolution eventually gained unanimous endorsement by the Club's board, and the idea has since received some public support and substantial press coverage. The proposal does have its critics, however, as was evident in the frosty reception it drew during congressional hearings in Page, Arizona, in September 1997, where Sen. Ben Nighthorse Campbell proclaimed the plan a "certifiable nut idea."[25]

If the modern West no longer appears fully to embrace the development-at-all-cost mind-set that Aspinall advocated, is he now irrelevant to understanding the West? Has the congressman become simply a pork-barrel relic from the past? The answer is clearly no. Aspinall's actions helped create the modern West. During the course of his career, the chairman foresaw and tried to forestall some of the current dilemmas confronting the West. He also made the state of Colorado a "player" in the political debates over the future development of the West. When the congressman died in 1983, Colorado Governor Richard Lamm remarked, "No one in our history has done more to win Colorado a place at the table in Washington."[26]

It was odd for an "environmentalist" like Lamm to praise Aspinall so highly, in light of their past differences, but by the late 1970s both of them shared certain concerns. Throughout his career the congressman had been a sharp critic of California's unquenchable thirst for Colorado River water and had warned that if left unchecked California would consume far in excess of its allotment. Lamm had similar concerns and even seemed willing to sacrifice his environmental beliefs over the issue. In 1982 he spoke in defense of the water projects that Aspinall had secured for the Western Slope. The governor remarked, "I like the outdoors and free-flowing water too. But the environmentalists apparently want all our water to go to California."[27]

Almost twenty years after the congressman's death, the federal government is still wrestling with the problem that Aspinall warned of: how to force California to live within the limits of the 1922 Colorado River Compact. Current estimates are that California is using 800,000 acre-feet of river water per year in excess of its annual 4.4 maf allotment. This despite all the legislative initiatives, executive edicts, court rulings, and reclamation projects specifically designed to solve the problem. The latest

Family and friends gather to see Colorado Governor Richard Lamm sign a proclamation declaring "Mr. Aspinall, Mr. Chairman Day," on October 12, 1984, a year after the congressman died. Left to right: Owen Aspinall, Joyce Aspinall, Richard Aspinall, Ival Goslin, Robert Thompson, Dick Martin, Tommy Thompson, Bill Cleary, Carol Edmonds Sullivan. Despite Lamm's clash with Aspinall on environmental issues in the 1960s, by the late 1970s the governor had become a supporter of Aspinall's water projects. (Courtesy of the Archives, University of Colorado at Boulder Libraries)

attempt was unveiled in December 2000 by outgoing Secretary of the Interior Bruce Babbit, who announced a fifteen-year plan to wean California from its addiction to the Colorado River surplus. While the plan was widely praised by water managers in the West, there were a few cynical observers who predicted that when the fifteen years had passed California would still be using the surplus.[28]

The reclamation projects that Aspinall pushed through Congress did physically preserve, as much as possible, Colorado's and the Upper Basin's share of the Colorado River. These dams and the water they hold, however, also produced an unexpected side effect. The water in these reservoirs is not just being used for such expected objectives as irrigation and hydroelectricity. Instead, over time the water has also been put to other uses, including recreation and such environmental goals as protecting endangered fish through the regulated release of stored water. This unexpected outcome has led one environmental writer to ask:

Is this revisionist history? Did the dam-builders, after all, know what they were doing? . . . Were Congressman Aspinall and his associates in Congress and in the Bureau [of Reclamation] visionaries, and not the porkbarrelers and villains they are painted in so many muck-raking books?

There are no answers to the questions. We can only say that their work, accidentally or deliberately, left in place an adaptable system of plumbing. Today, various upper basin interests and economies are striving to use that plumbing in ways not written in the original plans.

If Aspinall's actions ultimately end up helping to preserve the environment of the West, that would be an ironic outcome indeed.[29]

Aspinall not only shaped the landscape and waterscape of the modern West, he also played a role in establishing larger national priorities. In 1972 the journalist and political scholar Neil Peirce published a profile of the eight Rocky Mountain states. In his discussion of Colorado, Peirce noted the sharp conflicts over water between the Front Range and the Western Slope, and between Colorado and the rest of the West. Peirce also noted the success the state had in obtaining federally funded water projects. This high level of federal subsidies for reclamation prompted Peirce to comment, "An affluent America might be said to have seriously underinvested in programs to help its impoverished whites, blacks, Hispanos, and Indians, to safeguard the environment, restore the cities, and assure an adequate education and medical care for all. But no one could reasonably accuse it of selfishness in funding water and reclamation projects for Western states." It was Wayne Aspinall, perhaps more than any other man, who kept that funding flowing.[30]

So in the end, what should one make of Wayne Aspinall? When Aspinall was elected to Congress in 1948 he had one paramount goal in mind: promoting the economic development of Colorado's Western Slope. To do so, Aspinall believed it was necessary to secure a large and stable supply of water. He further believed that this infrastructure development could only occur through a federally subsidized program. The congressman was certainly not alone or unique in holding these goals and beliefs; numerous other politicians, before and after Aspinall, have also shared them. What was unique about Aspinall was that he ultimately rose to a position of power where he could effectively demand support for his projects from other people.

Aspinall, through the strength of his personality and position, was able to make the Western Slope a player in national politics and to force other groups and individuals to pay attention to the region's needs and wants— an impressive achievement for an elderly politician with a marginal hold on a largely rural district. While he achieved this position of power through a combination of luck and pluck, Aspinall did not view being Interior Committee Chair as simply a nice capstone to a long political career (as his successor on the committee, Rep. James Haley of Florida, did). Rather, he saw his acquiring this position as crucial to promoting the Western Slope's agenda. The way Aspinall promoted that agenda, however, was so heavy-handed that he ultimately drove away support and undermined his own efforts, and despite all his work he was unable to change two basic realities: California and the Front Range continue to dominate the Western Slope.

The congressman's biggest failing, however, was not that he could not keep his temper in check or that he did not economically liberate the Western Slope; rather, it was his refusal to acknowledge that the world had changed. The point of view Aspinall held was quite mainstream when he was first elected in 1948, and quite out of date by the time he was defeated in 1972. Had he been willing to embrace at least some aspects of the larger changes going on in American society, Aspinall might have been better able to help the Western Slope make the transition from the nineteenth to the twenty-first century. Ironically, the environmental movement Aspinall fought against has in many ways been far more effective in thwarting the imperial desires of Southern California and the Front Range than the congressman ever was. Instead Aspinall ultimately squandered his political capital on a series of ill-fated reclamation projects that did little to secure the long-term prosperity of the region and instead came to stand as monuments to his hubris rather than his vision.

This is not to say that we can or should simply dismiss people like Aspinall as irrelevant to modern times. The ongoing arguments about topics such as drilling for oil in the Arctic National Wildlife Refuge clearly indicate that the issues raised during the debates over the Echo Park and Grand Canyon dams are still current today. The Republican victories in the 1994 congressional elections presented an interesting postscript that dispels any notion about the apparent eclipsing of Wayne Aspinall's point of view or reputation. After the chairman's portrait ended up in storage in 1990, then-Rep. Ben Nighthorse Campbell eventually rescued the painting and sent it to a local museum in Aspinall's old district. There the picture remained on display, along with Aspinall's trademark Stetson, until the Republicans won control of the U.S. House of Representatives in the fall of 1994. Rep. Don Young of Alaska, the new Republican chair of the House Interior Committee (now renamed the House Resources Committee), at the behest of then Republican Colorado Rep. Wayne Allard, recalled the painting from the museum and reinstalled it in the committee room. "Mr. Chairman" was once again presiding in the House.[31]

Notes

For expanded citation information and commentary, please see the notes for Stephen C. Sturgeon, "Wayne Aspinall and the Politics of Western Water," Ph.D. diss., University of Colorado at Boulder, 1998.

Abbreviations

ASU	Arizona Collection, Department of Archives and Manuscripts, Arizona State University Libraries
Bancroft	The Bancroft Library, University of California, Berkeley
CPA	The Papers of Clinton P. Anderson, Library of Congress
CU	Wayne Aspinall Papers, Western Historical Collections, University of Colorado at Boulder
DPL	Western History Department, Denver Public Library
DU	Wayne N. Aspinall Papers, University of Denver Special Collections
JFK	John F. Kennedy Presidential Library
LBJ	Lyndon B. Johnson Presidential Library
MKU	Morris K. Udall Papers, Special Collections, University of Arizona Library
ROHO	Regional Oral History Office, The Bancroft Library, University of California, Berkeley
SC Members	Sierra Club Members Papers, BANC MSS 71/295 c, The Bancroft Library, University of California, Berkeley
SC NLO	Sierra Club National Legislative Office Records, BANC MSS 71/289 c, The Bancroft Library, University of California, Berkeley
SC Records	Sierra Club Records, BANC MSS 71/103 c, The Bancroft Library, University of California, Berkeley
SLU	Stewart L. Udall Papers, Special Collections, University of Arizona Library

Preface

1. U.S. Bureau of Reclamation, Department of the Interior, *Dams for Reclamation* 4 (1966), quoted in Andrews, *Who Runs the Rivers?*, 167.

2. Statistics on Aspinall's district come from McCarthy, "He Fought for His West," 34.

3. The term "environmental" replaced "conservation" in the late 1960s and early 1970s. The Brower quotation is from Dennis Farney, "U.S. Presidents Come and Go, but the Power of Rep. Aspinall Persists," *Wall Street Journal,* 21 January 1972, 1. The Aspinall comment is from Reisner, *Cadillac Desert,* 298.

4. "Aspinall Declines to Serve on House Ways, Means Unit," *Rocky Mountain News,* 15 December 1950.

5. Richard Tucker, "Aspinall Formally Launches His Campaign," *Rocky Mountain News,* 20 August 1972, 66; "Aspinall Opens Primary Drive," *Denver Post,* 20 August 1972, 30; Leonard Larsen, "Aspinall, Evans Will Run with McGovern—Loosely," *Denver Post,* 18 July 1972, 4.

6. For Aspinall's views on the Senate see Sparks, Interview by author. Owen Aspinall had already been working for the government of American Samoa for several years prior to his appointment to the governorship. For LBJ's role in this matter see Memo, Lyndon Johnson to James Jones, June 12, 1967, "Aspinall, Wayne (CONG)," White House Central File: Name File, LBJ; Bernstein, *Guns or Butter,* 266.

7. For "crusty" see Farney, "U.S. Presidents Come and Go, but the Power of Rep. Aspinall Persists," *Wall Street Journal,* 21 January 1972, 1; for "difficult" see Memo, Mike Manatos to Bill Moyers, March 3, 1964, Ex LE/NR 3, box 142, White House Central File, LBJ; for "abrasive" see Akin, transcript of oral history interview, 19; for "irascible" see Ehrlichman, transcript of oral history interview, 356; for "wily" see Udall, *Education of a Congressman,* 156; for "prickly" see Bernstein, *Guns or Butter,* 266; for "cantankerous" and "rigid" see Tom Gavin, "Wayne Norviel Aspinall: A Genuine Colorado Original," *Denver Post,* 14 February 1982, D1; for "autocratic" see Josephy, *American Heritage History of the Congress,* 375. (Pete) McCloskey, transcript of oral history interview, 309; John Rhodes, see "Personal Log," folder 7, box 1, Rich Johnson Papers, ASU, October 11, 1967; Udall, "Around the Plaza," 22; Wayne Norviel Aspinall, FOIPA Request # 390.117, Federal Bureau of Investigation, Department of Justice, Washington, D.C.

8. Wayburn, transcript of oral history interview, 71. Letter, Wayne Aspinall to Tom Gavin, February 19, 1982, "1982 Newspaper Clippings," folder 37, box 43, CU. For praise of Aspinall see memo, May 29, 1965, folder 12, box 5, Carl T. Hayden Papers, ASU; and Smith and Deering, *Committees in Congress,* 168.

9. Schulte, "He Never Met a Dam He Didn't Like" (conference paper).

Fenno, *Congressmen in Committees,* 57–64, 92–94. Worster, *Rivers of Empire,* 265, 277–278.

10. Ed Willis quote from Fradkin, *A River No More,* 108.

Chapter 1. The Water, the Land, and the People

1. Ferril, "Here is a Land Where Life is Written in Water," in *Trial by Time,* 87. This poem is inscribed in the rotunda of the Colorado State Capitol Building.

2. Don Worster quoted in Harvey, "Environment, Politics, and the Central Utah Project" (conference paper), 2.

3. Precipitation figures from Pisani, *To Reclaim a Divided West,* xiii–xix.

4. Dunbar, "The Adaptability of Water Law," 57.

5. Dunbar, "The Adaptability of Water Law," 58–60. For a discussion of the partial forfeiture clause, see Ballard, Devine, and associates, *Water and Western Energy,* 48. For an explanation of "beneficial use" see Engelbert and Sheuring, *Water Scarcity,* 55.

6. Collins, "Transmountain Diversion of Water from the Colorado River" (master's thesis), 13. El-Ashry and Gibbons, *Water and Arid Lands,* 34. Dunbar, "The Adaptability of Water Law," 64. For further information on Hispanic water practices in the Southwest, see Meyer, *Water in the Hispanic Southwest,* and Pisani, *Water, Land, and Law,* 18–20. For concise definitions of prior appropriation and riparian water law, see Bates et al., *Searching Out the Headwaters,* 205.

7. Vranesh, *Colorado Citizens' Water Law Handbook,* v, 7, 61; see also Fleming, *Legal and Institutional Issues in Colorado Water,* 16–19.

8. Vranesh, *Colorado Citizens' Water Law Handbook,* 20. For *Coffin v. Left Hand Ditch Company,* see Tyler, *The Last Water Hole in the West,* 3; also Radosevich et al., *Evolution and Administration of Colorado Water Law,* 25. For Front Range water project information see Leonard and Noel, *Denver: Mining Camp to Metropolis,* 458–459.

9. Silkensen, *Windy Gap,* 2. Diggs and Sweeney, *Who Owns the West,* 9. Ingram, Laney, and McCain, *A Policy Approach to Political Representation,* 106. Mehls, *The Valley of Opportunity,* 2; O'Rourke, *Frontier in Transition,* 6

10. Bates et al., *Searching Out the Headwaters,* 41–42. Silkensen, *Windy Gap,* 10. El-Ashry and Gibbons, *Water and Arid Lands,* 343.

11. Folk-Williams, Fry, and Hilgendorf, *Western Water Flows to the Cities,* 96–105, 109–115. For water figures see Diggs and Sweeney, *Who Owns the West,* 10; and Rennicke, *The Rivers of Colorado,* 94. Lavender, "The Role of Water in the History and Development of Colorado," 413. Silkensen, *Windy Gap,* 11. Tyler, *The Last Water Hole in the West,* 3. For the definition of an acre-foot see Marston, *Western Water Made Simple,* 190.

12. Coleman, "Water on Colorado's Western Slope" (Honors thesis), 4.

13. Silkensen, *Windy Gap*, 14–15; and Lochhead, *Transmountain Diversions in Colorado*, 5–8.

14. Howard McMullin, "A Western Slope View on Water," *Rocky Mountain News*, 13 March 1954, 25. Articles discussing the Glenwood crisis appeared in the *Rocky Mountain News* on March 5 (p. 13), March 8 (p. 34), and March 12 (p. 12).

15. Fleming, *Legal and Institutional Issues in Colorado Water*, 13–15; Goslin, "Interstate River Compacts," 416; and Getches, *Water and the American West*, 2. The nine states with which Colorado has signed compacts are Arizona, California, Nevada, New Mexico, Utah, Wyoming, Texas, Kansas, and Nebraska. For a brief summary of the compacts, see Radosevich et al., *Evolution and Administration of Colorado Water Law*, 212–222.

16. Rennicke, *The Rivers of Colorado*, 58, 60. Fradkin, *A River No More*, 35, 42–43, 321. Michelle Boorstein, "Reversing the Colorado's Course: Restoration, Conservation in Wake of Excess," *Contra Costa Times*, 25 May 1997, A13.

17. Rennicke, *The Rivers of Colorado*, 60. For the definitive history of the Colorado River Compact of 1922, see Hundley, *Water and the West*.

18. Radosevich et al., *Evolution and Administration of Colorado Water Law*, 212; El-Ashry and Gibbons, *Water and Arid Lands*, 179; Goslin, "Interstate River Compacts," 421–423; and Waters, *The Colorado*, 328.

19. Ingram, Laney, and McCain, *A Policy Approach to Political Representation*, 107–108; El-Ashry and Gibbons, *Troubled Waters*, 12; and Bates et al., *Searching Out the Headwaters*, 117. Clark, *Water in New Mexico*, 501. For a discussion of how the erroneous water assumptions in the Colorado River affect the Upper Basin's water use, see Ballard, Devine, and associates, *Water and Western Energy*, 28; Wahl, *Markets for Federal Water*, 271; Bates et al., *Searching Out the Headwaters*, 117; and Somma, "The Colorado River" (Ph.D. diss.), 56.

20. There is a sharp divide between scholars over the question of whether the Colorado River Compact protects the Upper Basin's water rights or leaves them vulnerable to appropriation by the Lower Basin. See Getches, *Water and the American West*, 158; Weatherford and Brown, *New Courses for the Colorado River*, 113–116.

21. Weatherford and Brown, *New Courses for the Colorado River*, 28–30; Radosevich et al., *Evolution and Administration of Colorado Water Law*, 217–220; Dunbar, *Forging New Water Rights*, 142; *Depletion of Water Supplies*, 9–12; Goslin, "Interstate River Compacts," 424–425; Collins, "Transmountain Diversion of Water from the Colorado River" (master's thesis), 27; and Clark, *Water in New Mexico*, 501–503.

22. Lavender, "The Role of Water in the History and Development of Colorado," 410; Dunbar, *Forging New Water Rights*, 46–57; and Collins, "Transmountain Diversion of Water from the Colorado River" (master's thesis), 30–32.

23. Clarke and McCool, *Staking Out the Terrain*, 133–134. See also Dawdy,

Congress in Its Wisdom; Robinson, *Water for the West;* and Warne, *The Bureau of Reclamation.* Swain, "The Bureau of Reclamation and the New Deal," 138. For how hydroelectricity saved the Bureau, see Nash and Etulain, *The Twentieth-Century West,* 278.

24. Coate, "The New School of Thought," 58–63; and Koppes, "Environmental Policy and American Liberalism," 30.

25. Worster, *Rivers of Empire.* White, *It's Your Misfortune,* 56; Diggs and Sweeney, *Who Owns the West?,* 10, 13, 19, 24, and 29.

26. Cronin and Loevy, *Colorado Politics & Government,* 17. For the quotation from David Lavender see Vandenbusche and Smith, *A Land Alone,* vii. For a discussion of the devastating impact the Exxon pullout had on the Western Slope see Gulliford, *Boomtown Blues.*

27. Gulliford, *Boomtown Blues,* 42–43; Underwood, *Town Building on the Colorado Frontier,* 52. Vandenbusche and Smith, *A Land Alone,* 188.

28. For a look at the role boosterism played in Grand Junction see Mehls, *The Valley of Opportunity,* 165; and Eastin, "The Little Empire of the Western Slope," 28–49. For a history of the development of northwestern Colorado see Athearn, *An Isolated Empire.* Raley, "Irrigation, Land Speculation, and the History of Grand Junction, Colorado" (conference paper). Vandenbusche and Smith, *A Land Alone,* 185.

29. Raley, "Irrigation, Land Speculation, and the History of Grand Junction, Colorado" (conference paper), 7. Vandenbusche and Smith, *A Land Alone,* 185–187; and O'Rourke, *Frontier in Transition,* 144.

30. Vandenbusche and Smith, *A Land Alone,* 160, 218, 264; and Mehls, *The Valley of Opportunity,* 198.

Chapter 2. The Accidental Congressman

1. Edmonds, *Mr. Chairman,* 38.

2. Ibid.; Mary Louise Giblin, "Wayne Aspinall, 1896–1983," *Daily Sentinel,* 10 October 1983, 8; and Letter, Neal Bishop to Wayne Aspinall, August 17, 1945, box 16, DU.

3. Aspinall, transcript of oral history interview by David McComb, 7. Robert Tweedell, "Wayne Aspinall: A Man to Remember," Empire Magazine, *Denver Post,* 4 May 1980, 10.

4. Aspinall, transcript of oral history interview by David McComb, 1; and Brown, *Aspinall: Centennial Edition,* 1. Robert Tweedell, "Wayne Aspinall: A Man to Remember," Empire Magazine, *Denver Post,* May 4, 1980, 10; "In Tribute to Wayne Aspinall," *Congressional Record,* 98th Cong., 1st sess., November 8, 1983, 129, pt. 22: 31520. Carol Edmonds, Wayne N. Aspinall biographic sketch, p. 3, "Aspinall Genealogy," folder 1, box 1, CU.

5. Ben Cole, "Rep. Aspinall Holds Water Key," *Arizona Republic,* 28 July 1963,

1B; Edmonds, *Mr. Chairman,* 112–114; Memo, J. W. Penfold to Bill Voigt, August 17, 1955, "Dinosaur National Monument (Colorado and Utah) Correspondence, Aug.–Sept. 1953," Conservation Department Records, 1891–1973, folder 21, box 64, SC Records. For an expanded discussion of Aspinall's childhood see my dissertation, "Wayne Aspinall and the Politics of Western Water," University of Colorado at Boulder, 1998.

6. Aspinall, oral history interview with Al Look. For specific examples of Aspinall's "God wants us to use it" theology see Wayne Aspinall, Speech, "Man's Demand on His Environment," September 24, 1966, "1966 Speeches," folder 5, box 23, CU; Letter, Wayne Aspinall to George Wheeler, April 26, 1974, "1974 Politics," folder 3, box 36, CU; and Wayne Aspinall, Speech to the Future of Public Lands State-Wide Natural Resource Conference, March 25, 1976, "1976 Speeches," folder 9, box 40, CU.

7. Letter, Wayne Aspinall to Debbie Briggs, September 12, 1972, "1972, Colorado Politics, 4th District Correspondence," File Pol 1c, box 463, DU. For voting pattern see Wayne Aspinall, "A Family Message to My Family," 1975 (?), "Aspinall Genealogy," folder 1, box 1, CU. On his endorsement of Ford, see Letter, Wayne Aspinall to Robert Hogsett, June 21, 1976, "1974–76 Narrows Project," folder 49, box 38, CU.

8. Aspinall, oral history interview with Al Look; Wayne Aspinall, Speech, "Irrigation and Federal Participation in Colorado," July 18, 1977, folder 19, box 39, CU.

9. Aspinall, oral history interview with Al Look; Aspinall, transcript of oral history interview by David McComb, 6; Tweedell, " A Man to Remember," 10; Carol Edmonds, "Young Wayne Aspinall Had a Good Head for Wrangling, a Good Hand for Gavels," Westworld Magazine, *Daily Sentinel,* 30 April 1978, 6.

10. Aspinall, oral history interview with Al Look; Aspinall, transcript of oral history interview by David McComb, 9, 15; Edmonds, "Young Wayne Aspinall," 6.

11. Aspinall, transcript of oral history interview by David McComb, 15; Mary Louise Giblin, "Wayne N. Aspinall Dies," *Daily Sentinel,* 10 October 1983, 5; and Aspinall, oral history interview with Al Look.

12. Letter, Wayne Aspinall to John Mellon, March 13, 1978, "1978–81 Western State College," folder 48, box 39, CU. McCarthy, "He Fought for His West," 33; Sparks, transcript summary of interview. Aspinall, transcript of oral history interview by David McComb, 15–17. For a detailed history of the Colorado–Big Thompson Project see Tyler, *The Last Water Hole in the West.*

13. Aspinall, oral history interview with Judy Prosser; Giblin, " Aspinall Dies," 5; Aspinall, oral history interview with Al Look; Carol Edmonds, "The Congressman: Wayne Aspinall Had Reputation of Being Flinty as Mountain Cliffs," Sunday Magazine, *Daily Sentinel,* 16 March 1975, 2. For his 1946 election decision

and the quote from "Big Ed" see letter, Neal Bishop to Wayne Aspinall, August 17, 1945, box 16, DU.

14. Edmonds, "The Congressman," 2.

15. Aspinall, oral history interview with Al Look; Edmonds, "Young Wayne Aspinall," 7; Aspinall, transcript of oral history interview by Nancy Whistler, 12.

16. Edmonds, "Young Wayne Aspinall," 7; Aspinall, oral history interview with Judy Prosser.

17. Vandenbusche and Smith, *A Land Alone,* 280; letter, Eugene Mast to Eugene Cervi, November 3, 1947, "Aspinall—County Chairman," box 19, DU. For Aspinall's comments about the race see Letter, Wayne Aspinall to Eugene Mast, August 3, 1948, same folder. For the article critical of Rockwell see Bernard DeVoto, "Sacred Cows and Public Lands," *Harper's Magazine,* July 1948, 44–55. For primary results see Charles T. O'Brien, "Demo Chairman Aspinall Enters Bid for Congress: Out to Lick Incumbent Rockwell," *Denver Post,* 24 July 1948, 1.

18. Noland, oral history presentation. Aspinall, transcript of oral history interview by Nancy Whistler, 12–13; Aspinall, oral history interview with Helen Hansen; Brown, *Aspinall: Centennial Edition,* 40.

19. Aspinall, oral history interview with Al Look; Tweedell, "A Man to Remember," 28; Aspinall, transcript of oral history interview by Nancy Whistler, 11; Edmonds, Aspinall biographic sketch. For election results see *Rocky Mountain News,* 4 November 1948, 16.

20. Edmonds, "The Congressman," 2; McCarthy, "He Fought for His West," 34. Edmonds, Aspinall biographic sketch; Aspinall, oral history interview with Al Look. For information on Aspinall's friendship with Ford, see Mary Louise Giblin, "Wayne Aspinall, 1896–1983," *Daily Sentinel,* 10 October 1983, 8. For Aspinall friendship with Kennedy, see Aspinall, transcript of oral history interview by Charles Morrissey.

21. Tweedell, "A Man to Remember," 40; Giblin, "Wayne Aspinall, 1896–1983," 8; Aspinall, transcript of oral history interview by Nancy Whistler, 35.

22. Brown, *Aspinall: Centennial Edition,* 11–12; "In Tribute to Wayne Aspinall," *Congressional Record,* 98th Cong., 1st sess., November 8, 1983, 129, pt. 22: 31519; and Dennis Farney, "U.S. Presidents Come and Go, but the Power of Rep. Aspinall Persists," *Wall Street Journal,* 21 January 1972, 22. For other comments on Aspinall's punctuality, see Tweedell, "A man to remember," 29; and Traylor, oral history interview with Alice Wright.

23. Drury, transcript of oral history interview, 618. The initial entry in Aspinall's FBI file was a clipping from the *Washington Post,* dated January 20, 1949, which gave a brief biographical sketch of the congressman. The file remained inactive for four years until 1953 when Aspinall complained to the FBI that one of his friends (unidentified) had been falsely accused of being a communist. During

the course of a meeting with FBI agents to discuss the matter, Aspinall made the mistake of criticizing J. Edgar Hoover. The record of this meeting noted "the congressman's obvious animosity toward the F.B.I.," and subsequent entries in Aspinall's file for the next eight years repeatedly refer to his criticism of Hoover. One record bears the handwritten notation, "I have a suspicion that he might be a source of trouble in the future." Information contained in Wayne Norviel Aspinall, FOIPA Request # 390.117 (Federal Bureau of Investigation, Department of Justice, Washington, D.C.).

24. Vandenbusche and Smith, *A Land Alone,* 281; Letter, Wayne Aspinall to Mike Perko, November 11, 1968, "1968, Department of Interior, National Park Service," File 45, box 299, DU. *The CWA News,* May 1954, 5, located in "1954 CWA News," folder 1, box 13, CU. Bernstein, *Guns or Butter,* 310.

25. Aspinall, transcript of oral history interview by Nancy Whistler, 6; Aspinall, oral history interview with Al Look; Aspinall, transcript of oral history interview by David McComb, 29; letter, Wayne Aspinall to Floyd Dominy, December 24, 1951, "Biographical Information, 1951–1969, Employment-Asst. Commr.," box 2, Papers of Floyd E. Dominy, American Heritage Center, University of Wyoming.

26. Edmonds, "Young Wayne Aspinall," 7; Edmonds, *Mr. Chairman,* 38; Giblin, "Wayne Aspinall, 1896–1983," 8. Aspinall's rapid rise in seniority on the Interior Committee was due to an odd combination of deaths, defeats, departures, and retirements. See Nelson, *Committees in the U.S. Congress, Vol. 1,* 557–559. For Senate bid, see Bob Whearley, "Aspinall to Seek Re-Election; Plays Coy on Senatorial Race," *Rocky Mountain News,* 26 April 1954, 5; "Aspinall Tells Young Democrats GOP Offers Little on Reclamation," *Rocky Mountain News,* 8 September 1955, 68; letter, Wayne Aspinall to James D'Arcy, November 16, 1972, "1967 Political, 4th District Correspondence," File Pol 1c, box 285, DU. For information about the House Ways and Means spot, see "Aspinall Declines to Serve on House Ways, Means Unit," *Rocky Mountain News,* 15 December 1950.

27. The close outcome of the 1952 election led to several months of speculation about whether the results would be reversed by Congress. Although state GOP officials encouraged Shults to contest the election in the House of Representatives, he declined to do so. For coverage of the controversy see "Shults-Aspinall Contest Awaits Precinct Recount," *Rocky Mountain News,* 6 November 1952, 5; Bert Hanna, "Aspinall Announced as Winner," *Denver Post,* 25 November 1952, 1; "Aspinall-Shults Recount Left Up to Congress," *Denver Post,* 26 November 1952, 2; Tom Gavin, "Shults Likely to Carry Recount Plea to Congress," *Rocky Mountain News,* 26 November 1952, 5; "Shults' Forces Urged to Demand Recount," *Rocky Mountain News,* 3 December 1952, 20.

28. The political scientists deemed Aspinall's seat "unsafe" because it did not meet their three-part criteria for determining Democratic "safe" seats: (1) won by

a Democrat in every election since 1940; (2) won by an average of 60 percent or more of the vote since 1944; and (3) won by not less than 55 percent of the vote since 1946. See Raymond E. Wolfinger and Joan Heifetz Hollinger, "Safe Seats, Seniority, and Power in Congress," in Peabody and Polsby, *New Perspectives on the House of Representatives,* 60.

29. Aspinall, transcript of oral history interview by Nancy Whistler, 29; U.S. Department of Interior, "Grand Valley Project," *Project Data Book.*

30. *Congressional Record,* 82d Cong., 2d sess., May 19, 1952, 98, pt. 4: 5510. For a detailed discussion of the Collbran Project see Raley, "The Collbran Project" (master's thesis).

31. Dominy, transcript of oral history interview by Brit Allan Storey, 22–24. On extended repayment period for the Uncompahgre, see Wayne Aspinall, Speech, "Irrigation and Federal Participation in Colorado," July 18, 1977, folder 19, box 39, CU.

32. Raley, "The Collbran Project" (master's thesis), 18–19, 72–73.

33. For national defense angle see Raley, "The Collbran Project" (master's thesis), 18, 41; and *Congressional Record,* 82d Cong., 2d sess., May 19, 1952, 98, pt. 4: 5510–5511.

34. "Congress Rules on Reclamation, Aspinall Warns," *Rocky Mountain News,* 17 November 1950, 25; John R. Murdock, "Address by Aspinall . . . ," *Congressional Record* (Appendix), 81st Cong., 2d sess., December 15, 1950, 96, pt. 18: A7718.

35. For an overview of the federal reclamation policies of the Truman and Eisenhower era, see Coate, "The New School of Thought," 58–63; Koppes, "Environmental Policy and American Liberalism," 17–53; and Richardson, Dams, Parks & Politics. For Aspinall's criticism of Eisenhower's policies see *Congressional Record,* 84th Cong., 1st sess., August 1, 1955, 101, pt. 10: 12764; Wayne Aspinall, Speech to the National Reclamation Association, October 25, 1955, folder 3, box 13, CU.

Chapter 3. This Is Dinosaur

1. Tocqueville, *Democracy in America,* 2: 50.

2. Carey, "The Application of Economic Criteria" (D.B.A. diss.), 79; Edmonds, *Mr. Chairman,* 68; Gary Weatherford and Phillip Nichols, "Summary of the Legislative History of the Colorado River Storage Project," in Mann, Weatherford, and Nichols, *Legal-Political History of Water Resource Development,* 5.

3. Moss, *The Water Crisis,* 82; Gary Weatherford and Phillip Nichols, "Summary of the Legislative History of the Colorado River Storage Project," in Mann, Weatherford, and Nichols, *Legal-Political History of Water Resource Development,* 5; "Law of the River," 1955, unlabeled background file, box 52, DU; and Moley and Watkins, *The Upper Colorado Reclamation Project,* 9.

4. Gary Weatherford and Phillip Nichols, "Summary of the Legislative History of the Colorado River Storage Project," in Mann, Weatherford, and Nichols, *Legal-Political History of Water Resource Development,* 6–7; Carey, "The Application of Economic Criteria" (D.B.A. diss.), 82; Moley and Watkins, *The Upper Colorado Reclamation Project,* 45; Harvey, *A Symbol of Wilderness,* 44; Mann, "Conflict and Coalition," 144; and Kenney, "River Basin Administration and the Colorado" (Ph.D. diss.), 258. The formal name of this report, nicknamed the "Blue Book," is *The Colorado River: A Comprehensive Report on the Development of Water Resources: A Natural Menace Becomes a Natural Resource.* The government citation for this report is House Doc. 419, 80th Cong., 1st sess. Martin, *A Story that Stands Like a Dam,* 48.

5. Kenney, "River Basin Administration and the Colorado" (Ph.D. diss.), 259; Mann, "Conflict and Coalition," 144–145.

6. Kenney, "River Basin Administration and the Colorado" (Ph.D. diss.), 259; Mann, "Conflict and Coalition," 144–145.

7. Resume of Activities of Wayne Aspinall, "Personal—Biography, 1961," file P-10, box 95, DU. Terrell, *War for the Colorado River,* 2: 12–14. Presentation at luncheon for twenty-fifth anniversary of the Colorado River Storage Project, folder 17, box 40, CU. Letter, Wayne Aspinall to Gary Hart, "1979–83 Gary Hart," folder 55, box 30, CU. "Aspinall Declines to Serve on House Ways, Means Unit," *Rocky Mountain News,* 15 December 1950, 13.

8. Moley and Watkins, *The Upper Colorado Reclamation Project,* 45–46; for a concise discussion of the "cash register dam" concept, see Carothers and Brown, *The Colorado River through the Grand Canyon,* 180–182.

9. Aspinall's congressional files contain a report explaining benefit-cost analysis and arguing, not surprisingly, that the Colorado River Storage Project passes this fiscal test. Yet in that same folder is a report discussing how certain proposed individual projects in the CRSP do not meet the benefit-cost analysis criteria. This second report recommends retaining these projects on the assumption that further study will yield a better benefit-cost return and because these projects have active local support. See *Benefit-Cost Analysis* and "Report of Committee on Selection of Projects for Detailed Study," both in unlabeled background file, box 52, DU.

10. Letter, Wayne Aspinall to R. W. Turner, "1963 Dept. of Interior-Rec'm San Juan-Chama," file 50f, box 129, DU; Wayne Aspinall, "Colorado River Problems," *Congressional Record (Appendix),* 83d Cong., 1st sess., May 13, 1953, 99, pt. 10: A2591; Robinson, *Water for the West,* 86. For Aspinall's views on "bundling" water projects together see letter, Wayne Aspinall to Michael Strauss, "Precinct Voting Record—1952," box 21, DU; and letter, Wayne Aspinall to Gary Hart, "1979–83 Gary Hart," folder 55, box 30, CU.

11. James M. Daniel, "Great Industrial Future Predicted for Colorado Basin," *Rocky Mountain News,* 3 March 1955, 13; Summary of the Colorado River Storage Project, unlabeled background file, box 52, DU; letter, George Kelley to Conservationists, "Dinosaur National Monument (Colorado and Utah) Correspondence, 1951," Conservation Department Records, 1891–1973, folder 17, box 64, SC Records.

12. Gary Weatherford and Phillip Nichols, "Summary of the Legislative History of the Colorado River Storage Project," in Mann, Weatherford, and Nichols, *Legal-Political History of Water Resource Development,* 8–9; also see "Rivals in Crime," chap. 6 in Reisner, *Cadillac Desert.* Wayne Aspinall, Statement to the Upper Colorado River Compact Commission, September 17, 1979, folder 3, box 38, CU.

13. For Aspinall's concern about the Eisenhower administration see Presentation at luncheon for twenty-fifth anniversary of the Colorado River Storage Project, folder 17, box 40, CU.

14. Richardson, *Dams, Parks & Politics,* 129–130. Harvey, *A Symbol of Wilderness,* 148–150. Kenney, "River Basin Administration and the Colorado" (Ph.D. diss.), 260. For a brief overview of federal water policy in the 1950s, see Milazzo, "Going with the Flow" (conference paper). For Eisenhower's attitudes toward reclamation, see Richardson, *The Presidency of Dwight D. Eisenhower,* 48–50.

15. McCarthy, "He Fought for His West," 37. Wayne Aspinall, "Talk is Cheap but Water Earns Money," *Congressional Record (Appendix),* 84th Cong., 1st sess., February 2, 1955, 1: A571. Wayne Aspinall, 1956 campaign statement, "1956 Campaign Pamphlet Info.," folder 4, box 13, CU.

16. Sparks, Transcript summary of interview. Wright, *You and Your Congressman,* 60–62.

17. For the unexpected support from the Eisenhower administration, see Scott, interview with author. Despite his active criticism of Eisenhower, Aspinall also later acknowledged the president's support of the CRSP. See letter, Wayne Aspinall to Duane Vandenbusche, August 9, 1978, folder 25, box 39, CU. For unexpected opposition from conservationists, see Dominy, telephone interview with author. In the 1950s the term "conservationist" replaced the earlier term, "preservationist," before eventually giving way in the 1970s to the term "environmentalist." For a discussion of this change in terminology, see Fox, *The American Conservation Movement,* 289–292.

18. For a detailed account of the Echo Park Dam controversy (which, however, offers only a limited discussion of Aspinall's role in it), see Harvey, *A Symbol of Wilderness.* Another useful, if shorter, account is Stratton and Sirotkin, *The Echo Park Controversy.* Bates et al., *Searching Out the Headwaters,* 45; Nash, *Wilderness and the American Mind,* 209; Fox, *The American Conservation Movement,* 281.

19. Harvey, *A Symbol of Wilderness,* 183–184; Kenney, "River Basin Administration and the Colorado" (Ph.D. diss.), 263; and Vandenbusche and Smith, *A Land Alone,* 268.

20. Martin, *A Story that Stands Like a Dam,* 51. Stephen Fox does mention that some conservationists did not automatically view Dinosaur as an arid wasteland; see Fox, *The American Conservation Movement,* 282; see also Cohen, *The History of the Sierra Club,* 145.

21. Bates et al., *Searching Out the Headwaters,* 45; Kenney, "River Basin Administration and the Colorado" (Ph.D. diss.), 263; Edmonds, *Mr. Chairman,* 81–82; Nash, *Wilderness and the American Mind,* 209–210; Harvey, *A Symbol of Wilderness,* 56–57, 238–239; Fradkin, *Sagebrush Country,* 246.

22. Harvey, *A Symbol of Wilderness,* 93–97; Senecah, "The Environmental Discourse of David Brower" (Ph.D. diss.), 58.

23. Nash, *Wilderness and the American Mind,* 212–213. Stegner, *This Is Dinosaur;* Fox, *The American Conservation Movement,* 285; Runte, *National Parks,* 187.

24. Neel, "Irreconcilable Differences" (Ph.D. diss.), 487; Fox, *The American Conservation Movement,* 284.

25. Memo, J. W. Penfold to Bill Voigt, August 17, 1953, "Dinosaur National Monument (Colorado and Utah) Correspondence, Aug.–Sept. 1953," Conservation Department Records, 1891–1973, folder 21, box 64, SC Records.

26. Ibid. Aspinall apparently did enjoy the trip; several years later he commented that the participants "had a wonderful time, and I got a great thrill out of it which stays with me to this day." Letter, Wayne Aspinall to Harry Woodward, May 13, 1963, "1963 Personal Correspondence, Invitations," folder P-8, box 145, DU.

27. Neel, "Irreconcilable Differences" (Ph.D. diss.), 487; Martin, *A Story that Stands Like a Dam,* 59; Fox, *The American Conservation Movement,* 285; and Richardson, *Dams, Parks & Politics,* 135.

28. Quotes are taken from the following letters from Aspinall: Arthur Carhart, June 29, 1955; and Horace Albright, April 14, 1955. All letters located in "Echo Park Project-1955," box 69, DU.

29. Quotes are taken from the following letters from Aspinall: James Cinnamon, July 29, 1955; and Thompson Marsh, April 25, 1955, box 69, DU.

30. Quotes are taken from the following letters from Aspinall: Thompson Marsh, April 25, 1955; and Mildred Shaw, April 25, 1955, box 69, DU.

31. Aspinall to Edward Groth, June 3, 1955, box 69, DU. KLZ Radio Address, "1956 Political Materials for 1956 District Campaign," folder 16, box 13, CU.

32. KLZ Radio Address. Correspondence between Aspinall and Horace Albright, April 14, 1955; Arthur Carhart, June 29, 1955, box 69, DU. For other conspiracy proponents, see Bingham, "Reclamation and the Colorado," 240; Scott, interview with author.

33. Letter, Richard Leonard to Joe Penfold, August 29, 1953, "Dinosaur National Monument (Colorado and Utah) Correspondence, Aug.–Sept. 1953," Conservation Department Records, 1891–1973, folder 21, box 64, SC Records.

34. Richardson, *Dams, Parks & Politics,* 137, 148; and Neel, "Irreconcilable Differences" (Ph.D. diss.), 496–497. Floyd Dominy later maintained that the reclamationists could have defeated the conservationists if the Echo Park supporters had launched their PR campaign earlier. See Dominy, telephone interview with author.

35. Nash, *Wilderness and the American Mind,* 215; Martin, *A Story that Stands Like a Dam,* 61. For a complete transcript of the hearings see House Committee on Interior and Insular Affairs, *Hearings on H.R. 4449 et al. on CRSP* (1954). For Brower's memories of his testimony see Brower, *For Earth's Sake,* 325–341.

36. Martin, *A Story that Stands Like a Dam,* 61. Brower testimony, House Committee on Interior and Insular Affairs, *Hearings on H.R. 4449 et al. on CRSP* (1954), 789–799, 824–828; Terrell, *War for the Colorado River,* 2: 95–96. For the significance of this change in tactics, see Senecah, "The Environmental Discourse of David Brower" (Ph.D. diss.), 59.

37. Brower testimony, House Committee on Interior and Insular Affairs, *Hearings on H.R. 4449 et al. on CRSP* (1954), 824–826; Martin, *A Story that Stands Like a Dam,* 62.

38. Brower testimony, House Committee on Interior and Insular Affairs, *Hearings on H.R. 4449 et al. on CRSP* (1954), 831–832.

39. Cohen, *The History of the Sierra Club,* 160.

40. Kenney, "River Basin Administration and the Colorado" (Ph.D. diss.), 264.

41. Wayne Aspinall, "The Upper Colorado River Storage and Development Project," *Congressional Record,* 83d Cong., 2d sess., August 16, 1954, 100, pt. 11: 14698–14700.

42. Ibid.; memo, Joe Penfold to Howard Zahniser, David Brower, et al., November 16, 1954, "Echo Park, Dinosaur National Monument, Izaak Walton League, 1950–1956," Correspondence Sites 4: 500, The Wilderness Society Papers, DPL.

43. James Daniel, "Colorado River Project Called 'Boondoggle,'" *Rocky Mountain News,* 20 April 1955, 43; Mann, "Conflict and Coalition," 148; Scott, interview with author. See also Moley and Watkins, *The Upper Colorado Reclamation Project.*

44. Wayne Aspinall, "The Economics of the Upper Colorado Storage Project," *Congressional Record (Appendix),* 84th Cong., 1st sess., May 16, 1955, 13: A3543–3544. Letter, Wayne Aspinall to John Dingell, June 6, 1955, "Echo Park Project—1955," box 69, DU.

45. Letter, Aspinall to Dingell, June 6, 1955, "Echo Park Project—1955," box 69, DU.

46. Ibid.

47. Traylor, Oral History Interview with Alice Wright; Neal, transcript summary of interview. Undated speech, unlabeled background file, box 52, DU.

48. Mann, "Conflict and Coalition," 145–146.

49. Ibid.; Kenney, "River Basin Administration and the Colorado" (Ph.D. diss.), 264–265; Robert Perkin, "Colorado Ends Long Delay by OK of Upper River Project," *Rocky Mountain News,* 12 December 1953, 3; Bill Miller, "Water Boils Over in Statehouse," *Rocky Mountain News,* 2 March 1955, 5; memo, J. W. Penfold to "Cooperators," December 18, 1953, "Dinosaur National Monument (Utah) Izaak Walton League of America, 1953," Edgar Wayburn Papers, 1932–1985, folder 45, box 228, SC Members.

50. For a more detailed discussion of Aspinall's role in the debate over the Fryingpan-Arkansas Project, see chapter 4. Letter, Harold Christy to Gordon Allott, June 11, 1958, "Nat. Res. 5 A Plan for Reclamation," box 44, Series V Gordon Allott Papers, Western Historical Collections, University of Colorado at Boulder; Wayne Aspinall, Congressional testimony and speeches, "Fryingpan–Arkansas Project, 1949–1956 and undated material," File 1, box 20, DU.

51. Gary Weatherford and Phillip Nichols, "Summary of the Legislative History of the Colorado River Storage Project," in Mann, Weatherford, and Nichols, *Legal-Political History of Water Resource Development,* 12; Carey, "The Application of Economic Criteria" (D.B.A. diss.), 84; Mann, "Conflict and Coalition," 154–155; Nash, *Wilderness and the American Mind,* 216; Terrell, *War for the Colorado River,* 2: 116–123; Fenno, *Congressmen in Committees,* 267; James Daniel, "House Defeats Frying Pan; Basin Storage Bill in Danger," *Rocky Mountain News,* 29 July 1954, 5.

52. Wayne Aspinall, Congressional testimony before subcommittee on CRSP, 1955, unlabeled background file, box 52, DU.

53. Terrell, *War for the Colorado River,* 2: 222–229; Martin, *A Story that Stands Like a Dam,* 67–68.

54. Terrell, *War for the Colorado River,* 2: 220–221; Gary Weatherford and Phillip Nichols, "Summary of the Legislative History of the Colorado River Storage Project," in Mann, Weatherford, and Nichols, *Legal-Political History of Water Resource Development,* 16.

55. Letter, Howard Zahniser to A. T. Steele, November 12, 1954, "Echo Park, Dinosaur National Monument, July–Dec. 1954," Correspondence Sites 4: 500, The Wilderness Society Papers, DPL; Secretary's Report for the Colorado Citizens' Committee for the Development and Protection of Natural Resources—Northwestern Colorado Chapter, 1954, "Dinosaur National Monument (Colorado and Utah) Colorado Citizens' Committee, 1954–1955," Conservation

Department Records, 1891–1973, folder 12, box 67, SC Records. By the time the hearings ended in 1955, Aspinall seemed resigned to dropping Echo Park Dam (see letter, Aspinall to Thomas Marsh, April 25, 1955, "Echo Park Project—1955," box 69, DU). While both the Reclamation Subcommittee and the full Interior Committee favored the CRSP bill, neither would approve a bill including Echo Park (see Martin, *A Story that Stands Like a Dam,* 69; Terrell, *War for the Colorado River,* 2: 237), nor would the full House of Representatives (see Edmonds, *Mr. Chairman,* 93; Mann, "Conflict and Coalition," 155; letter, Aspinall to James Cinnamon, July 29, 1955, "Echo Park Project—1955," box 69, DU). For the sacrifice quote see letter, Wayne Aspinall to John Dingell, June 6, 1955, "Echo Park Project—1955," box 69.

56. Edmonds, *Mr. Chairman,* 94, 96; Martin, *A Story that Stands Like a Dam,* 69; Mann, "Conflict and Coalition," 155; Cosco, *Echo Park,* 88. Barnet Nover, "Hope Still Seen for Echo Park Dam: Study Plan Hold Up Proposal," *Denver Post,* 14 June 1955, 44, and "Colorado River Project Gets Committee Okay," *Denver Post,* 28 June 1955, 8.

57. Edmonds, *Mr. Chairman,* 96–97; Cosco, *Echo Park,* 88. Martin, *A Story that Stands Like a Dam,* 69; Mann, "Conflict and Coalition," 155; Aspinall participated actively in the negotiations over a compromise on the power revenues issue (see Presentation at luncheon for twenty-fifth anniversary of the Colorado River Storage Project, folder 17, box 40, CU). For Aspinall's conclusion that the bill could not pass see letter, Aspinall to Clifford Kester, July 26, 1955, "Echo Park Project—1955," box 69, DU. L. A. Chapin, "Death Knell Sounded for This Session," *Denver Post,* 26 July 1955, 1; "Upper Basin Plan Put Off Until Next Year," *Rocky Mountain News,* 27 July 1955, 5; Editorial, "Still Vital to Our Future," *Rocky Mountain News,* 28 July 1955, 36. Comments to the Upper Colorado River Commission, September 19, 1955, "Colorado River, Current, General," box 44, DU.

58. Gary Weatherford and Phillip Nichols, "Summary of the Legislative History of the Colorado River Storage Project," in Mann, Weatherford, and Nichols, *Legal-Political History of Water Resource Development,* 18; Cosco, *Echo Park,* 88. For brief accounts of the Denver summit, see Nash, *Wilderness and the American Mind,* 219; Martin, *A Story that Stands Like a Dam,* 71; Mann, "Conflict and Coalition," 155; Neel, "Irreconcilable Differences" (Ph.D. diss.), 499; Richardson, *Dams, Parks & Politics,* 150; Harvey, *A Symbol of Wilderness,* 277–278; and Baird, "The Politics of Echo Park" (Ph.D. diss.), 517–519.

59. "An Open Letter . . . ," *Denver Post,* 31 October 1955, 20. For a discussion of the ad, see Cohen, *The History of the Sierra Club,* 171–172; Cosco, *Echo Park,* 88. For McKay's flip-flop, see Harvey, *A Symbol of Wilderness,* 277–278; Carey, "The Application of Economic Criteria" (D.B.A. diss.), 85.

60. "Aspinall Not Advised of River Talks," *Daily Sentinel,* 21 October 1955, 1; Anderson, *Outsider in the Senate,* 241; Notes on Echo Park, December 2, 1955,

"Dinosaur National Monument (Colorado and Utah) Echo Park Dam, 1950–1962," Conservation Department Records, 1891–1973, folder 4, box 70, SC Records.

61. Neel, "Irreconcilable Differences" (Ph.D. diss.), 500–501.

62. Memo, "Notes on Echo Park," December 12, 1955, "Dinosaur National Monument (Colorado and Utah) Echo Park Dam, 1950–1962," Conservation Department Records, 1891–1973, folder 4, box 70, SC Records. For a brief discussion of the role Brower played in negotiations with Aspinall, see Leonard, transcript of oral history interview, 129–130. Aspinall's staff assistant, Tommy Neal, recalls that Brower and Aspinall had several meetings in January 1956; see Neal, e-mail interview with author.

63. The participants at the CRSP congressional caucus included Senators Gordon Allott, Clinton Anderson, and Frank Barrett, and Representatives Aspinall and Dawson; see memo, Gordon Allott to himself, January 17, 1956, "Colo. River Storage Project, departmental reports," folder 3, box 71, Series VI Gordon Allott Papers, Western Historical Collections, University of Colorado at Boulder. James Daniel, "Rewritten Upper Basin Bill to Satisfy All," *Rocky Mountain News,* 21 January 1956, 17.

64. Letter, Wayne Aspinall & William Dawson to Edgar Wayburn, January 26, 1956, "Dinosaur National Monument (Utah), 1953–1955," Edgar Wayburn Papers, 1932–1985, folder 44, box 228, SC Members. Edmonds, *Mr. Chairman,* 98; Gary Weatherford and Phillip Nichols, "Summary of the Legislative History of the Colorado River Storage Project," in Mann, Weatherford, and Nichols, *Legal-Political History of Water Resource Development,* 18–19; Baird, "The Politics of Echo Park" (Ph.D. diss.), 522.

65. James Daniel, "House Unit OKs Upper Colorado," *Rocky Mountain News,* 9 February 1956, 10; Baird, "The Politics of Echo Park" (Ph.D. diss.), 524–525. For opposition see Mann, "Conflict and Coalition," 156. For Aspinall and Engle's pledge, see Terrell, *War for the Colorado River,* 2: 251; Wayne Aspinall, Congressional testimony and speeches, 1956, "Small Projects, Conference Comm," box 44, DU.

66. Wayne Aspinall, Speech to the House of Representatives, *Congressional Record,* 84th Cong., 2d sess., February 28, 1955, 102, pt. 3: 3473–3475, 3503–3513. Terrell, *War for the Colorado River,* 2: 257.

67. For the story about Northcutt Ely, see Gilmore, transcript summary of interview; Scott, interview with author. Letter, David Brower to Wayne Aspinall, June 29, 1960, "1960—Department of the Interior, National Park Service, Dinosaur-Echo Park," file 44-b, box 79, DU. Brower later referred to Aspinall as an "enemy," but he did consider Aspinall to be "the architect of the Colorado River Storage Project"; see Brower, transcript of oral history, 269. Letter, Stewart Udall to Larry Mehren, April 1, 1965, "April–May 1965," folder 5, box 168,

SLU; see also, memo, Arizona Authority and Power Program Meeting, February 7, 1963, "Jan.–Feb. 1963," folder 6, box 166, SLU. Letter, Wayne Aspinall to Duane Vandenbusche, November 9, 1978, folder 25, box 39, CU; Carol Edmonds, "The Congressman: Wayne Aspinall Had Reputation of Being Flinty as Mountain Cliffs," *Daily Sentinel,* March 16, 1975, 4; Aspinall, transcript of oral history interview by Nancy Whistler, 30. Epitaph for Aspinall and wife, "Aspinall Genealogy," folder 1, box 1, CU.

68. Pamphlet, Major Legislation, 2nd Session, 84th Congress . . . 1956, "1956 Campaign Pamphlet Info.," folder 4, box 13, CU; 1956 Radio Election Ad, "1956 Advertising—Radio," folder 25, box 4, CU; Telegram, Wayne Aspinall to Carson Lyman, November 7, 1956, "1956 Correspondence Sept.–Nov.—Letters Written in Grand Junction," folder 5, box 13, CU. Larry Ingram, "3 Colorado Congressmen Win, 4th Has Narrow Lead," *Denver Post,* 7 November 1956, 29. Neal, transcript summary of interview.

Chapter 4. *The River Went over the Mountain*

1. Ferril, "Here Is a Land Where Life Is Written in Water," in *Trial by Time,* 88.

2. For a discussion and useful graphic depiction of the numerous water diversions to the Front Range, see Riebsame, *Atlas of the New West,* 92–93. Letter, Wayne Aspinall to Orest Gerbaz, June 30, 1954, box 49, DU.

3. Mehls, "Into the Frying Pan" (Ph.D. diss.), 87–89, 108–111, 116–120; Milenski, *Water: The Answer to a Desert's Prayer,* 27, 30; Sherow, *Watering the Valley,* 59. U.S. Department of Interior, *Colorado: Bureau of Reclamation Projects,* 14.

4. Vandenbusche and Smith, *A Land Alone,* 264; letter, Wayne Aspinall to Duane Vandenbusche, November 9, 1978, folder 25, box 39, CU.

5. Vandenbusche and Smith, *A Land Alone,* 266; Milenski, *Water: The Answer to a Desert's Prayer,* 30; Collins, "Transmountain Diversion of Water from the Colorado River" (master's thesis), 58.

6. Neal, e-mail interview with author. Collins, "Transmountain Diversion of Water from the Colorado River" (master's thesis), 55, 57.

7. Neal, e-mail interview with author. Wayne Aspinall, undated congressional testimony, "Fryingpan-Arkansas Project, 1949–1956 and undated material," file 1, box 20, DU.

8. Aspinall, undated testimony, "Fryingpan-Arkansas Project, 1949–1956 and undated material," file 1, box 20, DU.

9. Ibid.

10. Ibid. Fenno, *Congressmen in Committees,* 261; James Daniel, "House Defeats Frying Pan; Basin Storage Bill in Danger," *Rocky Mountain News,* 29 July 1954, 5.

11. 1954 radio script, folder 2, box 4; 1954 TV script, "1954 Advertising Radio," folder 11, box 4, both at CU.

12. "Aspinall Answers," *Daily Sentinel,* 30 October 1954, 3; Nello Cassai, "Colorado's Congress Delegation Reelected," *Denver Post,* 3 November 1954, 39; "Rep. Aspinall to Push Irrigation Project," *Rocky Mountain News,* 11 November 1954, 21.

13. Milenski, *Water: The Answer to a Desert's Prayer,* 31; Letter, Wayne Aspinall to Orest Gerbaz, June 30, 1954, box 49, DU.

14. Only scattered references to Saylor's victory exist. A *Pueblo Chieftain* editorial dated 30 September 1954 mentions it, as does a *Daily Sentinel* article dated 4 September 1960 in which Saylor endorsed Aspinall for re-election. Stewart Udall also mentioned the incident during an interview and claimed that Aspinall, as a result of this political embarrassment, dropped his support for the storage reservoir near Aspen. See Udall, telephone interview with author. Nello Cassai, "Colorado's Congress Delegation Reelected," *Denver Post,* 3 November 1954, 39; "Rep. Aspinall to Push Irrigation Project," *Rocky Mountain News,* 11 November 1954, 21. Numerous former associates of Aspinall recalled his hostile relationship with Aspen. See Traylor, Oral History Interview with Alice Wright; Sparks, transcript summary of interview; Cleary, interview with author; Tommy Neal, e-mail interview with author.

15. Memo, J. W. Penfold to Bill Voigt, September 17, 1953, "Dinosaur National Monument (Colorado and Utah) Correspondence, Aug.–Sept. 1953," Conservation Department Records, 1891–1973, folder 21, box 64, SC Records; David Brower materials located in "Frying Pan Transmountain Water Diversion Project (Colo.), 1951–1955," David R. Brower Papers, 1933–1983, folder 12, box 19, SC Members. In addition to opposing the Fry-Ark, local conservationists also were puzzled as to why Aspinall would help pass the project. See letter, Art Carhart to Joe Anderson, February 14, 1959, "Correspondence, 12/15/67–12/19/58," box 78, Arthur H. Carhart Collection, DPL.

16. House Committee on Interior and Insular Affairs, *Hearings on H.R. 412 on Fryingpan-Arkansas Project* (1955), 32–33, 36, 64, 263, 420.

17. Letter, Frank Hoag to Joseph Martin, June 19, 1956, "Public Works, Fryingpan-Arkansas, S. 300," folder 9, box 72, Series VI Gordon Allott Papers, Western Historical Collections, University of Colorado at Boulder. *Congressional Record,* 84th Cong., 2d sess., July 26, 1956, 102, pt. 11: 14795–14802. "House Kills Frying Pan Measure," *Denver Post,* July 26, 1956, 1; Fenno, *Congressmen in Committees,* 261.

18. Letter, Wayne Aspinall to Flint Holmes, September 10, 1956, "1956 Correspondence Sept.–Nov.—Letters Written in Grand Junction," folder 5, box 13, CU.

19. Letter, Harold Christy to Gordon Allott, June 11, 1958, "Nat. Res. 5 A Plan for Reclamation," box 44, Series V Gordon Allott Papers, Western Historical Collections, University of Colorado at Boulder.

20. House Committee on Interior and Insular Affairs, *Hearings on H.R. 594 on Fryingpan-Arkansas Project* (1957), 15, 23, 119. Gene Wortsman, "Fryingpan-Arkansas Defeat Will Come as an Anticlimax," *Rocky Mountain News,* 21 August 1958, 40.

21. Gene Wortsman, "Failure of Fryingpan Is Blamed on State," *Rocky Mountain News,* 21 August 1958, 40. Sparks, interview with author.

22. Sparks, interview with author.

23. Ibid.; Milenski, *Water: The Answer to a Desert's Prayer,* 31; Mehls, "Into the Frying Pan" (Ph.D. diss.), 196–198. Like most successful ideas, everybody now takes credit for it. Sparks said he and his staff came up with the new reservoir proposal, Milenski suggests it was his idea, and Mehls attributes it to Chenoweth. "Historic Water Pact Signed," *Rocky Mountain News,* 1 May 1959, 5; Peirce, *The Mountain States of America,* 55. Brown, *Aspinall: Centennial Edition,* 18. Vandenbusche and Smith, *A Land Alone,* 266; letter, Wayne Aspinall to Duane Vandenbusche, November 9, 1978, folder 25, box 39, CU.

24. Nelson, *Committees in the U.S. Congress, Vol. 1,* 557–568. Representative Joel Hefley became chair of the House Committee on Standards of Official Conduct (better known as the House Ethics Committee) in January 2001.

25. Fenno, *Congressmen in Committees,* 60, 92, 118–119; Brown, *Aspinall: Centennial Edition,* 6–13; Edmonds, *Mr. Chairman,* 20–24; Sparks, interview with author. Aspinall is often described as the model for autocratic chairmen and as an example of the dangers of the seniority system. See Josephy, *The American Heritage History of the Congress,* 375; Smith and Deering, *Committees in Congress,* 168, 176; Morrow, *Congressional Committees,* 40, 206; Hibbing, *Congressional Careers,* 82, 205; Vogler, *The Politics of Congress,* 184–185; McCubbins and Sullivan, *Congress: Structure and Policy,* 159, 176; Bolling, *House Out of Order,* 103, 107; McCurdy, "When Committees Change" (Ph.D. diss.).

26. Fenno, *Congressmen in Committees,* 120–121. It should be noted that the congressmen Fenno quotes were speaking without attribution. Only a few representatives ever publicly criticized Aspinall, and then only in the last few years of his congressional career when some Interior Committee members rebelled against Aspinall's strict controls. (See chapter 7 for further discussion.)

27. Aspinall, transcript of oral history interview by Nancy Whistler, 32–33; Aspinall, transcript of oral history interview by Charles Morrissey, 4–5. Stewart Udall maintains that Aspinall was considered for the Interior post. See Udall, transcript of oral history interview by William Moss, 34–35; Udall, transcript of oral history interview by Charles Morrissey, 29; Udall, transcript of interview by Charles Coate; Udall, telephone interview with author. However, one of Aspinall's staff, Tommy Neal, doubts that the congressman was under consideration for the position or that Aspinall had any interest in it. See Neal, transcript summary of interview; Neal, e-mail interview with author. Aspinall's own comments

are ambiguous. See letter, Wayne Aspinall to Herbert Allen, November 21, 1960, "1960 Correspondence A–B," folder 13, box 15; letter, Wayne Aspinall to Leslie Savage, December 19, 1960, "1960 Correspondence S–T," folder 19, box 15, both located at CU. In the latter letter, Aspinall claims to have said "no" to the position, but this may have been a preemptive move because there is no evidence it was ever formally offered to him.

28. While relations between Aspinall and the White House were officially friendly, internal memos suggest that Aspinall and his requests were frequently handled with kid gloves to keep the congressman happy. See letter, Wayne Aspinall to Kenneth O'Donnell, March 5, 1963, Gen IV I/1963/ST 6, box 428, White House Central File: Subject Files, JFK; letter, Wayne Aspinall to Kenneth O'Donnell, February 27, 1961, "Aspinall, Wayne (Cong)", White House Central File: Names File, JFK.

29. Stewart Udall, transcript of oral history interview by William Moss, 117–118. Smith, "John Kennedy, Stewart Udall, and New Frontier Conservation," 341.

30. Letter, Aspinall to Albert Campbell, December 2, 1958, "1958 Alphabetical File of Letters Written from Grand Junction office, A–D," folder 1, box 14, CU.

31. Cooley and Wandesforde-Smith, *Congress and the Environment*, 55, 58; Gene Wortsman, "Wilderness Bill Failure Blamed on Aspinall," *Rocky Mountain News*, 17 October 1962, 34; Anderson and Viorst, *Outsider in the Senate*, 234; Bendiner, *Obstacle Course on Capitol Hill*, 61. Aspinall would use this "strategic withdrawal" trick again during debate over the Central Arizona Project (see chap. 6).

32. While the negative press rapidly escalated after Aspinall killed the Wilderness Bill in October 1962, he had already come under criticism before then; see Editorial, "Strange Liberalism," *Washington Daily News*, 2 September 1962. The most famous public criticism of Aspinall was in Paul Brooks's essay, "Congressman Aspinall vs. The People of the United States," *Harper's Magazine*, March 1963, 60–63. For an example of negative local press, see Editorial, "Aspinall's Wilderness Abortion," *Glenwood Springs Sage*, 27 September 1962.

33. Smith, "John Kennedy, Stewart Udall, and New Frontier Conservation," 349–350; Cooley and Wandesforde-Smith, *Congress and the Environment*, 58–59. Aspinall announced his request for what came to be called the Public Land Law Review Commission in a letter to President Kennedy, with a simultaneous press release, dated October 15, 1962. See press release by Aspinall on public land management, Ex LE/NR1-LE/NR 6-1, box 489, White House Central File: Subject Files, JFK. Both John Carver and Stewart Udall agreed that the Commission was Aspinall's pound of flesh for passing the Wilderness Bill. See Carver, transcripts of oral history interviews by John Stewart and William Moss, 5th

interview, 50; Stewart Udall, transcript of oral history interview by William Moss, 101.

34. For White House optimism about the Wilderness Bill, see memo, Lee White to John Kennedy, November 12, 1963, White, Lee C 1961–1962, box 67, Presidential Office Files, JFK. For the final conversation between Aspinall and Kennedy, see Edmonds, *Mr. Chairman,* 166; Brown, *Aspinall: Centennial Edition,* 31.

35. Smith, "John Kennedy, Stewart Udall, and New Frontier Conservation," 333, 353. For Aspinall's assessment of the delays in consideration see letter, Wayne Aspinall to William Nelson, February 26, 1960, "1960—Department of Interior, Bureau of Reclamation, Upper Colorado River Storage Project," File 62, box 80, DU.

36. Letter, Wayne Aspinall to Eugene Bond, February 2, 1960, "1960—Department of Interior, Bureau of Reclamation, Gunnison Arkansas (Fryingpan)," file 69, box 81, DU. Letter, Wayne Aspinall to James Moore, April 4, 1961; letter, Wayne Aspinall to George Larson, April 11, 1961, both in "1961—Department of Interior, Bureau of Reclamation, Gunnison-Arkansas (Fryingpan)," file 69, box 89, DU. McCarthy, "He Fought for His West," 37; Bert Hanna, "Aspinall Pledges 'Do or Die' Effort," *Denver Post,* 10 January 1962, 1; Bert Hanna, "Aspinall, Udall at Odds on Water Project Strategy," *Denver Post,* 10 January 1962, 13. Letter, Aspinall to Philip Smith, January 29, 1962, "1962 Department of Interior, Colorado River Water Conservation District," DU. *Colorado Water Congress Newsletter,* 26 January 1962, 1–2.

37. *Colorado Water Congress Newsletter,* 26 February 1962, 5–6, and 26 March 1962, 2. Bert Hanna, "Arkansas Valley's Economic Future Rests on Saving Pan-Ark Bill," *Denver Post,* 15 April 1962, 1AAA; Editorial, "Front Burner for the Fryingpan," *Denver Post,* 18 April 1962, 22. Mann, "Conflict and Coalition," 157.

38. Sparks, interview with author; Sparks, transcript summary of interview. Richard Fenno examined Aspinall's strategy of lining up votes before taking legislation to the floor—see Fenno, *Congressmen in Committees,* 122–123.

39. Sparks, interview with author. Letter, Wayne Aspinall to House colleagues, June 6, 1962, "Fryingpan-Arkansas History, Correspondence with Members of Congress," box 49, DU.

40. *Congressional Record,* 87th Cong., 2d sess., June 12, 1962, 108, pt. 8: 10147–10148.

41. Ibid.

42. Ibid., 10171–10174; Fenno, *Congressmen in Committees,* 262. Gene Wortsman, "House Quickly Okays Fryingpan Project," *Rocky Mountain News,* 14 June 1962, 5; "Colo. Lawmakers Beam over Fryingpan Success," *Rocky Mountain News,* 14 June 1962, 42. Mehls, "Into the Frying Pan" (Ph.D. diss.), 218, 220.

Chapter 5. The High-Water Mark

1. In 1934 Arizona posted its National Guard on the east bank of the Colorado River in an attempt to halt construction of Parker Dam. See Fradkin, *A River No More*, 108–109; Berkman and Viscusi, *Damming the West*, 106–108. For a discussion of the 1940s version of the Central Arizona Project, see Weatherford, *Water and Agriculture in the Western U.S.*, 149–154.

2. Robinson, *Water for the West*, 104; Pearson, "Salvation for Grand Canyon," 159; Fradkin, *A River No More*, 250; Johnson, *The Central Arizona Project*, 78; Terrell, *War for the Colorado River*, 1: 253–255; Ben Cole, "West Has Strong Friend in Rep. John Saylor," *Arizona Republic*, 1963, "Undated 1963–1964," folder 9, box 170, SLU. Aspinall, transcript of oral history interview by Ross R. Rice, 10.

3. Fradkin, *A River No More*, 250. Weatherford and Brown, *New Courses for the Colorado River*, 22–24,31. Edmonds, *Mr. Chairman*, 125; Bingham, "Reclamation and the Colorado," 245.

4. Chief Justice Earl Warren, a former governor of California, removed himself from the case. (For California's argument, see Robinson, *Water for the West*, 104.) Weatherford and Brown, *New Courses for the Colorado River*, 31–35; and Holmes, *History of the Federal Water Resources Programs and Policies*, 55–57. For a more detailed discussion of the issues contested in the case, see Mann, *The Politics of Water in Arizona*, 89–96; Kenney, "River Basin Administration and the Colorado" (Ph.D. diss.), 267–273.

5. Letter, Wayne Aspinall to Stewart Udall, November 27, 1962, "1963, Department of Interior, Lower Basin States," file 63, box 130, DU; copies are also located in "1962–63 Correspondence U–Z," folder 37, box 18, CU; and "Jan.–Feb. 1963," folder 6, box 166, SLU.

6. Holmes, *History of the Federal Water Resources Programs and Policies*, 57–58; Clark, *Water in New Mexico*, 526–527; Weatherford, *Water and Agriculture in the Western U.S.*, 154; Dean, " 'Dam Building Still Had Some Magic Then,' " 84.

7. Wayne Aspinall, Speech to the Arizona State Reclamation Association, September 28, 1963, folder 9, box 15, Central Arizona Project Association Records, ASU. Newspaper coverage of Aspinall's visit and speech were quite laudatory. See "Quiet, Powerful Lawmaker in Spotlight," *Phoenix Gazette*, 26 September 1963, 15; "Aspinall Favors Area Water Plan," *Arizona Republic*, 28 September 1963; "No Project This Year, Predicts Rep. Aspinall," *Arizona Republic*, 28 September 1963. Later analysis of Aspinall's speech was less effusive. See Johnson, *The Central Arizona Project*, 147.

8. Ben Cole, "Rep. Aspinall Holds Water Key," *Arizona Republic*, 28 July 1963, 1B. For the Udall quote see Stewart Udall, article on lessons learned from the passage of the Upper Colorado Storage Project, April 5, 1956, "Echo Park, Dinosaur National Monument, Sierra Club Releases, 1950–1957," Correspondence

Sites 4: 501, The Wilderness Society Papers, DPL. For Hayden see Analysis of Circumstances Affecting the Central Arizona Project and Suggested Procedure, July 1963, folder 5A, box 788, Carl T. Hayden Papers, ASU.

9. Udall and Hayden were far more concerned about the opposition of California and the lack of unity among Arizonans. See Coate, "The Biggest Water Fight in American History," 82–83. Rhodes, transcript of oral history interview by Dean Smith, 17. Letter, Wayne Aspinall to Ed Johnson, October 9, 1963, "1963, Department of Interior, CRSP," File 62, box 130, DU.

10. Among the officials expressing their belief that Aspinall would help pass the CAP were Secretary Udall; his assistant, Orren Beaty; and Floyd Dominy. See Stewart Udall, handwritten minutes of meeting, "Feb.–March 1964," folder 6, box 167; memo, Orren Beaty to Stewart Udall, December 31, 1964, "Nov.–Dec. 1964," folder 2, box 168; Joseph Jensen, memo, Confidential Report to M.W.D. Directors on conference with Sec. Udall, December 15, 1964, "Nov.–Dec. 1964," folder 2, box 168, all located in SLU. Coate, "The Biggest Water Fight in American History," 83–85. Dean, " 'Dam Building Still Had Some Magic Then,' " 90; Reisner, Cadillac Desert, 305; Hundley, Water and the West, 324.

11. Dean, " 'Dam Building Still Had Some Magic Then,' " 90–91; Reisner, Cadillac Desert, 305; Hundley, Water and the West, 324; Mann, "Politics in the United States and the Salinity Problem of the Colorado River," 118–119; Tyler, The Last Water Hole in the West, 147.

12. Coate, "The Biggest Water Fight in American History," 81; Reisner, Cadillac Desert, 284–285; Peirce, The Mountain States of America, 144; Welsh, How to Create a Water Crisis, 105; For a map illustrating the various diversions schemes under consideration, see Tyler, The Last Water Hole in the West, 321.

13. Mann, "Politics in the United States and the Salinity Problem of the Colorado River," 117; Dean, " 'Dam Building Still Had Some Magic Then,' " 90–92; Somma, "The Colorado River" (Ph.D. diss.), 83–84. Jackson's active role in this issue contrasted sharply with his usually limited interest in matters before the Senate Interior Committee. See Baker, Conservation Politics.

14. Reisner, Cadillac Desert, 283–284; Coate, "The Biggest Water Fight in American History," 86; Palmer, Endangered Rivers, 82.

15. Coate, "The Biggest Water Fight in American History," 86; Somma, "The Colorado River" (Ph.D. diss.), 84; Dean, " 'Dam Building Still Had Some Magic Then,' " 84; Berkman and Viscusi, Damming the West, 117; Fradkin, A River No More, 229; Sparks, transcript summary of interview.

16. Holmes, History of the Federal Water Resources Programs and Policies, 58–59; Coate, "The Biggest Water Fight in American History," 86; Pearson, "Salvation for Grand Canyon," 160

17. Memo, Ed Weinburg to Stewart Udall, February 11, 1965, "Jan.–Feb. 1965," folder 3, box 168, SLU. Letter, Stewart Udall to Larry Mehren, April 1,

1965, "April–May 1965," folder 5, box 168, SLU. Memo for Files, May 29, 1965, folder 12, box 5, Carl T. Hayden Papers, ASU.

18. Indications of Aspinall's concerns began appearing in spring 1965. See *Colorado River Association Newsletter,* "March 1965," folder 4, box 168, SLU; Johnson, *The Central Arizona Project,* 153. Letter to Victor Paulek, May 13, 1965, folder 39 G 8, box 184, DU.

19. Letter, Stewart Udall to Wayne Aspinall, May 15, 1965, "1965 Department of Interior, Upper Basin Correspondence," file 39G(1), box 184, DU.

20. Ingram, *Water Politics,* 72; Coate, "The Biggest Water Fight in American History," 87; Johnson, *The Central Arizona Project,* 158. Memo for Files, May 29, 1965, folder 12, box 5, Carl T. Hayden Papers, ASU.

21. Letter, Morris Udall and John Rhodes to Wayne Aspinall, June 9, 1965, "April–June 1965," folder 1, box 476, MKU (emphasis in the original quote).

22. Ibid. Letter, Wayne Aspinall to Morris Udall, June 11, 1965, "April–June 1965," folder 1, box 476, MKU. Johnson, *The Central Arizona Project,* 160.

23. Letter, Carl Hayden to Floyd Dominy, June 10, 1965, "June–July 1965," folder 6, box 168, SLU. See also typed copy of this letter, dated June 16, 1965, Colorado River Water, box 710, CPA.

24. Coate, "The Biggest Water Fight in American History," 88. Memo from John Rhodes, July 7, 1965, folder 4, box 7, Carl T. Hayden Papers, ASU.

25. Memo, "The Arizona Water Situation as of July 22, 1965," "CAP: Legislative Correspond. July–September, 1965," folder 2, box 3, Central Arizona Project, 89th Congress, John J. Rhodes Papers, ASU.

26. Letter, Wayne Aspinall to Ed Johnson, July 30, 1965, file L-11(b)1-a, box 196, DU.

27. Johnson, *The Central Arizona Project,* 161.

28. House Committee on Interior and Insular Affairs, *Hearings on H.R. 4671 on Lower Colorado River Basin Project* (1965), 134.

29. Ibid., 245.

30. Ibid., 245–249; Johnson, *The Central Arizona Project,* 166. Years later Wayne Akin, a lobbyist for the CAP, was asked in an interview about Goddard's testimony and whether or not the governor had deliberately mispronounced Aspinall's name. Akin replied, "No. He was just stupid." See Akin, transcript of oral history interview, 19.

31. House Committee on Interior and Insular Affairs, *Hearings on H.R. 4671 on Lower Colorado River Basin Project* (1965), 388. Aspinall had legitimate reasons to mistrust New Mexico, since in fact the state was negotiating a separate agreement with Arizona concerning water flow between the two states. See Clark, *Water in New Mexico,* 529–530; Ingram, *Water Politics,* 90–91.

32. Letter, Aspinall to Mike Perko, February 5, 1964, "1964 Legislation, Interior Department, Irrigation and Reclamation, General," file L-11(b), box 165;

letter, Aspinall to Eleanor Mueller, November 19, 1964, "1964 Central Arizona Project," file L-11(b)1-b, box 165; letter, Aspinall to Ralph Culter, March 11, 1965, file L-11(b)1, box 196; letter, Aspinall to Robert King, April 21, 1965, "1965 Legislation, Central Arizona Project," file L11(b)1-a, box 196. All correspondence at DU.

33. Miles, *Guardians of the Parks,* 228; Bert Hanna, "Columbia River's Wasted Water Proposed for Colorado Basin," *Denver Post,* 18 July 1965, 86. For evidence of the growing public backlash against the dams see Bruce Stewart, "Think Big: An Open Letter to the Secretary of the Interior," *Harper's Magazine,* August 1965, 62–63. Johnson, *The Central Arizona Project,* 164; House Committee on Interior and Insular Affairs, *Hearings on H.R. 4671 on Lower Colorado River Basin Project* (1965), 80.

34. Johnson, *The Central Arizona Project,* 167–170; House Committee on Interior and Insular Affairs, *Hearings on H.R. 4671 on Lower Colorado River Basin Project* (1965), 802, 735.

35. Letter, John Geoffrey Will to Douglas J. Wall, November 22, 1965, folder 12, box 5, Carl T. Hayden Papers, ASU; Aspinall, transcript of oral history interview by Ross R. Rice, 11.

36. For descriptions of the projects see Vandenbusche and Smith, *A Land Alone,* 269–270. For newspaper quote see Gordon Gauss, "Aspinall Calls for Sharing of U.S. Natural Resources," *Daily Sentinel,* 28 September 1965, 1.

37. For "pound" quote, see Peirce, *The Mountain States of America,* 235. For *Science* quote, see O'Brien, "Cost Control and Authorization of Bureau of Reclamation Projects" (master's thesis), 121. For Stewart Udall quote, see Udall, telephone interview with author. For additional sources discussing the extortion theory, see Miles, *Guardians of the Parks,* 226; Hundley, *Water and the West,* 324; Mann, "Conflict and Coalition," 159; Somma, "The Colorado River" (Ph.D. diss.), 82.

38. Berkman and Viscusi, *Damming the West,* 115; Tyler, *The Last Water Hole in the West,* 323, 545n81.

39. Dominy, transcript of oral history interview by Brit Allan Storey; Reisner, *Cadillac Desert,* 303; Dominy, telephone interview with author.

40. Cleary, transcript of oral history interview by Alice Wright, 12; Cleary, interview with author. Letter, Wayne Aspinall to Gary Hart, September 16, 1980, "1979–83 Gary Hart," folder 55, box 30, CU.

41. Reisner, *Cadillac Desert,* 302.

42. Memo, L. M. Alexander to Lower Colorado River Basin File, December 9, 1965, folder 6, box 7, Carl T. Hayden Papers, ASU.

43. Ingram, *Water Politics,* 74–75.

44. For congressional meeting see memo, John Rhodes to CAP Files, March 9, 1966, folder 1, box 9, Carl T. Hayden Papers, ASU. For "blackmail" memo see

memo, Orren Beaty to Stewart Udall, March 9, 1966, "April–June 1965," folder 1, box 476, MKU.

45. The Dolores Project review was the only one that was finished. Johnson, *The Central Arizona Project,* 180; Ingram, *Water Politics,* 76. For a summary of the meeting see L. M. Alexander, Memo for Files, March 30, 1966, "CAP: Dallas Creek–West Divide & San Miguel Projects," folder 6, box 2, Central Arizona Project, 89th Congress, John J. Rhodes Papers, ASU.

46. Memo, John Rhodes to CAP Files, March 9, 1966, folder 1, box 9, Carl T. Hayden Papers, ASU.

47. Letter, Wayne Aspinall to Charles L. Schultze, March 14, 1966, folder 1, box 7, Carl T. Hayden Papers, ASU.

48. For a copy of the Interior Department's March 16 press release on the status of the Dallas Creek, San Miguel, and West Divide reports see "1966 Department of Interior, Information Materials and News Releases," file 34B, box 212. For a chronology of the rapid project approval, see "Project Supporters Are Furious with Aspinall," *Durango Daily Herald,* 11 April 1966, folder L-11b(1)a23, box 245. Both items are at DU.

49. Letter, Phillip Hughes to Stewart Udall, April 30, 1966, "Jan.–May 1966," folder 1, box 169, SLU.

50. Letter, Aspinall to David Wood Jr., May 10, 1966, file L-11b(1)a23, box 245; "Capitol Comments," May 13, 1966, "Southwestern Colorado Reclamation," box 516; both items at DU.

51. Johnson, *The Central Arizona Project,* 180, 183. For five-minute limit see "Witnesses Skip Real Purpose," *Daily Sentinel,* 18 May 1966, "1966 Certificate, Newspaper Clippings," folder 27, box 42, CU.

52. Memo, Morris Udall to Les Alexander, April 26, 1966, "CAP: Indians," folder 7, box 2, Central Arizona Project, 89th Congress, John J. Rhodes Papers, ASU.

53. House Committee on Interior and Insular Affairs, *Hearings on H.R. 4671 on Lower Colorado River Basin Project* (1966), 1260.

54. Ibid., 1071, 1269–1271.

55. Ibid., 1363.

56. House Committee on Interior and Insular Affairs, *Hearings on H.R. 4671 on Lower Colorado River Basin Project* (1966), 1361.

57. Ibid., 1428–1434, 1464. Approximately half the witnesses were federal, state, and local government officials, who tended to favor the project; only a fifth of the witnesses represented environmental groups. In his statement Brower was quick to note that his charges of suppression were against the Interior Department, not the House Interior Committee. For the materials the Sierra Club submitted to the Interior Committee see "A Compendium of Statements and Documents Presented . . . to the Congress with Respect to Hearings on H.R.

4671," May 19, 1966, "Grand Canyon: Lower Colorado River Basin Project Act, 1966," folder 22, box 125, SC NLO.

Chapter 6. Flooding the Sistine Chapel

1. Letter, Wayne Aspinall to Frank Plaut, July 13, 1966, folder L-11b(1)a, box 245, DU.

2. Note that Aspinall's support for the Bridge Canyon Dam reversed his position of two years earlier. See letter, Wayne Aspinall to John Holden, June 20, 1966, "1966 Legislation, Central Arizona, Project, Dec. 65–June 66," folder L-11b(1)a23, box 245, DU.

3. Letter, Aspinall to Julie Green, August 27, 1966, folder L-11b(1)a22, box 245, DU.

4. Ibid.

5. "Knight Errant to Nature's Rescue: Close-up California's David Brower, No. 1 Conservationist," *Life*, 27 May 1966, 39.

6. Pearson, "Salvation for Grand Canyon," 165; Nash, *Wilderness and the American Mind*, 229; Cohen, *The History of the Sierra Club*, 360.

7. Cohen, *The History of the Sierra Club*, 360; Nash, *Wilderness and the American Mind*, 230; Pearson, "Salvation for Grand Canyon," 166; Fox, *The American Conservation Movement*, 320; Berry, *Lobbying for the People*, 48.

8. Despite the increase in memberships, the Club did experience financial difficulties for the next several years, traceable in part to the loss of their tax-deductible status. Nash, *Wilderness and the American Mind*, 230–231; Miles, *Guardians of the Parks*, 228; Allin, *The Politics of Wilderness Preservation*, 180; Palmer, *Endangered Rivers*, 85; Wiley and Gottlieb, *Empires in the Sun*, 291. For Brower quote see Cohen, *The History of the Sierra Club*, 361. For the Sistine advertisement, see Pearson, "Salvation for Grand Canyon," 165; Brower, *For Earth's Sake*, 368; Cohen, *The History of the Sierra Club*, 363; Nash, *Wilderness and the American Mind*, 231.

9. Senecah, "The Environmental Discourse of David Brower" (Ph.D. diss.), 148. Letter, Aspinall to Ruth Wood, July 27, 1966, folder L-11b(1)a22; letter to James Rigg, June 27, 1966, folder L-11b(1)a23. Both letters are in box 245 DU.

10. "Aspinall Hits Sierra Club Lobby Tactics," *Daily Sentinel*, 6 July 1966, 1. Letter, Jeff Ingram to Wayne Aspinall, July 8, 1966, "Colorado River, June–Aug. 1966," Michael McCloskey Papers, 1950–1987, folder 100, box 27, SC Members.

11. Letter, Richard Lamm to Wayne Aspinall, June 26, 1966, folder L11-B-(1)a, box 245, DU.

12. Letter, Frank Plaut to Wayne Aspinall, July 7, 1966; letter, Aspinall to Plaut, July 13, 1966. Both letters are in folder L11-B-(1)a, box 245, DU.

13. Letter, Lamm to Aspinall, August 1, 1966, folder L11-B-(1)a, box 245, DU.

14. Letter, Aspinall to Lamm, August 4, 1966; letter, Lamm to Aspinall, August 12, 1966. Both letters are in folder L11-B-(1)a, box 245, DU.

15. Memo, Morris Udall to CAP File, June 2, 1966, folder 2, box 476, MKU. Senecah, "The Environmental Discourse of David Brower" (Ph.D. diss.), 150.

16. "Capitol Comments," May 13, 1966, "HR 4761 Colorado River Basin," box 516 DU; the column was split and published on two consecutive days in the *Daily Sentinel:* 11 August 1966, 4; and 12 August 1966, 4. Letter (copy), Wayne Aspinall to Richard Martin, August 29, 1966, "1966 Department of Interior, Bureau of Reclamation," file 39, box 216, DU.

17. Memo, L. M. Alexander to CAP files, August 31, 1966, folder 8, box 7, Carl T. Hayden Papers, ASU. Pearson, "Salvation for Grand Canyon," 168.

18. For last-minute strategy sessions see memo, Morris Udall to John Rhodes, September 22, 1966, "Sept.–Nov. 1966," folder 4, box 169, SLU. For Aspinall's "confession" see Latousek, "The Extinction of the Western Water Buffalo" (master's thesis), 93.

19. Wayne Aspinall, "Man's Demand on His Environment: Solving the Dilemma Between Man's Needs and His Wants," speech to the Third Open Space Conference, Vail, Colorado, September 24, 1966, located in "1966 Speeches," folder 5, box 23, CU.

20. Ibid.

21. Wayne Aspinall, "Colorado's Involvement in Westwide Water Planning," speech to the Colorado State Grange, Cortez, Colorado, October 1, 1966, located in "Sept.–Nov. 1966," folder 4, box 169, SLU.

22. Ibid.

23. Ibid.

24. Ibid.

25. Ibid.

26. Speech located in "Sept.–Nov. 1966," folder 4, box 169, SLU.

27. Ibid.

28. Bert Hanna, "Udall's Thermal Power Plan Nonsense, Aspinall Says," *Denver Post,* 18 November 1966, 29.

29. Senecah, "The Environmental Discourse of David Brower" (Ph.D. diss.), 114; *Colorado Water Congress Newsletter,* 1 December 1966, 4.

30. Senecah, "The Environmental Discourse of David Brower" (Ph.D. diss.), 114; Reisner, *Cadillac Desert,* 298. A photograph of the altercation was published on the front page of the *Albuquerque Tribune,* 18 November 1966.

31. For a quick summary of the different versions of the CRBP introduced in Congress, see Johnson, *The Central Arizona Project,* 196. For the details of Udall's plan see Holmes, *History of the Federal Water Resources Programs and Policies,* 147; and Dean, " 'Dam Building Still Had Some Magic Then,' " 96.

32. For details of Aspinall's bill, see Press Release, "Aspinall Introduces Bill to

Expand Grand Canyon National Park," February 27, 1967, folder L-11b(1)c, box 275, DU. Senecah, "The Environmental Discourse of David Brower" (Ph.D. diss.), 157–158; Pearson, "Salvation for Grand Canyon," 170.

33. Memo, Stewart Udall to Lyndon Johnson, March 14, 1967, folder 8, box 133, SLU; Coate, "The Biggest Water Fight in American History," 91.

34. House Committee on Interior and Insular Affairs, *Hearings on H.R. 3300 on Colorado River Basin Project* (1967), 249, 261, 263.

35. Ibid.

36. *Colorado Water Congress Newsletter,* March 1967, 6; Bert Hanna, "Aspinall Confident about His River Bill," *Denver Post,* 19 March 1967, 33.

37. Wayne Aspinall, speech at the Starvation Dam, Utah, Groundbreaking Ceremonies, May 31, 1967, folder Pub. 6, box 284, DU. Aspinall's speech was reprinted in *Congressional Record,* 90th Cong., 1st sess., June 7, 1967, 113, pt. 11: 15078–15081. Letter, Aspinall to I. W. Patterson, June 28, 1967, folder L-11b(1)b, box 274, DU.

38. Ibid.

39. Letter, Aspinall to Karl Carson, July 17, 1967; letter, Aspinall to Ed Johnson, July 27, 1967. Both letters are in folder 39B, box 256, DU.

40. *Colorado Water Congress Newsletter,* 1 August 1967, 5; Johnson, *The Central Arizona Project,* 205–206; Pearson, "Salvation for Grand Canyon," 173; William Blair, "Senate Debating Water Plan Bill," *New York Times,* 4 August 1967, 36.

41. Letter, Morris Udall to John McCormack, August 11, 1967, folder 3, box 1, Central Arizona Project, 90th Congress, John J. Rhodes Papers, ASU; Ingram, *Water Politics,* 61.

42. Letter, Aspinall to John McCormack, August 18, 1967, folder L-11(b)1a, box 274, DU; Ingram, *Water Politics,* 61.

43. Editorial, "Threat to SW Colorado," *Durango Herald,* 9 August 1967, 2. Letter, Aspinall to Arthur Ballantine, August 14, 1967, folder L-11b(1)a, DU.

44. Letter, Aspinall to Ballantine, August 14, 1967, folder L-11b(1)a, DU; letter, Aspinall to Mahlon White, August 17, 1967, folder L-11b(1)b; letter, Aspinall to Gilbert Slade, August 17, 1967, folder L-11b(1)a. All letters are in box 274, DU.

45. "Aspinall Lowers Demands on Colorado River Bill," *Daily Sentinel,* 28 August 1967, 1; for off-the-record remarks, see memo, Ray Killian to Congressional Delegation and Task Force, August 25, 1967, folder 3, box 5, Carl T. Hayden Papers, ASU.

46. For evidence of the split over Colorado's water strategy see Morley Fox, Central Arizona Project Association Situation Report, August 31, 1967, folder 3, box 5, Carl T. Hayden Papers, ASU; see also Editorial, "Support for Water," *Daily Sentinel,* 5 September 1967, 5. "Aspinall Casts Doubts of Water, Financing for Arizona Project," *Daily Sentinel,* 3 September 1967, 1. For quote see letter,

Aspinall to Allan Czillinger, August 30, 1967, folder L-11b(1)a, box 274, DU. Wayne Aspinall, speech to the National Conference of State and Federal Water Officials, September 6, 1967, folder 1, box 6, Central Arizona Project, 90th Congress, John J. Rhodes Papers, ASU; James Kelley, "Aspinall Blasts Water Pact Lag," *Denver Post,* 7 September 1967, 3; Coate, "The Biggest Water Fight in American History," 91.

47. Dick Thomas, "Aspinall Demands River Bill Changes," *Denver Post,* 8 September 1967, 20; "River Legislation Still Snagged," *Daily Sentinel,* 9 September 1967. "River-Silt Recreation Bonanza," *Daily Sentinel,* 8 September 1967; Dick Thomas, "Aspinall Speaks at Ceremony Dedicating Reservoir Project," *Denver Post,* 10 September 1967, 29.

48. Latousek, "The Extinction of the Western Water Buffalo" (master's thesis), 98; Report, Regional Director to Commissioner, September 15, 1967, "Professional File, 1967, Overseas Travel," box 28, Papers of Floyd E. Dominy, American Heritage Center, University of Wyoming. Senator Hayden had threatened the Fryingpan-Arkansas once before, in June 1965, but the threat this time seemed far more serious. "Fryingpan Funds Facing Trouble in Coming Year," *Pueblo Star-Journal,* 29 August 1967; James Kelley, "Coloradans Concerned at Threat to Fry-Ark," *Denver Post,* 22 September 1967.

49. Barnet Nover, "Hayden Acts to Get Project Bill onto Floor," *Denver Post,* 28 September 1967. For a copy of Hayden's press release announcing his plan, see "Hayden in New Move on Water Bill," September 28, 1967, XIII Interior Committee: Central Ariz. Project, box 736, CPA.

50. Letter, Floyd Dominy to Carl Hayden, September 6, 1966, folder 1, box 4. Dominy also discussed his idea during a CAP strategy meeting in September 1966. See memo, L. M. Alexander to CAP Task Force, September 15, 1966, folder 8, box 7. Both documents in Carl T. Hayden Papers, ASU. When asked later about his role in devising a way to make an end run around Aspinall, Dominy merely said that it was a difficult situation for him since he was friends with both men. See Dominy, telephone interview with author.

51. Rhodes, transcript of oral history interview, 18–20. For a similar account see Rhodes and Smith, *I Was There,* 95. Note: both these accounts give the wrong year, 1968 instead of 1967, for this event.

52. Aspinall wrote two letters within days of the committee's meeting in which he stated that he had always planned to bring the bill up in January, and that Senator Hayden had known about this since July. See letter, Wayne Aspinall to Al Czillinger, October 12, 1967; letter, Aspinall to Kenny Miller, October 11, 1967. Both letters are in "1967 Leg, Interior and Insular Affairs Committee, Colorado River Basin Project, Correspondence Aug–Sept.," file L-11b(1)a, box 274, DU.

53. Letter, Wayne Aspinall to John Love, October 11, 1967, "CAP: Colorado," folder 7, box 3, Central Arizona Project, 90th Congress, John J. Rhodes Papers, ASU.

54. Ibid. Letter, John Saylor to Everett Dirksen, October 6, 1967, folder 1, box 6, Central Arizona Project, 90th Congress, John J. Rhodes Papers, ASU.

55. Letter, Aspinall to Ken Browne, October 5, 1967; letter, Wayne Aspinall to Ed Johnson, November 10, 1967. Both letters are in "1967 Leg, Interior and Insular Affairs Committee, Colorado River Basin Project, Correspondence Aug–Sept.," file L-11b(1)a, box 274, DU. Bob Sweeney, "Future of Juniper Dam Appears Lengthy Aspinall Reports," *Northwest Colorado Daily Press,* 26 October 1967, 1.

56. Johnson, *The Central Arizona Project,* 212.

57. Memo on Conference between Udall and Aspinall, January 2, 1968, "1968," folder 11, box 169, SLU.

58. House Committee on Interior and Insular Affairs, *Hearings on H.R. 3300 on Colorado River Basin Project* (1968), 741; Johnson, *The Central Arizona Project,* 214. For Aspinall's goal for the hearings, see letter, Aspinall to Gale McGee, January 31, 1968, folder L-11b(1)a, box 308, DU.

59. House Committee on Interior and Insular Affairs, *Hearings on H.R. 3300 on Colorado River Basin Project* (1968), 714–715, 745–753, 788; Johnson, *The Central Arizona Project,* 214–216; "Water Enough to Run CAP, House Is Told," *Arizona Republic,* 31 January 1968. For Aspinall's motive in entering the statement, see letter, Aspinall to John Sherman, February 16, 1968, folder L-11b(1)a, box 308, DU.

60. Morris Udall, Summary of the Proceedings at Reclamation Subcommittee, February 8, 1963, folder 5, box 15, Carl T. Hayden Papers, ASU. For the vow of silence see Elmer Lammi, "Aspinall Introduces Own Arizona Plan," *Rocky Mountain News,* 8 February 1968, 5.

61. Johnson, *The Central Arizona Project,* 218. Morley Fox, Central Arizona Project Association Situation Report, March 8, 1968, folder 3, box 15, Carl T. Hayden Papers, ASU.

62. *Congressional Record,* 90th Cong., 2d sess., May 15, 1968, 114, pt. 10: 13407, 13411.

63. Ibid. For press coverage of the House vote see "House Authorizes Colorado River Project," *Wall Street Journal,* 17 May 1968, 7; "Colorado Stakes Remaining Water on Colorado R.," *Pueblo Chieftain,* 17 May 1968, 5B; *Colorado Water Congress Newsletter,* 1 June 1968.

64. Letter, Morris Udall to Wayne Aspinall, May 22, 1968, folder 3, box 15, Carl T. Hayden Papers, ASU. Letter, John Rhodes to Wayne Aspinall, May 17, 1968, folder L-11b(1)a, box 308, DU.

65. Letter, Wayne Aspinall to John Rhodes, May 21, 1968, folder L-11b(1)a, box 308, DU.

66. Johnson, *The Central Arizona Project,* 224–225; "Basin Bill Faces Tough Senate-House Test," *Daily Sentinel,* 26 May 1968, 12. For information on the conference negotiations see Rich Johnson, "Personal Log," folder 8, box 1, Rich Johnson Papers, ASU.

67. Bert Hanna, "At 72, Rep. Aspinall Hits Campaign Trail," *Denver Post,* 20 August 1968, 15. Despite Aspinall's optimism that the ten years would pass quickly, Congress in 1978 extended the ban for another ten years, and again in 1986. Coate, "The Biggest Water Fight in American History," 93. For a brief summary of the final contents of the CRBP bill see Bert Hanna, "State's Water Officials Praise Bill on Colorado River," *Denver Post,* 15 September 1960, 30; Holmes, *History of the Federal Water Resources Programs and Policies,* 147–148.

68. Edmonds, *Mr. Chairman,* 144; Brown, *Aspinall: Centennial Edition.*

Chapter 7. All the King's Men

1. Ian M. Thompson, "A Critical Appraisal of U.S. Rep. Wayne Aspinall," *Durango Herald,* 16 August 1970, 2.

2. Marjorie Hunter, "Persuasive Land Use Counselor," *New York Times,* 24 June 1970, 22; Philip Fradkin, "Rep. Aspinall, Boss of the West," *Washington Post,* 5 December 1971, E1 (quote on this page); Dennis Farnet, "Ruler of the Land," *Wall Street Journal,* 21 January 1972, 1. Morton's comments so outraged the Republican delegates that he was later forced to retract them. See "Solon Takes Back Aspinall Praise," *Daily Sentinel,* 8 August 1968, 1; Bert Hanna, "At 72, Rep. Aspinall Hits Campaign Trail," *Denver Post,* 20 August 1968, 15.

3. By the late 1960s the term "environmental" had replaced the earlier terms "conservation" and "preservation." For a discussion of this change in terminology, see Fox, *The American Conservation Movement,* 292. For elements of decline see McCarthy, "He Fought for His West," 41–42.

4. Letter, Aspinall to Frank Walek, November 30, 1959, "1959 Alphabetical File of Letters Written from Grand Junction office, M–Z," folder 13, box 14, CU; McCarthy, "He Fought for His West," 37; Bert Hanna, "Agencies Grappling with Basin Projects," *Denver Post,* 12 December 1965, 39; Notes from Ottis Peterson to Mr. Dominy, September 22, 1967, "Professional File, 1967, Overseas Travel," box 28, Papers of Floyd E. Dominy, American Heritage Center, University of Wyoming.

5. Letter, Aspinall to Arthur Ballantine, May 2, 1969, "1969 Aspinall-for-Congress Committee," folder Pol 4, box 356; letter, Wayne Aspinall to William Grant, June 29, 1965, "1965 Political, State Correspondence," File Pol 1b, box 205. Both letters are at DU.

6. Rendall Ayers, "Love Calls Lawmakers to Redistricting Session," *Denver*

Post, 21 April 1964, 12. "Here's Statistical Picture of Congressional Districts," *Rocky Mountain News,* 1 May 1964, 5.

7. "Here's Statistical Picture of Congressional Districts," *Rocky Mountain News,* 1 May 1964, 5; Schoenebaum, *Political Profiles: The Nixon/Ford Years,* 32; Lee Olson, "Aspinall Faces Fight," *Denver Post,* 19 June 1970, 22.

8. Letter, Wayne Aspinall to Robert McConnell, October 19, 1968, "1968 Correspondence M–N," folder 12, box 24, CU.

9. For Aspinall's involvement with the Narrows Project, see letter, H. P. Dugan to Floyd Dominy, July 19, 1965, "Correspondence, 1965, Blue Envelope Letter," box 4, Papers of Floyd E. Dominy, American Heritage Center, University of Wyoming; letter (copy), Wayne Aspinall to Ned Dermody, March 22, 1966, "1966 LEG The Narrows Project," File L-11b(3)a, box 233; Letter, Wayne Aspinall to Eric Wendt, August 25, 1967, "1967 Department of Interior, Bureau of Reclamation," file 39, box 256. Both letters are at DU. For congressional debate, see *Congressional Record,* 91st Cong., 2d sess., August 3, 1970, 116, pt. 20: 27029–27034; *Congressional Record,* 91st Cong., 2d sess., August 13, 1970, 116, pt. 21: 28804–28805. Reisner has a scathing discussion of the Narrows Project in *Cadillac Desert,* 425–451.

10. Letter, Aspinall to Richard Nixon, September 4, 1969, "1969 Executive Offices, White House," folder 1, box 323; letter, Aspinall to Eileen Crane, November 7, 1969, "1969 Executive Offices, Bureau of the Budget," folder 1-A box 323; letter, Aspinall to Clayton Cotten, November 24, 1969, "1969, Interior Department, Fruitland Mesa," folder 39G(6), box 330; Aspinall, speech to the Third Western Interstate Water Conference, August 27, 1969, "1969 Speeches," folder Pub-6, box 355; Aspinall, speech to National Reclamation Association, October 23, 1969, "1969 Speeches," folder Pub-6, box 355; Aspinall, Speech to the Irrigation Districts Association of California, December 5, 1969, "1969 Speeches," folder Pub-6, box 355. All items located at DU.

11. Jack Anderson, "Aspinall Host at a Lobby Party," *Washington Post,* 15 December 1969, D13; Jack Anderson, "Western Roundup in Washington," *Daily Sentinel,* 15 February 1970, 4; Jack Anderson, "Pacific Isles Have Smell of Scandal," *Washington Post,* 20 October 1971, A29; letter, Aspinall to Carl Brown, January 14, 1970, folder 49, box 370, DU.

12. William Steif, "Nader Force Seeks to End Colo. River Water Project," *Rocky Mountain News,* 7 November 1971, 3; Robert Threlkeld, "Nader Scores Aspinall, Climate Project," *Rocky Mountain News,* 7 November 1971, 5. Nader's group eventually published their findings in Berkman and Viscusi, *Damming the West.*

13. Wayne Aspinall, Press Release, November 9, 1971, folder I-11b, box 420, DU; Leonard Larsen, "Water Project Attack Assailed," *Denver Post,* 10 December 1971, 54. Letter, Aspinall to Felix Sefcovic, November 12, 1971, folder 39A, box

404, DU. For subsequent criticisms of Aspinall see Green, Fallows, and Zwick, *Ralph Nader Congress Project,* 21; Sussman, *Citizens Look at Congress;* Ralph Nader Congress Project, *The Environment Committees.*

14. Jacobs, *A Rage for Justice,* 141; Edgar Wayburn, transcript of oral history interview, 319.

15. Jacobs, *A Rage for Justice,* 141; Frances Melrose, "Wayne Aspinall, 82, Strives to Stay in the Water Picture," *Rocky Mountain News,* 24 November 1978, 8; Dennis Farnet, "Ruler of the Land," *Wall Street Journal,* 21 January 1972, 22.

16. Jacobs, *A Rage for Justice,* 220–221.

17. Schoenebaum, *Political Profiles,* 32.

18. Jacobs, *A Rage for Justice,* 221. After the reforms had been in effect for a year, both Aspinall and the rebels agreed that the changes had not, apart from the increased staff sizes, radically changed the workings of the committee, although Aspinall complained that things took longer now. See Dennis Farnet, "Ruler of the Land," *Wall Street Journal,* 21 January 1972, 22; Fenno, *Congressmen in Committees,* 285–286.

19. Gilmore, transcript summary of interview.

20. Traylor, Oral History Interview with Alice Wright; Neal, transcript summary of interview; Sparks, interview with author; Dennis Farnet, "Ruler of the Land," *Wall Street Journal,* 21 January 1972, 22.

21. "Aspinall's Win Overwhelming," *Denver Post,* 4 November 1964, 77; "Win Gives Aspinall 10th Term," *Denver Post,* 9 November 1966, 73; "Rep. Aspinall Re-elected To 11th Term in House," *Denver Post,* 6 November 1968, 44. Aspinall's frequently weak margin of victory during his twenty-four-year House career led one writer to note that the congressman was an oddity among House chairmen, who normally came from ultra-safe seats. See Weaver, *Both Your Houses,* 74. For the public's awareness that Aspinall was vulnerable in 1970, see "MNC's Marginal Districts," *National Journal,* 15 August 1970, 1767.

22. For rumors, see *Rocky Mountain News* clipping, dated 16 February 1970, in folder Pub 7, box 388, DU. Leonard Larsen, "Aspinall 'Confirms' Candidacy," *Denver Post,* 31 March 1970, 2. Letters to Aspinall's campaign manager, indicating surprise that he ran again, are located in "1970 General File," folder 29, box 10, CU.

23. Letter, Aspinall to Mrs. Carl Newlon, April 28, 1970, folder 49, box 370, DU. For Larimer and Weld concerns, see letter, Aspinall to Claude Crane, June 23, 1970, "1970 Pub & Pol, 4th District Corresp.," folder Pol-1c, box 389; letter, Wayne Aspinall to Ellis Lupton, September 16, 1970, box 430; both letters are in the DU collection. For concerns about Vietnam as an issue in the election, see letters in folder Pol-1c, box 389, DU.

24. Leonard Larsen, "Dem and GOP Enter Race Against Aspinall," *Denver Post,* 16 June 1970, 2.

25. Chuck Green, "4th Dist. Race a Different Campaign: Richard Perchlik," *Denver Post,* 3 September 1978, 80. For the assessment of Perchlik's campaign see Marion Edey, "Aspinall's Re-election Chances," 1972 "Elections Political Parties 1972," Conservation Department Records, 1891–1973, folder 9, box 162, SC Records. For Perchlik's water diversion comment, see undated newspaper clipping from the [Montrose?] *Daily Press* located in folder 4A, box 390, DU. For Aspinall's Vietnam shift, see Chuck Green, "4th Dist. Race a Different Campaign: Wayne Aspinall," *Denver Post,* 3 September 1978, 80; 1970 Election Campaign pamphlet, "1970 Advertising-General," folder 11, box 10, CU.

26. Letter, Aspinall to Tom Kassler, September 15, 1970, "1970 Pub & Pol, State Corresp.," folder Pol-1b, box 389, DU.

27. Charles Traylor to Bill Cleary, August 5, 1970, "Political, Aspinall for Congress," folder Pol-4(1), box 430, DU. For further evidence of local dissatisfaction, see Ian M. Thompson, "A Critical Appraisal of U.S. Rep. Wayne Aspinall," *Durango Herald,* 16 August 1970, 2.

28. "Aspinall Victor in Fourth," *Denver Post,* 9 September 1970, 79. Lawrence Walsh, "Aspinall Campaigns 'on My Record,' " *Rocky Mountain News,* 19 October 1970, 22; Monk Tyson, "Mutual Understanding Advocated by Aspinall," *Denver Post,* 22 October 1970, 69.

29. "Wayne Aspinall Defeats Gossard, Wins 12th Term," *Denver Post,* 4 November 1970, 77. Letter, Aspinall to David Miller, October 1, 1970, "1970 Pub & Pol, Aspinall for Congress Comm. Oct.–Dec.," folder Pol-4, box 390, DU.

30. "Special Session for Reapportion Gains," *Rocky Mountain News,* 25 June 1971, 6; Sussman, *Citizens Look at Congress,* 4; letter, Bill Cleary to Thelma Farhar, November 17, 1971, "1971 Political, Aspinall for Congress," folder Pol-4, box 430, DU.

31. Charles Roos, "GOP Leaders Compete with Redistricting Bills," *Denver Post,* 5 March 1972, 50; for Aspinall's lobbying attempt see letter, Aspinall to Dan Noble, March 9, 1971, folder Pol-1a, box 463, DU. The GOP tried to claim that the redistricting was not being done in a partisan manner. See "Gerrymandering in Colorado Done Scientifically," *Daily Sentinel,* 16 July 1972, 11. Robert Burns, "Love Unhappy with Reapportionment Plan," *Rocky Mountain News,* 29 April 1972, 8; Charles Carter, "Redistrict Bill Becomes Law," *Denver Post,* 12 May 1972, 3.

32. Letter, Aspinall to Edmund Hennelly, May 11, 1972, folder Pol-4, box 465; letter, Aspinall to A. Hills, May 25, 1972, "1972 Colorado Politics, Redistricting," folder Pol-1a, box 463. Both letters are in DU. Sussman, *Citizens Look at Congress,* 4; Michael Barone, "Campaign '72 Report/High Turnover Expected in House Seats But No Major Party Realignments," *National Journal,* 27 May 1972, 912.

33. Leonard Larsen, "Aspinall Declares for Congress Again," *Denver Post,* 16 June 1972, 50. For younger voter demographics see Warren Weaver, "Young

Voters May Change Make-up of Congress in 1972," *New York Times*, 20 September 1971, 14.

34. Letter, Aspinall to J. L. Cefkin, April 17, 1972, "1972, Colorado Politics, 4th District Correspondence," file Pol 1c, box 463. Letter, Aspinall to James Shelton, May 22, 1972, file Pol 4, box 465. Letter, Aspinall to Al Whatley, June 8, 1972, file Pol 4, box 465. All letters are in DU. "Aspinall's Aides Urge Him to Seek Re-election," *Rocky Mountain News*, 15 June 1972, 111; Leonard Larsen, "Aspinall Declares for Congress Again," *Denver Post*, 16 June 1972, 50. For a copy of the press release announcing Aspinall's candidacy, see letter, Aspinall to Amos Allard, "1972 Political," folder 4a, box 464, DU. For Aspinall's insistence that he had no choice but to be a candidate, see letter, Aspinall to Kenneth Monfort, June 21, 1972, "1972, Aspinall for Congress Committee," file Pol 4, box 465; letter, Aspinall to Virginia Herrle, October 13, 1972, "Campaign-Condolences," box 466; letter, Aspinall to Jack Vickers, October 17, 1972, "Campaign-Condolences," box 466. All letters are at DU.

35. "Harvard Law Student to Oppose Aspinall," *Denver Post*, 5 June 1972, 2; "CSU Graduate to Challenge Aspinall for Demo Spot," unidentified newspaper clipping; Tom Gavin, "Aspinall May Face New Dem Opponent," *Denver Post* [no date]. Both clippings located in folder Pol-4, box 465, DU. "Aspinall of Colorado Faces a Major Test in Primary Tuesday," *New York Times*, 10 September 1972, 54; "Aspinall's Primary: The Land-Use Issue," *National Journal*, 22 July 1972, 1196; 1972 Election Newspaper ad for Merson, *Ouray Gazette*, 7 September 1972.

36. Leonard Larsen, "Aspinall Declares for Congress Again," *Denver Post*, 16 June 1972, 50. For "Mersin" reference see letter, Aspinall to Amos Allard, April 10, 1972, folder Pol-1c, box 463; letter, Aspinall to Al Whatley, June 8, 1972, folder Pol-4, box 465. For questions about Phelps see letter, Aspinall to Gordon Ibbotson, May 24, 1972, folder Pol-4, box 465. Letter, Aspinall to Forrest Kelley, June 23, 1972, folder Pol-1c, box 463; letter, Aspinall to Wyatt Wood, June 16, 1972, folder Pol-1c, box 463. All letters are located at DU.

37. Robert Threlkeld, "Aspinall 'Heading' 'Dirty Dozen' List," *Rocky Mountain News*, 8 June 1972, 5; Leonard Larsen, "Aspinall Makes Environmental 'Dirty Dozen,' " *Denver Post*, 7 June 1972, 43. In addition to the "dirty dozen," Aspinall was also identified as one of the "deadly dozen" representatives targeted for defeat by an anti–Vietnam War group. See "Representatives Listed as Foes by Antiwar and Ecology Groups," *New York Times*, 12 June 1972, 32. For more information on Environmental Action see Lacey, *Government and Environmental Politics*, 91; Berry, *Lobbying for the People*, 242. Schrepfer, *The Fight to Save the Redwoods*.

38. Editorial, "The 'Dirty' Dozen," *Rocky Mountain News*, 13 June 1972, 34; Pasquale Marranzino, "The Pollution of Rash Words," *Rocky Mountain News*, 13 June 1972, 35; Editorial, "Attack on Aspinall," *Daily Sentinel*, 14 June 1972, 4. See Marion Edey, "Aspinall's Re-election Chances," June 1972, "Elections Political

Parties 1972," Conservation Department Records, 1891–1973, folder 9, box 162, SC Records. Letter, Gordon Allott to Clark MacGregor, September 14, 1971, Congressional Correspondence, 1971 [4 of 4], box 39, White House Central Files: Staff Member and Office Files: John C. Whitaker, Nixon Presidential Materials, National Archives at College Park. (Pete) McCloskey, transcript of oral history interview, 298.

39. Letter, Aspinall to Kenneth Johnson, June 19, 1972, "1972, Aspinall for Congress Comm.," folder Pol-4, box 465, DU; transcript of interview with NBC Radio, June 7, 1972, "1972 Primary News Releases & Statements 2," folder 16, box 11, CU. Confidential Memorandum, John Swanner to Aspinall, July 18, 1972, "Political 1972," folder 4b, box 464, DU. "Ecology Group Tries to Unseat Rep. Aspinall," *Los Angeles Times,* 7 September 1972, 14.

40. Jack Frank and Sam Lusky, 1972 Election Strategy Memo, August 8, 1972, "1972 Primary—General File," folder 7, box 11, CU.

41. For 1972 Election Advertising Materials see the following: "1972 Advertising-Flyers," folder 40, box 10; "1972 Advertising—Testimonials," folder 44, box 10. For gun quote see open letter, Wayne Aspinall to voters, August 24, 1972, "1972 Primary News Releases & Statements 1," folder 15, box 11. All the preceding items are located at CU.

42. Letter, Aspinall to W. D. Farr, June 26, 1972, folder Pol-4, box 465; letter, Wayne Aspinall to H. A. True Jr., June 25, 1972, "Campaign Spending WNA-72," box 464; letter, Aspinall to Gordon Ibbotson, June 22, 1972, folder Pol-4, box 465. All letters are at DU.

43. Letter, Wayne Aspinall to Debbie Briggs, September 12, 1972, "1972, Colorado Politics, 4th District Correspondence," file Pol 1c, box 463, DU. Cleary, interview with author.

44. Cleary, interview with author; Marion Edey, "Aspinall's Re-election Chances," June 1972, "Elections Political Parties 1972," Conservation Department Records, 1891–1973, folder 9, box 162, SC Records. "Conservation Leader Sends Thanks to Aspinall," *Rocky Mountain News,* 27 August 1972, 10; Press Release: Sierra Club Sets the Record Straight, August 28, 1972, "Elections Political Parties 1972," Conservation Department Records, 1891–1973, folder 9, box 162, SC Records.

45. Editorial, "A Primary to Watch," *New York Times,* 7 September 1972, 42; Press Release: Rebuttal to *New York Times* Editorial, September 8, 1972, "1972 Primary—General File," folder 7, box 11, CU.

46. Michael Frome, "Rate Your Candidate," *Field & Stream,* September 1972, 65. When the magazine first started rating congressional members in 1968, it gave Aspinall a mixed review, but by 1970 the review had become a negative one. See *Field & Stream,* September 1968, 106; September 1970, 62. James Nathan Miller, "The Outdated Law that Ravages the West," *Reader's Digest,* September 1972,

178. Letter, Wayne Aspinall to C. W. Hymar, September 21, 1972, "1972, Political" file 4a, box 464, DU.

47. Richard Tucker, "Aspinall Facing Toughest Fight of His Career," *Rocky Mountain News,* 10 September 1972, 5. Letter, Wayne Aspinall to John Wold, September 12, 1972, "Campaign Spending WNA-72," box 464, DU. Richard Tucker, "Merson Dumps Aspinall in 4th District," *Rocky Mountain News,* 13 September 1972, 5; Charles Roos, "Aspinall's 50-year Career Ends," *Denver Post,* 13 September 1972, 49.

48. Lee Olson, "Wayne Served the West Well," *Denver Post,* "1972 Condolences Messages," box 466, DU; Leonard Larsen, "A Farewell Look at Aspinall," *Denver Post,* 17 September 1972; Barclay Jameson, "Defeat Doesn't Dim Aspinall's Fine Record," *Daily Sentinel,* 17 September 1972, 4; Editorial, "Aspinall's Achievements Will Stand the Test of Time," *Denver Post,* 17 September 1972, 23; Tom Gavin, "They're Sorry Aspinall Lost," *Denver Post,* 18 September 1972, 19; Pat Oliphant, political cartoon, *Denver Post,* 18 September 1972, 20.

49. Editorial, "Defeat for Slope," *Daily Sentinel,* 17 September 1972, 4.

50. Charles Roos, "Dems Quit over Loss by Aspinall," *Denver Post,* 24 September 1972, 21; Jeff Roberts, "Allard Revs Up for Close Struggle," *Denver Post,* 20 October 1996, 1A. Letter, Howard Scott to Wayne Aspinall, September 16, 1972, "1972, Campaign Condolences," box 466, DU.

51. Over the next several months and years Aspinall wrote numerous letters, and made comments in the press, in which he listed (with slight variations) the same four reasons why he lost the primary. Letter, Wayne Aspinall to Leo Bouret, September 21, 1972, "1972, Colorado Politics, 4th District Correspondence," file Pol 1a; letter, Wayne Aspinall to David Miller, October 6, 1972, "1972, Colorado Politics, 4th District Correspondence," file Pol 1c. Both items located in box 463, DU.

52. "How the Ecologists Defeated Aspinall," *Business Week,* 23 September 1972, 27.

53. Ibid.

54. Abbott, Leonard, and McComb, *Colorado: A History of the Centennial State,* 310–311.

55. Juan Cameron, "Growth Is a Fighting Word in Colorado's Mountain Wonderland," *Fortune,* October 1973, 148; Leonard Larsen, "Interior Voices Are Lost," *Denver Post,* 12 November 1972; Wiley and Gottlieb, *Empires in the Sun,* 131–134. Letter, Aspinall to Donald Dawson, November 15, 1972; letter, Aspinall to Ralph Mecham, November 20, 1972. Both letters are located in "1972, Campaign Condolences," box 466, DU.

56. Letter, Morris Udall to Wayne Aspinall, November 15, 1972, "1972, Campaign Condolences," box 466, DU. For the two sides of the Dominy story, see Reisner, *Cadillac Desert,* 260; Dominy, transcript of oral history interview by

Brit Allan Storey. Chelf, *Congress in the American System,* 54; Fishel, *Party & Opposition,* 207.

57. Wayburn, transcript of oral history interview, 320.

58. Letter, Wayne Aspinall to the *Rocky Mountain News,* May 13, 1974, "1974 Land Use and Land Use Conference," folder 41, box 31, CU. Edmonds, *Mr. Chairman,* 25.

59. For Aspinall's involvement with Club 20, see letter, Wayne Aspinall to Ted Adamczyk, February 12, 1976, "1976 Club 20—General Correspondence," folder 1, box 28; letter, Wayne Aspinall to Henry Faussone, May 6, 1977, "1977 Club 20—General," folder 27, box 27; letter, Wayne Aspinall et. al. to members of Congress, July 12, 1979, "1978–80 Club 20—General," folder 29, box 27, CU. Brown, *Aspinall: Centennial Edition,* 42–43; Wiley and Gottlieb, *Empires in the Sun,* 128–130. For his involvement with the Mountain State Legal Foundation, see letter, Wayne Aspinall to Al Cornelison, July 31, 1978, folder 18, box 29, CU. Wiley and Gottlieb, *Empires in the Sun,* 136. "Water for Troubled Shale Oil Developers," *Colorado Business,* June 1974, 15. "Silicon Firm to Be Headed by Aspinall," *Rocky Mountain News,* 25 July 1974, 5. For a brief summary of his lobbying affiliations, see "Aspinall Has Busy Retirement," *Rocky Mountain News,* 2 October 1973, 39; Frances Melrose, "Wayne Aspinall, 82, Strives to Stay in the Water Picture," *Rocky Mountain News,* 24 November 1978, 8.

60. "Ex-Rep. Aspinall Supporting Ford," *Rocky Mountain News,* 26 October 1976, 6. Robert Tweedell, "Wayne Aspinall: A Man to Remember," *Denver Post,* 4 May 1980, Empire Magazine, 27.

61. The five Colorado projects were the Narrows, Dallas Creek, Dolores, Fruitland Mesa, and the Savery–Pot Hook. For a detailed discussion of the Carter administration's botched attempt to cut reclamation projects, see Reisner, *Cadillac Desert,* 317–343. Aspinall, transcript of oral history interview by Nancy Whistler, 5. Letter to the Editor of *National Water Life,* November 1978, "1977–80 National Water Resources Assn.," folder 1, box 39; letter (copy), Wayne Aspinall to F. M. Starbuck, March 9, 1977, "1977 Water Projects—Carter's Purge," folder 48, box 37. Both letters are located at CU.

62. Statement by Wayne Aspinall for the Review Committee of the Department of Interior, Grand Junction, Colorado, March 21, 1977, "1977 Water Projects—Carter's Purge," folder 48, box 37, CU; "Aspinall Clarifies Comment Made during Water Hearing," *Rocky Mountain News,* 23 March 1977, 6. Letter, Wayne Aspinall to Charles Thomson, March 29, 1977, "1977 Water Projects—Carter's Purge," folder 48, box 37, CU. Letter, Wayne Aspinall to Jimmy Carter, April 28, 1977, "NR 7-1 5/1/77–5/31/77" folder, box NR 15, WHCF—Subject File, Jimmy Carter Library.

63. Letter, Wayne Aspinall to Mr. & Mrs. C. L. Archer, May 29, 1980, "1979–82 Western State College," folder 46, box 39, CU.

64. Letter, Wayne Aspinall to Rich Johnson, December 1, 1980, "1980 Colorado River—Arizona Water Commission," folder 51, box 37. Letter, Wayne Aspinall to Bill Armstrong, August 26, 1981, "1980–83 Armstrong, William M. C.," folder 22, box 26. Letters are located at CU. Kenneth Walsh, "Colorado's Animas–LaPlata Project 'Top Project' Priority," *Denver Post,* 1 October 1981, B5. Letter, Wayne Aspinall to Charles Luce, October 12, 1981. Letter, Wayne Aspinall to Walter Hickel, October 12, 1981. Both letters located in "1981 Denver University—Dinner Honoring WNA," folder 38, box 29. Letters are located at CU.

65. Letter, Wayne Aspinall to James Watt, August 16, 1982, "1981–82, Watt, James," folder 30, box 39, CU.

66. For the link between water and oil shale see Leonard Larsen, "Aspinall Joins Call for West's Water," *Denver Post,* 19 July 1979, 19; Ann Schmidt, "Carter Adviser Hears of West and Water," *Denver Post,* 2 March 1980, 34; and Wayne Aspinall, "Remarks to the Fifth Annual Water Workshop of the West, Colorado Rural Communities Institute," August 1, 1980, "1980 Western Colorado Rural Communities Institute," folder 37, box 39, CU. Carol Edmonds, "Wayne N. Aspinall: 'I Fitted the Epoch,'" *Shale Country,* December 1982, 16–17. For a more detailed discussion of Aspinall's role in promoting oil shale development see Sturgeon, "Tainted Pork: Wayne Aspinall and the Colorado Oil Shale Debacle" (conference paper).

67. For information on Aspinall's congressional contacts see letter, Harry Pforzhelmer to Wayne Aspinall and others, July 3, 1978, 1978 Paraho Development Cap., folder 41, box 33, CU; and letter, Wayne Aspinall to Dan Rostenkowski, March 12, 1982, 1981–83 Oil Shale—Paraho Development Corp.—General, folder 44, box 33, CU. The head of the Paraho Corporation, a subsidiary of SOHIO, recommended that SOHIO donate $5,000 to Club 20 in honor of Aspinall's work on oil shale—letter, Harry Pforzhelmer to R. M. Donaldson, March 25, 1975, 1975–76 Paraho Oil Shale Demonstration, Inc., folder 39, box 33, CU. The Paraho Corporation itself donated $20,000 to the Wayne Aspinall Foundation at Mesa State College, in Grand Junction, and $7,000 to the Aspinall Conference Center at Western State College in Gunnison. Minutes of a meeting of the Board of Directors of Paraho Development Corporation, January 4, 1983, 1981–83 Oil Shale—Paraho Development Corp.—General, folder 44, box 33, CU. Edmonds, "Wayne N. Aspinall: Long-Time Shale Watcher," 19; presentation to the Western Mining Congress, January 12, 1982, 1982 Oil Shale—Western Mining Congress, folder 10, box 34, CU.

68. Presentation to the Western Mining Congress, January 12, 1982, 1982 Oil Shale—Western Mining Congress, folder 10, box 34, CU; Carol Edmonds, "Wayne N. Aspinall: 'I Fitted the Epoch,'" *Shale Country,* December 1982, 17.

69. Letter, Aspinall to Harry Pforzhelmer, February 10, 1975, 1975–76 Shale

Country, folder 5, box 34, CU; Gulliford, *Boomtown Blues,* 105. Memo, John B. Jones to Wayne Aspinall, February 8, 1982, 1976 Paraho Oil Shale Demonstration, Inc., folder 38, box 33, CU.

70. Gulliford, *Boomtown Blues,* 151–157. For population information see Evans, "Analysis of a Boom/Bust Cycle," 25–27.

71. Carol Edmonds, "Wayne N. Aspinall: 'I Fitted the Epoch,'" *Shale Country,* December 1982, 19.

72. Letter, Wayne Aspinall to Harry Pforzhelmer, October 7, 1982, 1981–83 Oil Shale—Paraho Development Corp.—General, folder 44, box 33, CU; letter, Wayne Aspinall to Larry Lukens, March 7, 1983, 1981–83 Oil Shale—Paraho Development Corp.—General, folder 44, box 33, CU.

Chapter 8. With Every Drop We Drink

1. Ellen Haddow, "More Than 500 Attend Service for Aspinall," *Denver Post,* 14 October 1983, 5B.

2. "Wayne Aspinall," *Denver Post,* 11 October 1983, 2B; Joan Lowy, "Former House Baron Aspinall Dies at 87," *Rocky Mountain News,* 10 October 1983, 6; Ellen Haddow, "More Than 500 Attend Service for Aspinall," *Denver Post,* 14 October 1983, 5B; Joan Lowy, "Colorado Lawmaker Left Mark on West's History," *Rocky Mountain News,* 10 October 1983, 10; William R. Ritz and George Lane, "Ex-Rep. Aspinall, 'Mr. West,' Dies," *Denver Post,* 10 October 1983, 1A.

3. Traylor, Oral History Interview with Alice Wright; Julia Angwin, "Aspinall Portrait Now Back," *Denver Post,* 8 April 1995, 6A.

4. Aspinall, Oral History Interview with Judy Prosser. For information about the Aspinall Center, see Editorial, "Gunnison Project Honors Aspinall," *Denver Post,* 19 May 1981, 18. For Wayne Aspinall Unit, see Robert Tweedell, "Colorado Water Projects All Financially Feasible, Aspinall Says," *Denver Post,* 11 February 1980, 10; Leonard Larsen, "Curecanti Unit Renaming Urged to Honor Aspinall," *Denver Post,* 21 February 1980, 23; "Reservoirs Named for Aspinall," *Denver Post,* 17 July 1981.

5. Mary Louise Giblin, "Wayne N. Aspinall Dies," 10 October 1983, 1. Vandenbusche and Smith, *A Land Alone,* 281. For a typed copy of Aspinall's grave inscription see Epitaph for Aspinall and wife, "Aspinall Genealogy," folder 1, box 1, CU.

6. For the controversy surrounding the origins of the PLLRC see Paul Brooks, "Congressman Aspinall vs. The People of the United States," *Harper's Magazine,* March 1963, 60–63; Udall, transcript of oral history interview by Joe Frantz, 11; Carver, transcripts of oral history interviews by William Moss, 50.

7. Leonard, transcript of oral history interview, 270. Cawley, *Federal Land Western Anger,* 28. Gates, "Pressure Groups and Recent American Land Politics," 111.

8. Cawley, *Federal Land Western Anger,* 33, 35–36; Gates, "Pressure Groups and Recent American Land Politics," 112–113. For additional discussion about the PLLRC and its recommendations, see Allin, *The Politics of Wilderness Preservation,* 194–195; Wyant, *Westward in Eden,* 141–151; Clark, *Water in New Mexico,* 575.

9. Editorial, "Land Use—Or Giveaway?" *New York Times,* 10 July 1972, 30; Lee Olson, "Aspinall to Get His Day in Court," *Denver Post,* 8 August 1972, 23. For the demise of the PLLRC's reforms, see Cawley, *Federal Land Western Anger,* 38; Gates, "Pressure Groups and Recent American Land Politics," 118; Watkins and Watson, *The Land No One Knows,* 156–157; Klyza, *Who Controls Public Lands?,* 117–118. For Aspinall's prediction that public land reform would fail following his defeat, see letter (copy), Wayne Aspinall to A. Andrew Hauk, November 10, 1972, "1972, Campaign Condolences," box 466, DU; "U.S. Stumbles from Crisis to Crisis, Aspinall Says," *Denver Post,* 10 January 1973, 37. For Aspinall's support of the Sagebrush Rebellion see Wayne Aspinall, Sagebrush Rebellion testimony before the Colorado General Assembly Legislative Council's Interim Committee on Agriculture and Natural Resources, September 3, 1980, "1980 Colorado Legislative Council," folder 30, box 28; letter, Wayne Aspinall to Veron Ravenscroft, July 6, 1981, "1980–81 Sagebrush Rebellion," folder 47, box 31. Both documents at CU. Aspinall attended a national Sagebrush Rebellion conference in 1980, where he made the bizarre/hypocritical claim that "he doesn't like subsidies, no matter who receives them." See Joan Nice, "Rebels Revel in New Power, Polish," *High Country News,* 12 December 1980, 2.

10. Clark, *Water in New Mexico,* 515.

11. Ibid., 516. For a detailed discussion of the politics surrounding the passage of the ALP, see Ingram, *Water Politics,* chap. 5. For further discussion of the economic viability of the ALP, see O'Brien, "Cost Control and Authorization of Bureau of Reclamation Projects" (master's thesis). Gottlieb, *A Life of Its Own,* 55.

12. Karp, "Whose Water Is It Anyway?" 6–7.

13. For comment about Indians, see "Season's Bearish for Rivers," *Daily Sentinel,* May 1966, located in "1966 Certificate, Newspaper Clippings," folder 27, box 42, CU. For efforts on compromise, see letter, Wayne Aspinall to Scott Jacket, March 29, 1966, "1966 LEG Animas–LaPlata Project," File L-11b(2)a, box 233, DU.

14. Karp, "Whose Water Is It Anyway?" 8–12; Gail Schoettler, "Oasis or Mirage?" *Denver Post,* 15 June 1997, 1E.

15. Karp, "Whose Water Is It Anyway?" 13–14.

16. For Bureau confession see Karp, "Whose Water Is It Anyway?" 15. For evidence of Campbell's continued defense of the project, see Ellen Miller, "Leaders Wage Fight for Animas," 3 February 1997, 2B; Adriel Bettelheim, "30 Years of Pork," June 15, 1997, 1E; H. Joseph Hebert, "Senate Funds Animas Project," 16

July 1997, 1B; Editorial, "Honor the 473rd Treaty," 17 July 1997, 6B; "House Blocks Attack on Animas Project," 26 July 1997, 7A. All articles in the *Denver Post.*

17. For a description of the latest version of the ALP, see Tom Sluis, "A-LP Hits Its Peak in 2000," *Durango Herald,* 27 December 2000. The *Durango Herald* maintains an on-line archive of articles pertaining to the Animas–La Plata project at www.durangoherald.com/index__alp.asp.

18. William James quote from Patricia Nelson Limerick, "Uneasy Thoughts from Uneasy Places," in Forsman, *Arrested Rivers,* 36–37.

19. Aspinall, transcript of oral history interview by Nancy Whistler, 5, 12. Memo by Wayne Aspinall, "1976 Club 20-Natural Resources Committee, Chairman's File," folder 6, box 28. Wayne Aspinall, speech, "Does Washington Really Understand the People of the West?" May 15, 1978, folder 7, box 27. Both items are located at CU.

20. Letter, Wayne Aspinall to John Dingell, June 6, 1955, "Echo Park Project—1955," box 69, DU. Letter, Wayne Aspinall to William Shaw, April 14, 1978, "1973–78 Fruitland Mesa Water Conservancy District," folder 31, box 38, CU. Kenney, "River Basin Administration and the Colorado" (Ph.D. diss.), 280. "Ranchers Fear Curecanti Dam Perils Gunnison," *Rocky Mountain News,* 12 June 1951, 12.

21. Marston, *Western Water Made Simple,* 219; "Knight Errant to Nature's Rescue: Close-up California's David Brower, No. 1 Conservationist," *Life,* 27 May 1966, 39. Wayburn, transcript of oral history interview, 319–320.

22. House Committee on Interior and Insular Affairs, *Hearings on H.R. 4449 et al. on CRSP* (1954), 831–832. Letter, Aspinall to Julie Green, August 27, 1966, folder L-11b(1)a22, box 245, DU. Harvey, "Defending the Park System," 59.

23. Letter, Wayne Aspinall to Jane Anderson, February 23, 1970, folder 49, box 370; letter, Wayne Aspinall to Arthur Hyde, August 11, 1970, "1971 Aspinall for Congress," folder Pol-4(2), box 431; letter, Wayne Aspinall to Barbara Duprey, April 30, 1970, folder 49, box 370. All letters are located at DU. Letter, Wayne Aspinall to Carl Boyd, November 8, 1965, "1965 Interior and Insular Affairs Committee—General," folder 1, box 22, CU.

24. "New Rules Create New World for Dam," *Denver Post,* 10 October 1996, 15A. Doug Swanson, "Revamped River Unkind to Fish," *Denver Post,* 13 March 1997, 31A. Wilkinson, *Crossing the Next Meridian,* 281; Al Knight, "A Cool Glass of Conservation?" 29 September 1996, 1G; Bill Hornby, "A 'Wild and Scenic' South Platte Would Threaten Water Supply," 26 April 1997, 7B; Charlie Meyers, "South Platte Protection Plan," 18 March 1998, 12D. All articles in the *Denver Post.*

25. Matthew Brown, "Sierra Club Plan: Drain Lake Powell," *Contra Costa Times,* 26 January 1997, 5B; James Brooke, "Audacious Plan to Drain Lake Powell

Arouses Foes," *Denver Post,* 22 September 1997, 1A; Charlie Meyers, "Sierra Club Off Course in Lake Powell Debate," *Denver Post,* 3 October 1997, 2D; Vicki Michaelis, "Blazing Trail," *Denver Post,* 12 October 1997, Empire Magazine, 12; Ed Marston, "Drain Debate Exhilarating"; Penelope Purdy, "Erosion Never Sleeps," both articles in *Denver Post,* 21 December 1997, 1G.

26. "Ex-Congressman Aspinall Dies; Leader on West's Water Projects," *New York Times,* 10 October 1983, B8.

27. Lawrence Mosher, "Water-Short Colorado May Be Dammed If It Builds, Dammed If It Doesn't," *National Journal,* 17 July 1982, 1257.

28. Tony Perry, "Plan Targets South State's Use of River," *Contra Costa Times,* 12 August 1997; Ed Marston, "Quenching the Big Thirst," *High Country News,* 21 May 2001, 1.

29. Ellen Miller, "Revamping Water Right for Fish Proposed," *Denver Post,* 3 February 1998, 4B; Marston, *Western Water Made Simple,* 163.

30. Peirce, *The Mountain States of America,* 56.

31. Julia Angwin, "Aspinall Portrait Now Back," *Denver Post,* 8 April 1995, 6A.

Bibliography

Primary Source Materials
  Archives, Libraries, Museums and Special Collections

American Heritage Center, University of Wyoming
  Papers of Floyd E. Dominy
Arizona State University Libraries, Department of Archives and Manuscripts
  ASU Oral History Project
  Central Arizona Project Association Records
  Carl T. Hayden Papers
  Rich Johnson Papers
  John J. Rhodes Papers
  Ross R. Rice Collection
The Bancroft Library, University of California, Berkeley
  David R. Brower Papers
  Phillip Burton Papers
  Michael McCloskey Papers
  Sierra Club National Legislative Office Records
  Sierra Club Oral History Series
  Sierra Club Records
  Edgar Wayburn Papers
Bureau of Reclamation Library, Federal Center, Denver
  Historic Reclamation Projects Series
  Bureau of Reclamation Oral History Program
Jimmy Carter Presidential Library
  White House Central File: Subject File
Center for American History, University of Texas, Austin
  Sam Rayburn Papers
Colorado Historical Society, Denver
  Oral History of Colorado Project
  State Newspaper Project
Denver Public Library, Western History Department
  Arthur H. Carhart Collection
  Izaak Walton League of America, Front Range Chapter Papers

George Kelly Papers
The Wilderness Society Papers
Dwight D. Eisenhower Presidential Library
White House Central Files: Alpha File
Federal Bureau of Investigation, Department of Justice, Washington, D.C.
Wayne Norviel Aspinall, FOIPA Request no. 390.117
Gerald R. Ford Presidential Library
Electronic Daily Diary
Lyndon B. Johnson Presidential Library
Confidential File
Papers of DeVier Pierson
White House Central File
White House Central File: Name File
John F. Kennedy Presidential Library
Presidential Office Files
White House Central File: Names File
White House Central File: Subject File
White House Staff Files: Lawrence O'Brien
White House Staff Files: Lee White
Library of Congress, Manuscript Division
Papers of Clinton P. Anderson
Former Members of Congress Oral History Project
Mesa County Public Library, Grand Junction, Colorado
Mesa County Oral History Project
Museum of Western Colorado, Grand Junction, Colorado
Mesa County Oral History Project
Nixon Presidential Materials, National Archives at College Park,
    Maryland
White House Special Files: Central Files
WHCF: Staff Member and Office Files: John C. Whitaker
White House Central Files: Subject Files
Harry S. Truman Presidential Library
Papers of Oscar Chapman
Papers of Harry S. Truman: General File
Papers of Harry S. Truman: President's Personal File
Papers of Harry S. Truman: President's Secretary's File
Papers of Harry S. Truman: Official File
University of Arizona Library, Special Collections
Morris K. Udall Papers
Stewart L. Udall Papers

University of Colorado at Boulder, Western Historical Collections
  Gordon Allott Papers
  Wayne Aspinall Papers
University of Denver Special Collections
  Wayne N. Aspinall Papers

Published Government Documents

Congressional Record, 1949–1972, 1983.

U.S. Congress, House. Committee on Interior and Insular Affairs. *Hearings on H.R. 4449, 4443, and 4463 on Colorado River Storage Project.* 83d Cong., 2d sess., 1954.

——. *Hearings on H.R. 270, 2839, 3383, 3384, 4488 on Colorado River Storage Project, Parts 1 & 2.* 84th Cong., 1st sess., 1955.

——. *Hearings on H.R. 412 on Fryingpan-Arkansas Project.* 84th Cong., 1st sess., 1955.

——. *Hearings on H.R. 594 on Fryingpan-Arkansas Project.* 85th Cong., 1st sess., 1957.

——. *Hearings on H.R. 4671 on Lower Colorado River Basin Project.* 89th Cong., 1st sess., 1965.

——. *Hearings on H.R. 4671 on Lower Colorado River Basin Project.* 89th Cong., 2d sess., 1966.

——. *Hearings on H.R. 3300 on Colorado River Basin Project.* 90th Cong., 1st sess., 1967.

——. *Hearings on H.R. 3300 on Colorado River Basin Project.* 90th Cong., 2d sess., 1968.

U.S. Department of Interior, Bureau of Reclamation. *Colorado: Bureau of Reclamation Projects.* Denver, 1978.

——. *Project Data Book.* Washington, D.C., 1984.

Periodicals

NEWSPAPERS
Albuquerque Journal
Aspen Illustrated News
Aspen Times
Boulder Daily Camera
Contra Costa (County, California) *Times*
Colorado State University *Collegian*
Denver Post
Durango-Cortez Herald

Flagstaff, Arizona, *Daily Sun*
Fort Collins Coloradoan
Glenwood Springs Sage
Grand Junction *Daily Sentinel*
Greeley Tribune
Logan Herald Journal
High Country News
Los Angeles Times
Montrose *Daily Press*
New York Times
Northern Virginia Sun
Craig *Northwest Colorado Daily Press*
Ottawa (Kansas) *Herald*
Ouray Gazette
Phoenix, *Arizona Republic*
Phoenix Gazette
Pueblo Chieftain
Pueblo Star-Journal
Rifle Telegram
Rocky Mountain News
Sacramento Bee
Sterling *Journal-Advocate*
The CWA (Communication Workers of America) *News*
The Portland Oregonian
Tucson, *Arizona Daily Star*
USA Weekend
Wall Street Journal
Washington *Daily News*
Washington Post
Westword
Wyoming State Tribune

MAGAZINES
Atlantic Monthly
Business Week
Cervi's Rocky Mountain Journal
Colorado Business
Colorado Life
Colorado Outdoors
Colorado Water Congress Newsletter
Colorado Water Rights

Field & Stream
Flatirons Magazine
Fortune
Harper's Magazine
Life
McCall's
Mining Congress Journal
National Journal
Newsweek
Outdoor Life
Parade Magazine
Reader's Digest
Shale Country
Skier's Gazette
Sunset Magazine
Time Magazine
U.S. News & World Report

Interviews and Oral Histories

Akin, Wayne. Transcript of oral history interview by Jack August Jr. Arizona Collection, Department of Archives and Manuscripts, Arizona State University Libraries, September 14, 1982.

Allott, Gordon. Transcript summary of interview with Gordon Allott. ("1977 Edmonds, Carol," folder 16, box 45, Wayne Aspinall Papers.) Western Historical Collections, University of Colorado at Boulder, July 7, 1977.

Aspinall, Wayne. Transcript of oral history interview by Charles Morrissey. John Kennedy Presidential Library, November 10, 1965.

———. Transcript of oral history interview by Ross R. Rice. (Folder 5, Ross R. Rice Collection.) Arizona Collection, Department of Archives and Manuscripts, Arizona State University Libraries, October 23, 1973.

———. Transcript of oral history interview by David McComb. Oral History of Colorado Project, Colorado Historical Society, Denver, June 11, 1974.

———. Transcript of oral history interview by Joe Frantz. Lyndon Johnson Presidential Library, June 14, 1974.

———. Oral history interview by Al Look. Mesa County Oral History Project: Mesa County Public Library, Grand Junction, Colorado, January 1978.

———. Transcript of oral history interview by Nancy Whistler. (Folder 1, container 1.) Former Members of Congress Oral History Project, Library of Congress, February 15, 1979.

———. Oral history interview by Helen Hansen. Mesa County Oral History Project, Mesa County Public Library, Grand Junction, Colorado, August 10, 1981.

———. Oral history interview by Judy Prosser. Mesa County Oral History Project, Mesa County Public Library, Grand Junction, Colorado, August 17, 1982.

Behr, Peter. "Marin County Environmentalist and Political Leader: Spearheading the Save Our Seashore Campaign." Transcript of oral history interview by Ann Lage, 1990, in *Saving Point Reyes National Seashore, 1969–1970: An Oral History of Citizen Action in Conservation*. Regional Oral History Office, The Bancroft Library, University of California, Berkeley, 1993.

Brower, David R. "Environmental Activist, Publicist, and Prophet." Transcript of oral history interview by Susan Schrepfer, 1974–1978. Sierra Club History Series: Regional Oral History Office, The Bancroft Library, University of California, Berkeley, 1980.

Brown, Edmund G. Sr. "Years of Growth, 1939–1966: Law Enforcement, Politics, and the Governor's Office." Transcript of oral history interview by Malca Chall, 1979. Governmental History Documentation Project (Goodwin Knight/Edmund Brown Sr. Era), Regional Oral History Office, The Bancroft Library, University of California at Berkeley, 1982.

Carver, John. Transcripts of oral history interviews by John Stewart and William Moss. John Kennedy Presidential Library, September 20, 1968–December 22, 1969.

Cleary, William. Interview by author. Grand Junction, Colorado, June 9, 1997.

———. Transcript of oral history interview by Alice Wright. Mesa County Oral History Project, Museum of Western Colorado, Grand Junction, Colorado, May 16, 1987.

Desautels, Claude. Transcript of oral history interview by Louis Oberdorfer. John Kennedy Presidential Library, May 16, 1964.

Dolan, Joseph. Transcript of oral history interview by Charles Morrissey. John Kennedy Presidential Library, December 1, 1964.

Dominy, Floyd. Telephone interview by author. November 1, 1997.

———. Transcript of oral history interview by Joe Frantz. Lyndon Johnson Presidential Library, November 14, 1968.

———. Transcript of oral history interview by Brit Allan Storey. Bureau of Reclamation Library, Denver, April 6, 1994.

Drury, Newton Bishop. "Parks and Redwoods, 1919–1971." Transcript of oral history interview by Amelia Roberts Fry and Susan Schrepfer. Regional Oral History Office, The Bancroft Library, University of California, Berkeley, 1972.

Ehrlichman, John D. "Presidential Assistant with a Bias for Parks." Transcript of oral history interview by William J. Duddleson, 1991, in *Saving Point Reyes National Seashore, 1969–1970: An Oral History of Citizen Action in Conservation*.

Regional Oral History Office, The Bancroft Library, University of California, Berkeley, 1993.

Ellis, Clyde. Transcript of oral history interview by Ronald Grele. John Kennedy Presidential Library, April 5, 1965.

Evans, Brock. "Environmental Campaigner: From the Northwest Forests to the Halls of Congress." Transcript of oral history interview by Ann Lage, 1982, in *Building the Sierra Club's National Lobbying Program, 1967–1981*. Sierra Club History Series. Regional Oral History Office, The Bancroft Library, University of California, Berkeley, 1985.

Gilmore, John, and Patricia Gilmore. Transcript summary of interview with John and Patricia Gilmore. ("1977 Edmonds, Carol," folder 16, box 45, Wayne Aspinall Papers.) Western Historical Collections, University of Colorado at Boulder, May 16, 1977.

Goldsworthy, Patrick D. "Protecting the North Cascades, 1954–1983." Transcript of oral history interview by Ann Lage, 1983, in *Pacific Northwest Conservationists*. Sierra Club History Series. Regional Oral History Office, The Bancroft Library, University of California, Berkeley, 1985.

Hartzog, George B. "The National Parks, 1965." Transcript of oral history interview by Amelia Roberts Fry. Regional Oral History Office, The Bancroft Library, University of California, Berkeley, 1973.

Johnson, Katy Miller. "Catalyst and Citizen-Lobbyist in Washington." Transcript of oral history interview by Ann Lage, 1990, in *Saving Point Reyes National Seashore, 1969–1970: An Oral History of Citizen Action in Conservation*. Regional Oral History Office, The Bancroft Library, University of California, Berkeley, 1993.

Leonard, Richard M. "Mountaineer, Lawyer, Environmentalist." Transcript of oral history interview by Susan Schrepfer. Sierra Club History Series. Regional Oral History Office, The Bancroft Library, University of California, Berkeley, 1975.

Livermore, Norman B., Jr. "Man in the Middle: High Sierra Packer, Timberman, Conservationist, and California Resources Secretary." Transcript of oral history interview by Ann Lage and Gabrielle Morris, 1981–1982. Sierra Club History Series. Regional Oral History Office, The Bancroft Library, University of California, Berkeley, 1983.

Mallet, Jerry. Transcript summary of interview with Jerry Mallet. ("1977 Edmonds, Carol," folder 16, box 45, Wayne Aspinall Papers.) Western Historical Collections, University of Colorado at Boulder, June 28, 1977.

McCloskey, Michael. "Sierra Club Executive Director: The Evolving Club and the Environmental Movement, 1961–1981." Transcript of oral history interview by Susan Schrepfer, 1981. Sierra Club History Series. Regional Oral History Office, The Bancroft Library, University of California, Berkeley, 1983.

McCloskey, Paul (Pete) N., Jr. "An Environmentalist in Congress: Urging Presidential Action on Point Reyes." Transcript of oral history interview by Ann Lage, 1990, in *Saving Point Reyes National Seashore, 1969–1970: An Oral History of Citizen Action in Conservation.* Regional Oral History Office, The Bancroft Library, University of California, Berkeley, 1993.

McFarland, Sid. Telephone interview by author. November 1, 1997.

Neal, Tommy. E-mail interview by author. November 6–7, 1997.

——. Transcript summary of interview with Tommy Neal. ("1977 Edmonds, Carol," folder 16, box 45, Wayne Aspinall Papers.) Western Historical Collections, University of Colorado at Boulder, May 10, 1977.

Noland, Alta Leach. Oral History Presentation. Mesa County Oral History Project, Mesa County Public Library, Grand Junction, Colorado, March 1, 1989.

O'Brien, Lawrence. Transcript of oral history interview by Michael L. Gillette. Lyndon Johnson Presidential Library, December 4, 1985.

Pierson, DeVier. Transcript of oral history interview by Dorothy Pierce McSweeny. Lyndon Johnson Presidential Library, March 19, 1969.

Rhodes, John J. Transcript of oral history interview by Dean Smith. ASU Oral History Project, Arizona Collection, Department of Archives and Manuscripts, Arizona State University Libraries, May 1, 1991.

Sanders, Barefoot. Transcript of oral history interview by Joe B. Frantz. Lyndon Johnson Presidential Library, March 24, 1969.

Scott, Howard. Interview by author. Fruita, Colorado, June 10, 1997.

Sparks, Felix. Interview by author. Lakewood, Colorado, November 21, 1997.

——. Transcript summary of interview with Felix "Larry" Sparks. ("1977 Edmonds, Carol," folder 16, box 45, Wayne Aspinall Papers.) Western Historical Collections, University of Colorado at Boulder, July 5, 1977.

Traylor, Charles. Oral history interview with Alice Wright. Mesa County Oral History Project, Mesa County Public Library, Grand Junction, Colorado, March 1, 1987.

Tupling, W. Lloyd. "Sierra Club Washington Representative, 1967–1973." Transcript of oral history interview by Ann Lage, 1984, in *Building the Sierra Club's National Lobbying Program, 1967–1981.* Sierra Club History Series. Regional Oral History Office, The Bancroft Library, University of California, Berkeley, 1985.

Udall, Stewart. Telephone interview by author. November 11, 1997.

——. Transcript of oral history interview by Joe Frantz. Lyndon Johnson Presidential Library, October 31–December 16, 1969.

——. Transcript of oral history interview by William Moss. John Kennedy Presidential Library, February 16, 1970.

——. Transcript of oral history interview by Charles Morrissey. Former Members of Congress Oral History Project, Library of Congress, Washington, D.C., March 15, 1979.

———. Transcript of interview by Charles Coate. Author's personal copy, April 23, 1997.

Warne, William E. "Administration of the Department of Water Resources, 1961–1966." Transcript of oral history interview by Malca Chall, 1979, in *California Water Issues, 1950–1966*. Governmental History Documentation Project (Goodwin Knight/Edmund Brown Sr. Era). Regional Oral History Office, The Bancroft Library, University of California, Berkeley, 1981.

Wayburn, Edgar. "Sierra Club Statesman, Leader of the Parks and Wilderness Movement: Gaining Protection for Alaska, the Redwoods, and Golden Gate Parklands." Transcript of oral history interview by Ann Lage and Susan Schrepfer, 1976–1981. Sierra Club History Series. Regional Oral History Office, The Bancroft Library, University of California, Berkeley, 1985.

Weaver, Bob. Transcript summary of interview with Bob Weaver. (folder 17, box 45, Wayne Aspinall Papers.) Western Historical Collections, University of Colorado at Boulder, July 6, 1977.

Secondary Materials
Theses and Dissertations

Baird, Richard Edward. "The Politics of Echo Park and Other Water Development Projects in the Upper Colorado River Basin, 1946–1956." Ph.D. diss., University of Illinois, Urbana-Champaign, 1960.

Brittan, Margaret Regina. "A Probability Model for Integration of Glen Canyon Dam into the Colorado River System." Ph.D. diss., University of Colorado, Boulder, 1960.

Brodeur, Brian Robert. "Physical Constraints and Implications for Supplementing Arkansas River Flows for Recreation with the Fryingpan-Arkansas Project." Master's thesis, University of Colorado, Boulder, 1988.

Carey, Omer L. "The Application of Economic Criteria for Government Investment in National Parks—The Dinosaur National Monument Controversy." D.B.A. diss., Indiana University, 1962.

Coleman, Jon T. "Water on Colorado's Western Slope: Reactions to the Colorado Big-Thompson Project 1933 to 1937." Honors thesis, University of Colorado, Boulder, 1992.

Collins, Kay. "Transmountain Diversion of Water from the Colorado River: A Legal-Historical Study." Master's thesis, University of New Mexico, 1965.

Eddy, Frank Warren. "Culture Ecology and the Prehistory of the Navajo Reservoir District." Ph.D. diss., University of Colorado, Boulder, 1968.

Frost, James. "Projecting the Future of the Yampa River Basin in Northwest Colorado: An Examination of the Socio-Economic and Land Use Effects of Different Levels of Water Supply and Water Demand." Master's thesis, University of Colorado, Denver, 1981.

Johnson, Christopher G. "The Significance of Rainbow Bridge: From Prehistory to the Present." Master's thesis, Northern Arizona University, 1996.

Kenney, Douglas S. "River Basin Administration and the Colorado: Past Practices and Future Alternatives." Ph.D. diss., University of Arizona, 1993.

Kirk, Andrew Glenn. "Conservationists and Wilderness Preservation in Colorado." Master's thesis, University of Colorado, Denver, 1992.

Latousek, Thomas A. "Holding a River for Ransom; or, The Extinction of the Western Water Buffalo: Wayne Aspinall and the Colorado River Basin Act of 1968." Master's thesis, Colorado State University, 1998.

Livingston, Kenneth S. "A Case Study: The Effects of a Powerful Committee Chair on the Passage of the Wilderness Bill." Master's thesis, University of Richmond, 1996.

Mann, Roger. "Welfare Implications of Regional Economic Models with Application to the Animas–LaPlata Project." Ph.D. diss., Colorado State University, 1988.

Mayo, Dwight Eugene. "Arizona and the Colorado River Compact." Master's thesis, Arizona State University, 1964.

McCurdy, Karen Marie. "When Committees Change: The House Interior and Insular Affairs Committee Confronting Environmental Politics (1955–1986)." Ph.D. diss., University of Wisconsin-Madison, 1989.

Mehls, Carol Jean Drake. "Into the Frying Pan: J. Edgar Chenoweth and the Fryingpan-Arkansas Reclamation Project." Ph.D. diss., University of Colorado, Boulder, 1986.

Neel, Susan Rhoades. "Irreconcilable Differences: Reclamation, Preservation, and the Origins of the Echo Park Dam Controversy." Ph.D. diss., University of California, Los Angeles, 1990.

O'Brien, Jimmy Steven. "Cost Control and Authorization of Bureau of Reclamation Projects: Five Colorado River Storage Projects in Colorado." Master's thesis, University of Colorado, Boulder, 1980.

Pearson, Byron Eugene. "People above Scenery: The Struggle over the Grand Canyon Dams, 1963–1968." Ph.D. diss., University of Arizona, 1998.

Powers, Aleta Davis. "The Best Fruit Place in the World." Honors thesis, University of Northern Colorado, 1993.

Raley, Bradley. "The Collbran Project and the Bureau of Reclamation, 1937–1963: A Case Study in Western Resource Development." Master's thesis, University of Houston, 1992.

Senecah, Susan Louise. "The Environmental Discourse of David Brower: Using

Advocacy Advertising to Save the Grand Canyon." Ph.D. diss., University of
Minnesota, 1992.

Somma, Mark S. "The Colorado River: A Dynamic Study of the Dependence of
Politics on the Initial Conditions of Ecology." Ph.D. diss., University of Iowa,
1992.

Thomas, Thomas A. "Roads to an Uncertain Future: Colorado's Interstate High-
way System, 1945–95." Ph.D. diss., University of Colorado, Boulder, 1996.

Wilson, Joy. "An Analysis of the Rhetoric of Agitation and Control in the Sierra
Club Campaign to Protect the Grand Canyon." Master's thesis, North Texas
State University, 1974.

Conference Papers

Coate, Charles. "Vision, Politics, and Compromise: Stewart Udall and the Department of Interior." Paper presented at the annual meeting of the Western
History Association, St. Paul, Minnesota, October 17, 1997.

Harvey, Mark W. T. "Environment, Politics, and the Central Utah Project."
Paper presented at the environmental history conference sponsored by the
University of Montana, Missoula, April 9, 1994.

———. "Paying the Taxpayer: The Internal Revenue Service and the Environmental Movement." Paper presented at the biennial meeting of the American
Society for Environmental History, Baltimore, Maryland, March 1997.

Milazzo, Paul C. "Going with the Flow: Congress, Expertise, and Information in
Federal Water Policy." Paper presented at the biennial meeting of the American Society for Environmental History, Baltimore, Maryland, March 7, 1997.

Raley, Brad. "Irrigation, Land Speculation, and the History of Grand Junction,
Colorado." Paper presented at the annual meeting of the Western History
Association, Lincoln, Nebraska, October 1996.

Schulte, Steven. "He Never Met a Dam He Didn't Like: Explaining Congressman Wayne Aspinall." Paper presented at the annual meeting of the Western
Social Science Association, Reno, Nevada, April 20, 1996.

Sturgeon, Stephen C. "Tainted Pork: Wayne Aspinall and the Colorado Oil Shale
Debacle." Paper presented at the annual meeting of the American Historical
Association, New York, N.Y., January 3, 1997. Available in *Proceedings of the
American Historical Association, 1997,* reference # 10485. Ann Arbor, Mich.:
University Microfilms.

Articles

Arnold, Thomas Clay. "Theory, History, and the Western Waterscape: The Mar-
ket Culture Thesis." *Journal of the Southwest* 38, no. 2 (summer 1996): 215–240.

August, Jack L., Jr. "Carl Hayden, Arizona, and the Politics of Water Development in the Southwest, 1923–1928." *Pacific Historical Review* 58, no. 2 (May 1989): 195–216.

Baker, Richard Allan. "The Conservation Congress of Anderson and Aspinall, 1963–64." *Journal of Forest History* (July 1985): 104–119.

Bingham, Jay R. "Reclamation and the Colorado." *Utah Historical Quarterly* 28, no. 3 (July 1960): 232–249.

Coate, Charles. "The New School of Thought: Reclamation and the Fair Deal, 1945–1953." *Journal of the West* 22, no. 2 (April 1983): 58–63.

——. "The Biggest Water Fight in American History: Stewart Udall and the Central Arizona Project." *Journal of the Southwest* 37, no. 1 (spring 1995): 79–101.

Dana, Marshall N. "Reclamation, Its Influence and Impact on the History of the West." *Utah Historical Quarterly* 27, no. 1 (January 1959): 38–49.

Dean, Robert. " 'Dam Building Still Had Some Magic Then': Stewart Udall, the Central Arizona Project, and the Evolution of the Pacific Southwest Water Plan, 1963–1968." *Pacific Historical Review* 66, no. 1 (February 1997): 81–98.

Dunbar, Robert G. "The Adaptability of Water Law to the Aridity of the West." *Journal of the West* 24, no. 1 (January 1985): 57–65.

Eastin, Michael. "The Little Empire of the Western Slope: Boosterism in the Early Grand Valley." *Journal of the Western Slope* 3, no. 2 (spring 1988): 28–49.

Emmons, David M. "Constructed Providence: History and the Making of the Last American West." *Western Historical Quarterly* 25, no. 4 (winter 1994): 437–486.

Evans, Jim. "Analysis of a Boom/Bust Cycle: How Severe Was the Oil Shale Bust in Northwest Colorado?" *Colorado School of Mines Quarterly Review* 92, no. 3 (1992): 25–27.

Gates, Paul W. "Pressure Groups and Recent American Land Politics." *Agricultural History* 55, no. 2 (April 1981): 103–127.

Goslin, Ival V. "Interstate River Compacts: Impacts on Colorado." *Denver Journal of International Law and Policy* 6, Special Issue (1976): 415–438.

Harvey, Mark. "Defending the Park System: The Controversy over Rainbow Bridge." *New Mexico Historical Review* 58, no. 1 (January 1998): 45–67.

Hundley, Norris, Jr. "Clio Nods: Arizona v. California and the Boulder Canyon Act—A Reassessment." *Western Historical Quarterly* 3, no. 1 (January 1972): 17–51.

——. "Water and the West in Historical Imagination." *Western Historical Quarterly* 27, no. 1 (spring 1996): 5–31.

Karp, Leslie. "Whose Water Is It Anyway? Bureaucrats, the Animas–La Plata Project, and the Colorado Utes." *Journal of the Western Slope* 9, no. 3 (summer 1994): 1–20.

Koelzer, Victor. "New Growth Centers—A Role for the Bureau of Reclamation?" *Journal of the Water Resources Planning and Management Division, ASCE* 102, #WR2, Proc. Paper 12576 (November 1976): 311–326.

Koppes, Clayton R. "Environmental Policy and American Liberalism: The Department of Interior, 1933–1953." *Environmental Review* 7, no. 1 (spring 1983): 17–53.

Lamm, Richard D. "Colorado, Water, and Planning for the Future." *Denver Journal of International Law and Policy* 6, Special Issue (1976): 441–447.

Langbein, W. B. "L'Affaire LaRue." *Journal of the West* 22, no. 2 (April 1983): 39–47.

Lavender, David. "The Role of Water in the History and Development of Colorado." *Denver Journal of International Law and Policy* 6, Special Issue (1976): 407–414.

Lear, Linda J. "Boulder Dam: A Crossroads in Natural Resource Policy." *Journal of the West* 24, no. 4 (October 1985): 82–94.

Lee, Lawrence. "100 Years of Reclamation Historiography." *Pacific Historical Review* 47, no. 4 (November 1978): 507–564.

Lewis, Anne L. "Floor Success as a Measure of Committee Performance in the House." *Journal of Politics* 40, no. 2 (May 1978): 460–467.

Mann, Dean E. "Politics in the United States and the Salinity Problem of the Colorado River." *Natural Resources Journal* 15, no. 1 (January 1975): 113–128.

——. "Conflict and Coalition: Political Variables Underlying Water Resource Development in the Upper Colorado River Basin." *Natural Resources Journal* 15, no. 1 (January 1975): 141–169.

McCarthy, Michael. "He Fought for His West: Colorado Congressman Wayne Aspinall." *Colorado Heritage* 1 (1988): 33–44.

Moses, Raphael J. "Transmountain Diversions of Water in Colorado." *Denver Journal of International Law and Policy* 6, Special Issue (1976): 329–335.

Neel, Susan Rhoades. "A Place of Extremes: Nature, History, and the American West." *Western Historical Quarterly* 25, no. 4 (winter 1994): 489–505.

Pearson, Byron E. "Salvation for Grand Canyon: Congress, the Sierra Club, and the Dam Controversy of 1966–1968." *Journal of the Southwest* 36, no. 2 (summer 1994): 159–175.

Pisani, Donald J. "Deep and Troubled Waters: A New Field of Western History?" *New Mexico Historical Review* 63, no. 4 (October 1988): 311–331.

Reich, Peter L. "Studies in Western Water Law: Historiographical Trends." *Western Legal History* 9, no. 1 (winter/spring 1996): 1–7.

Righter, Robert W. "National Monuments to National Parks: The Use of the Antiquities Act of 1906." *Western Historical Quarterly* 20, no. 3 (August 1989): 281–301.

Sherman, Harris D. "The Role of the State in Water Planning, Research, and Administration." *Denver Journal of International Law and Policy* 6, Special Issue (1976): 449–453.

Smith, Thomas G. "John Kennedy, Stewart Udall, and New Frontier Conservation." *Pacific Historical Review* 64, no. 3 (August 1995): 329–362.

Steinberg, Theodore. " 'That World's Fair Feeling': Control of Water in 20th–Century America." *Technology and Culture* 34, no. 2 (April 1993): 401–409.

Stevens, Dale J. "The Colorado River System, Corridor or Barrier to Development?" *Journal of the West* 33, no. 3 (July 1994): 45–58.

Swain, Donald C. "The Bureau of Reclamation and the New Deal, 1933–1940." *Pacific Northwest Quarterly* 61, no. 3 (July 1970): 137–146.

Udall, Stewart. "Around the Plaza: An Anchor to Windward." *El Palacio* 100, no. 2 (spring 1995): 22.

Wickens, James F. "The New Deal in Colorado." *Pacific Historical Review* 38, no. 3 (August 1969): 275–291.

Books

Abbott, Carl, Stephen J. Leonard, and David McComb. *Colorado: A History of the Centennial State*. Rev. ed. Niwot: University Press of Colorado, 1982.

Allin, Craig W. *The Politics of Wilderness Preservation*. Westport, Conn.: Greenwood Press, 1982.

America's Water: Current Trends and Emerging Issues. Washington, D.C.: The Conservation Foundation, 1984.

Anderson, Clinton, and Milton Viorst. *Outsider in the Senate: Senator Clinton Anderson's Memoirs*. New York: World Publishing Company, 1970.

Anderson, Terry L., ed. *Water Rights: Scarce Resource Allocation, Bureaucracy, and the Environment*. San Francisco: Pacific Institute in Public Policy, 1983.

Anderson, Terry L., and Peter J. Hill, eds. *Water Marketing—The Next Generation*. Boulder, Colo.: Rowman & Littlefield, 1997.

Andrews, Barbara. *Who Runs the Rivers? Dams and Decisions in the New West*. Stanford, Calif.: Stanford Environmental Law Society, 1983.

Arrandale, Tom. *The Battle for Natural Resources*. Washington, D.C.: Congressional Quarterly, Inc., 1983.

Ashby, LeRoy, and Rod Gramer. *Fighting the Odds: The Life of Senator Frank Church*. Pullman: Washington State University Press, 1994.

Ashworth, William. *Nor Any Drop to Drink*. New York: Summit Books, 1982.

Aspinall, Wayne. *The Milward L. Simpson Lectures in Political Science*. Laramie: Department of Political Science, University of Wyoming, 1975.

Athearn, Frederic J. *An Isolated Empire: A History of Northwest Colorado*. Denver: U.S. Department of Interior, Bureau of Land Management, 1976.

Athearn, Robert G. *The Coloradans*. Albuquerque: University of New Mexico Press, 1976.

August, Jack L., Jr. *Vision in the Desert: Carl Hayden and Hydropolitics in the American Southwest*. Forth Worth: Texas Christian University Press, 1999.

Baker, Richard Allan. *Conservation Politics: The Senate Career of Clinton P. Anderson*. Albuquerque: University of New Mexico Press, 1985.

Ballard, Steven C., Michael D. Devine, and associates. *Water and Western Energy: Impacts, Issues, and Choices*. Boulder, Colo.: Westview Press, 1982.

Bates, Sarah F., David H. Getches, Lawrence J. MacDonnell, and Charles F. Wilkinson. *Searching Out the Headwaters: Change and Rediscovery in Western Water Policy*. Washington, D.C.: Island Press, 1993.

Bendiner, Robert. *Obstacle Course on Capitol Hill*. New York: McGraw-Hill, 1964.

Berkman, Richard L., and W. Kip Viscusi. *Damming the West: Ralph Nader's Study Group Report on the Bureau of Reclamation*. New York: Grossman Publishers, 1973.

Bernstein, Irving. *Guns or Butter: The Presidency of Lyndon Johnson*. New York: Oxford University Press, 1996.

Berry, Jeffrey M. *Lobbying for the People*. Princeton, N.J.: Princeton University Press, 1977.

Berry, Joyce K., and John C. Gordon, eds. *Environmental Leadership: Developing Effective Skills and Styles*. Washington, D.C.: Island Press, 1993.

Bingham, Sam. *The Last Ranch: A Colorado Community and the Coming Desert*. New York: Pantheon Books, 1996.

Biographical Directory of the United States Congress, 1774–1989. Washington, D.C.: United States Government Printing Office, 1989.

Bolling, Richard. *House Out of Order*. New York: E. P. Dutton & Co., 1965.

Brower, David R. *For Earth's Sake: The Life and Times of David Brower*. Salt Lake City, Utah: Peregrine Smith Books, 1990.

———. *Work in Progress*. Salt Lake City, Utah: Peregrine Smith Books, 1991.

Brown, F. Lee, and Helen M. Ingram. *Water and Poverty in the Southwest*. Tucson: University of Arizona Press, 1987.

Brown, Larry. *Aspinall: Centennial Edition*. Gunnison, Colo.: Western State College Foundation, 1996.

Carothers, Steven W., and Bryan T. Brown. *The Colorado River through the Grand Canyon: Natural History and Human Change*. Tucson: University of Arizona Press, 1991.

Carrier, Jim. *West of the Divide: Voices from a Ranch and a Reservation*. Golden, Colo.: Fulcrum Publishing, 1992.

Carson, Donald W., and James W. Johnson. *Mo: The Life and Times of Morris K. Udall*. Tucson: University of Arizona Press, 2001.

Cawley, R. McGreggor. *Federal Land Western Anger: The Sagebrush Rebellion & Environmental Politics.* Lawrence: University Press of Kansas, 1993.

Chelf, Carl P. *Congress in the American System.* Chicago: Nelson-Hall, 1977.

Clark, Ira G. *Water in New Mexico: A History of Its Management and Use.* Albuquerque: University of New Mexico Press, 1987.

Clark, Joseph S. *Congress: The Sapless Branch.* New York: Harper & Row, 1964.

Clarke, Jeanne Nienaber, and Daniel C. McCool. *Staking Out the Terrain: Power and Performance among Natural Resource Agencies.* Albany: State University of New York Press, 1996.

Coddington, Dean C., Harold L. Davis, and J. Gordon Milliken. *The Federal Reclamation Program: Its Impacts, Issues and Future Considerations.* Denver: U.S. Department of Interior, Bureau of Reclamation, 1972.

Cohen, Michael P. *The History of the Sierra Club, 1892–1970.* San Francisco: Sierra Club Books, 1988.

Colorado Forum. *The Upper Colorado River Basin and Colorado's Water Interests.* Denver: Colorado Forum, 1982.

Cooley, Richard, and Geoffrey Wandesforde-Smith, eds. *Congress and the Environment.* Seattle: University of Washington Press, 1970.

Cooper, Erwin. *Aqueduct Empire: A Guide to Water in California, Its Turbulent History, and Its Management Today.* Glendale, Calif.: Arthur H. Clark Company, 1968.

Cosco, Jon. *Echo Park: Struggle for Preservation.* Boulder, Colo.: Johnson Books, 1995.

Cronin, Thomas E., and Robert D. Loevy. *Colorado Politics & Government: Governing the Centennial State.* Lincoln: University of Nebraska Press, 1993.

Cronon, William, ed. *Uncommon Ground: Toward Reinventing Nature.* New York: W. W. Norton, 1995.

Cronon, William, George Miles, and Jay Gitlin, eds. *Under an Open Sky: Rethinking America's Western Past.* New York: W. W. Norton, 1992.

Davidson, Roger H., and Walter J. Oleszek. *Congress against Itself.* Bloomington: Indiana University Press, 1977.

Dawdy, Doris Ostrander. *Congress in Its Wisdom: The Bureau of Reclamation and the Public Interest.* Boulder, Colo.: Westview Press, 1989.

deBuys, William, and Alex Harris. *River of Traps: A Village Life.* Albuquerque: University of New Mexico Press, 1990.

Depletion of Water Supplies Allocated to State of Colorado by Colorado River Compacts. Los Angeles: Leeds, Hill and Jewett, Consulting Engineers, 1953.

Dickerman, Alan R., George E. Radosevich, and Kenneth C. Nobe. *Foundations of Federal Reclamation Policies: An Historical Review of Changing Goals and Objectives.* Fort Collins: Department of Economics, Colorado State University, 1970.

Diggs, David M., and Patrick Sweeney, eds. *Who Owns the West? Sixteen Case Studies on Natural Resource Ownership*. Montrose, Colo.: Western Organization of Resource Councils, 1985.

Divine, Robert A. *The Johnson Years, Volume Two: Vietnam, the Environment, and Science*. Lawrence: University Press of Kansas, 1987.

Dunbar, Robert G. *Forging New Rights in Western Waters*. Lincoln: University of Nebraska Press, 1983.

Edmonds, Carol. *Wayne Aspinall: Mr. Chairman*. Englewood, Colo.: Crown Point, Inc., 1980.

El-Ashry, Mohamed T., and Diana C. Gibbons. *Troubled Waters: New Policies for Managing Water in the American West*. Washington, D.C.: World Resources Institute, 1986.

——, eds. *Water and Arid Lands of the Western United States*. New York: Cambridge University Press, 1988.

Engelbert, Ernest A., and Ann Foley Sheuring, eds. *Water Scarcity: Impacts on Western Agriculture*. Berkeley: University of California Press, 1984.

Farmer, Jared. *Glen Canyon Dammed: Inventing Lake Powell & the Canyon Country*. Tucson: University of Arizona Press, 1999.

Fenno, Richard F., Jr. *Congressmen in Committees*. Boston: Little, Brown, 1973.

Ferril, Thomas Hornsby. *Trial by Time*. New York: Harper & Brothers, 1944.

Fishel, Jeff. *Party & Opposition: Congressional Challengers in American Politics*. New York: David McKay, 1973.

Fleming, Anthony H. *Legal and Institutional Issues in Colorado Water Resources Management*. Madison: Institute for Environmental Studies, University of Wisconsin-Madison, 1986.

Folk-Williams, John A., Susan C. Fry, and Lucy Hilgendorf. *Western Water Flows to the Cities*. Washington, D.C.: Island Press, 1985.

Foreman, Dave. *Confessions of an Eco-Warrior*. New York: Harmony Books, 1991.

Forsman, Chuck. *Arrested Rivers*. Niwot: University Press of Colorado, 1994.

Foster, Mark S. *Henry J. Kaiser: Builder in the Modern American West*. Austin: University of Texas Press, 1989.

Fox, Stephen. *The American Conservation Movement: John Muir and His Legacy*. Madison: University of Wisconsin Press, 1981.

Fradkin, Philip L. *A River No More: The Colorado River and the West*. Tucson: University of Arizona Press, 1981.

——. *Sagebrush Country: Land and the American West*. New York: Alfred A. Knopf, 1989.

Frederick, Kenneth D., and James C. Hanson. *Water for Western Agriculture*. Washington, D.C.: Resources for the Future, 1982.

Gertzog, Irwin N. *Congressional Women: Their Recruitment, Integration, and Behavior*. 2d ed. Westport, Conn.: Praeger, 1995.

Getches, David H., ed. *Water and the American West: Essays in Honor of Raphael J. Moses*. Boulder: Natural Resources Law Center, University of Colorado Law School, 1988.

Gottlieb, Robert. *A Life of Its Own: The Politics and Power of Water*. San Diego: Harcourt Brace Jovanovich, 1988.

Gómez, Arthur R. *Quest for the Golden Circle: The Four Corners and the Metropolitan West, 1945–1970*. Albuquerque: University of New Mexico Press, 1994.

Gould, Lewis. *Lady Bird Johnson and the Environment*. Lawrence: University Press of Kansas, 1988.

Graf, William L. *The Colorado River: Instability and Basin Management*. Washington, D.C.: Association of American Geographers, 1985.

——. *Wilderness Preservation and the Sagebrush Rebellions*. Savage, Md.: Rowman & Littlefield Publishers, 1990.

Green, Mark J., James M. Fallows, and David R. Zwick. *Ralph Nader Congress Project: Who Runs Congress?* New York: Bantam / Grossman, 1972.

Gulliford, Andrew. *Boomtown Blues: Colorado Oil Shale, 1885–1985*. Niwot: University Press of Colorado, 1989.

Gunther, John. *Inside U.S.A.* Rev. ed. New York: Harper & Row, 1951.

Harden, Blaine. *A River Lost: The Life and Death of the Columbia*. New York: W. W. Norton, 1996.

Harvey, Mark W. T. *A Symbol of Wilderness: Echo Park and the American Conservation Movement*. Albuquerque: University of New Mexico Press, 1994.

Haveman, Robert H. *Water Resource Investment and the Public Interest*. Nashville, Tenn.: Vanderbilt University Press, 1965.

Hays, Samuel P. *Beauty, Health, and Permanence: Environmental Politics in the United States, 1955–1985*. New York: Cambridge University Press, 1987.

Heuvelmans, Martin. *The River Killers*. Harrisburg, Pa.: Stackpole Books, 1974.

Hewston, John G., and Donald R. Franklin. *Recreational Use Patterns at Flaming Gorge Reservoir, 1963–65*. Washington, D.C.: U.S. Department of Interior, Bureau of Sport Fisheries and Wildlife, 1969.

Hibbing, John R. *Congressional Careers: Contours of Life in the U.S. House of Representatives*. Chapel Hill: University of North Carolina Press, 1991.

Hogan, Richard. *Class & Community in Frontier Colorado*. Lawrence: University Press of Kansas, 1990.

Hollon, W. Eugene. *The Great American Desert: Then and Now*. New York: Oxford University Press, 1966.

Holmes, Beatrice Hort. *History of the Federal Water Resources Programs and Policies, 1961–1970*. Washington, D.C.: U.S. Department of Agriculture; Economics, Statistics, and Cooperatives Service, 1979.

Holthaus, Gary, Patricia Nelson Limerick, Charles F. Wilkinson, and Eve Stryker

Munson, eds. *A Society to Match the Scenery: Personal Visions of the Future of the American West*. Niwot: University Press of Colorado, 1991.

Howe, Charles W. *Natural Resource Economics: Issues, Analysis, and Policy*. New York: John Wiley & Sons, 1979.

Howe, Charles W., and K. William Easter. *Interbasin Transfers of Water: Economic Issues and Impacts*. Washington, D.C.: Resources for the Future, 1971.

Hrebenar, Ronald J., and Ruth K. Scott. *Interest Group Politics in America*. Englewood Cliffs, N.J.: Prentice-Hall, 1982.

Hundley, Norris, Jr. *Dividing the Waters: A Century of Controversy between the United States and Mexico*. Berkeley: University of California Press, 1966.

———. *The Great Thirst: Californians and Water, 1770s–1990s*. Berkeley: University of California Press, 1992.

———. *Water and the West: The Colorado River Compact and the Politics of Water in the American West*. Berkeley: University of California Press, 1975.

Hunt, Constance Elizabeth. *Down by the River: The Impact of Federal Water Projects and Policies on Biological Diversity*. Washington, D.C.: Island Press, 1988.

Ingram, Helen M. *Water Politics: Continuity and Change*. Albuquerque: University of New Mexico Press, 1990.

Ingram, Helen M., Nancy K. Laney, and John R. McCain. *A Policy Approach to Political Representation: Lessons from the Four Corners States*. Baltimore, Md.: Johns Hopkins University Press, 1980.

Jacobs, John. *A Rage for Justice: The Passion and Politics of Phillip Burton*. Berkeley: University of California Press, 1995.

Johnson, Cathy Marie. *The Dynamics of Conflict between Bureaucrats and Legislators*. Armonk, N.Y.: M. E. Sharpe, 1992.

Johnson, Rich. *The Central Arizona Project, 1918–1968*. Tucson: University of Arizona Press, 1977.

Josephy, Alvin M., Jr. *The American Heritage History of the Congress of the United States*. New York: American Heritage Publishing Co., 1975.

Klyza, Christopher McGrory. *Who Controls Public Lands?* Chapel Hill: University of North Carolina Press, 1996.

Kneese, Allen V., and F. Lee Brown. *The Southwest under Stress: National Resource Development Issues in a Regional Setting*. Baltimore, Md.: Johns Hopkins University Press, 1981.

Lacey, Michael J., ed. *Government and Environmental Politics: Essay on Historical Developments since World War Two*. Washington, D.C.: The Woodrow Wilson Center Press, 1991.

Lamar, Howard Roberts. *The Far Southwest, 1846–1912: A Territorial History*. New Haven, Conn.: Yale University Press, 1966.

Lamm, Richard D., and Michael McCarthy. *The Angry West: A Vulnerable Land and Its Future*. Boston: Houghton Mifflin, 1982.

Lavender, David. *The Rockies*. New York: Harper & Row, 1968.

———. *The Southwest*. Albuquerque: University of New Mexico Press, 1980.

Leonard, Stephen J., and Thomas J. Noel. *Denver: Mining Camp to Metropolis*. Niwot: University Press of Colorado, 1990.

Lichtenstein, Nelson, and Eleanora Schoenebaum, eds. *Political Profiles*. New York: Facts on File, 1976.

Limerick, Patricia Nelson. *Desert Passages: Encounters with the American Deserts*. Niwot: University Press of Colorado, 1989.

———. *The Legacy of Conquest: The Unbroken Past of the American West*. New York: W. W. Norton, 1987.

Limerick, Patricia Nelson, Clyde A. Milner II, and Charles E. Rankin, eds. *Trails: Toward a New Western History*. Lawrence: University Press of Kansas, 1991.

Lochhead, James S. *Transmountain Diversions in Colorado*. Occasional paper, University of Colorado Law School, Natural Resource Law Center, 1987.

Lorch, Robert S. *Colorado's Government*. 4th ed. Boulder: Colorado Associated University Press, 1987.

Lowitt, Richard. *The New Deal and the West*. Norman: University of Oklahoma Press, 1984.

———, ed. *Politics in the Postwar American West*. Norman: University of Oklahoma Press, 1995.

Maass, Arthur, and Raymond L. Anderson. *. . . and the Desert Shall Rejoice: Conflict, Growth, and Justice in Arid Environments*. Cambridge, Mass.: MIT Press, 1978.

Malone, Michael P., and Richard W. Etulain. *The American West: A Twentieth-Century History*. Lincoln: University of Nebraska Press, 1989.

Mann, Dean E. *Interbasin Water Transfers: A Political and Institutional Analysis*. Washington, D.C.: National Water Commission, 1972.

———. *The Politics of Water in Arizona*. Tucson: University of Arizona Press, 1963.

Mann, Dean E., Gary Weatherford, and Phillip Nichols. *Legal-Political History of Water Resource Development in the Upper Colorado River Basin*. Lake Powell Research Project Bulletin 4. Los Angeles: National Science Foundation, 1974.

Marine, Gene. *America the Raped: The Engineering Mentality and the Devastation of a Continent*. New York: Simon and Schuster, 1969.

Markusen, Ann. *Regions: The Economics and Politics of Territory*. Totowa, N.J.: Rowman & Littlefield, 1987.

Marston, Ed, ed. *Reopening the Western Frontier*. Washington, D.C.: Island Press, 1989.

———. *Western Water Made Simple*. Washington, D.C.: Island Press, 1987.

Martin, Russell. *A Story that Stands Like a Dam: Glen Canyon and the Struggle for the Soul of the West*. New York: Henry Holt and Co., 1989.

McCool, Daniel. *Command of the Waters: Iron Triangles, Federal Water Development, and Indian Water*. Berkeley: University of California Press, 1987.

McCubbins, Mathew D., and Terry Sullivan, eds. *Congress: Structure and Policy*. New York: Cambridge University Press, 1987.

McPhee, John. *Encounters with the Archdruid*. New York: Noonday Press, 1971.

Mehls, Steven F. *The Valley of Opportunity: A History of West-Central Colorado*. Denver: U.S. Department of Interior, Bureau of Land Management, 1982.

Meyer, Michael C. *Water in the Hispanic Southwest: A Social and Legal History, 1550–1850*. Tucson: University of Arizona Press, 1984.

Milenski, Frank. *Water: The Answer to a Desert's Prayer*. Boone, Colo.: Trails Publishing, 1990.

Miles, John C. *Guardians of the Parks: A History of the National Parks and Conservation Association*. Washington, D.C.: Taylor & Francis, 1995.

Moley, Raymond, and Sen. Arthur V. Watkins. *The Upper Colorado Reclamation Project: Pro and Con*. Washington, D.C.: American Enterprise Association, 1956.

Monnett, John H., and Michael McCarthy. *Colorado Profiles: Men and Women Who Shaped the Centennial State*. Evergreen, Colo.: Cordillera Press, 1987.

Morgan, Arthur E. *Dams and Other Disasters: A Century of the Army Corps of Engineers in Civil Works*. Boston: Porter Sargent, 1971.

Morrow, William L. *Congressional Committees*. New York: Charles Scribner's Sons, 1969.

Moss, Frank E. *The Water Crisis*. New York: Frederick A. Praeger, 1967.

Murphy, Thomas P. *The New Politics Congress*. Lexington, Mass.: D. C. Heath and Company, 1974.

Nash, Gerald D., and Richard W. Etulain, eds. *Researching Western History: Topics in the Twentieth Century*. Albuquerque: University of New Mexico Press, 1997.

——. *The Twentieth-Century West: Historical Interpretations*. Albuquerque: University of New Mexico Press, 1989.

Nash, Roderick. *Wilderness and the American Mind*. 3d ed. New Haven, Conn.: Yale University Press, 1982.

Nelson, Garrison. *Committees in the U.S. Congress, 1947–1992*. 2 vols. Washington, D.C.: Congressional Quarterly, 1993–94.

O'Rourke, Paul M. *Frontier in Transition: A History of Southwestern Colorado*. Denver: U.S. Department of Interior, Bureau of Land Management, 1980.

Palmer, Tim. *Endangered Rivers and the Conservation Movement*. Berkeley: University of California Press, 1986.

Peabody, Robert L., and Nelson W. Polsby, eds. *New Perspectives on the House of Representatives*. 2d ed. Chicago: Rand McNally & Company, 1969.

Peacock, Deborah A. *Bureau of Reclamation Irrigation Subsidies: Legislative History* and *Congressional Knowledge*. Denver: U.S. Department of Interior, Bureau of Reclamation, 1985.

Pearson, Drew, and Jack Anderson. *The Case against Congress: A Compelling Indictment of Corruption on Capitol Hill*. New York: Simon and Schuster, 1968.

Peffer, E. Louise. *The Closing of the Public Domain: Disposal and Reservation Policies, 1900–50*. Stanford, Calif.: Stanford University Press, 1951.

Peirce, Neal R. *The Mountain States of America: People, Politics, and Power in the Eight Rocky Mountain States*. New York: W. W. Norton, 1972.

Peterson, Dean F., and A. Berry Crawford, eds. *Values and Choices in the Development of the Colorado River Basin*. Tucson: University of Arizona Press, 1978.

Pierce, John C., and Harvey R. Doerksen. *Water Politics and Public Involvement*. Ann Arbor, Mich.: Ann Arbor Science Publishers, 1976.

Pisani, Donald J. *To Reclaim a Divided West: Water, Law, and Public Policy 1848– 1902*. Albuquerque: University of New Mexico Press, 1992.

———. *Water, Land, and Law in the West: The Limits of Public Policy, 1850–1920*. Lawrence: University Press of Kansas, 1996.

Polsby, Nelson W. *Congress and the Presidency*. Englewood Cliffs, N.J.: Prentice-Hall, 1971.

Price, David E. *Policymaking in Congressional Committees: The Impact of "Environmental" Factors*. Tucson: University of Arizona Press, 1979.

Radosevich, G. E., K. C. Nobe, D. Allardice, and C. Kirkwood. *Evolution and Administration of Colorado Water Law, 1876–1976*. Fort Collins, Colo.: Water Resources Publications, 1976.

Ralph Nader Congress Project. *The Environment Committees: A Study of the House and Senate Interior, Agriculture, and Science Committees*. New York: Grossman Publishers, 1975.

Reisner, Marc. *Cadillac Desert: The American West and Its Disappearing Water*. New York: Penguin Books, 1986.

Reisner, Marc, and Sarah Bates. *Overtapped Oasis: Reform or Revolution for Western Water*. Washington, D.C.: Island Press, 1990.

Rennicke, Jeff. *The Rivers of Colorado*. Billings, Mont.: Falcon Press Publishing, 1985.

Rhodes, John J., and Dean Smith. *I Was There*. Salt Lake City, Utah: Northwest Publishing, 1995.

Richardson, Elmo. *Dams, Parks & Politics: Resource Development & Preservation in the Truman-Eisenhower Era*. Lexington: University Press of Kentucky, 1973.

———. *The Presidency of Dwight D. Eisenhower*. Lawrence: The Regents Press of Kansas, 1979.

Riebsame, William, James Robb, et al., eds. *Atlas of the New West: Portrait of a Changing Region*. New York: W. W. Norton, 1997.

Rieselbach, Leroy N. *Congressional Politics: The Evolving Legislative System.* 2d ed. Boulder, Colo.: Westview Press, 1995.

Ripley, Randall B. *Congress: Process and Policy.* New York: W. W. Norton, 1975.

Ripley, Randall B., and Grace A. Franklin. *Congress, the Bureaucracy, and Public Policy.* 3d ed. Homewood, Ill.: Dorsey Press, 1984.

Robbins, William G. *Colony and Empire: The Capitalist Transformation of the American West.* Lawrence: University Press of Kansas, 1994.

Robinson, Michael C. *Water for the West: The Bureau of Reclamation, 1902–1977.* Chicago: Public Works Historical Society, 1979.

Rockwell, Wilson. *Uncompahgre Country.* Denver: Sage Books, 1965.

Rothman, Hal. *Preserving Different Pasts: The American National Monuments.* Urbana: University of Illinois Press, 1989.

——, ed. *Reopening the American West.* Tucson: University of Arizona Press, 1998.

Runte, Alfred. *National Parks: The American Experience.* 2d ed., revised. Lincoln: University of Nebraska Press, 1987.

Sadler, Richard W., and Richard C. Roberts. *The Weber River Basin: Grass Roots Democracy and Water Development.* Logan: Utah State University Press, 1994.

Schaller, Michael, Virginia Scharff, and Robert D. Schulzinger, eds. *Present Tense: The United States since 1945.* Boston: Houghton Mifflin, 1992.

Schoenebaum, Eleanora, ed. *Political Profiles: The Nixon / Ford Years.* New York: Facts on File, Inc., 1979.

Schrepfer, Susan R. *The Fight to Save the Redwoods: A History of Environmental Reform, 1917–1978.* Madison: University of Wisconsin Press, 1983.

Sherow, James Earl. *Watering the Valley: Development along the High Plains Arkansas River, 1870–1950.* Lawrence: University Press of Kansas, 1990.

Silkensen, Gregory M. *Windy Gap: Transmountain Water Diversion and the Environmental Movement.* Fort Collins: Colorado Water Resources Research Institute, Colorado State University, 1994.

Simonds, Wm. Joe. *The Pine River Project.* Denver: U.S. Department of Interior, Bureau of Reclamation History Program, 1994.

Smith, Duane A. *Rocky Mountain West: Colorado, Wyoming, & Montana, 1859–1915.* Albuquerque: University of New Mexico Press, 1992.

Smith, Judith G., ed. *Political Brokers: Money, Organizations, Power, and People.* New York: Liveright, 1972.

Smith, Steven S., and Christopher J. Deering. *Committees in Congress.* Washington, D.C.: Congressional Quarterly, 1984.

Smythe, William E. *The Conquest of Arid America.* Rev. ed. New York: Macmillan, 1907.

Spofford, Walter O., Jr., Alfred L. Parker, and Allen V. Kneese, eds. *Energy Development in the Southwest: Problems of Water, Fish and Wildlife in the Upper*

Colorado River Basin, vol. 2. Washington, D.C.: Resources for the Future, 1980.

Starr, Kevin. *Material Dreams: Southern California through the 1920s.* New York: Oxford University Press, 1990.

Stegner, Wallace. *The American West as Living Space.* Ann Arbor: University of Michigan Press, 1987.

———. *Beyond the Hundredth Meridian: John Wesley Powell and the Second Opening of the West.* New York: Penguin Books, 1954.

———. *The Sound of Mountain Water.* Garden City, N.Y.: Doubleday, 1969.

———. *Where the Bluebird Sings to the Lemonade Springs: Living and Writing in the West.* New York: Wing Books, 1992.

———, ed. *This is Dinosaur: Echo Park Country and Its Magic Rivers.* Boulder, Colo.: Roberts Rinehart, 1985.

Stratton, Owen, and Phillip Sirotkin. *The Echo Park Controversy.* University: University of Alabama Press, 1959.

Straus, Michael W. *How to Meet the West's Needs for Water and Power.* Washington, D.C.: Public Affairs Institute, 1962.

Sundquist, James L. *Politics and Policy: The Eisenhower, Kennedy, and Johnson Years.* Washington, D.C.: The Brookings Institution, 1968.

Sussman, Robert. *Citizens Look at Congress: Wayne N. Aspinall, Democratic Representative from Colorado.* New York: Ralph Nader Congress Project/Grossman Publishers, 1972.

Terrell, John Upton. *War for the Colorado River,* vol. 1: *The California-Arizona Controversy.* Glendale, Calif.: Arthur H. Clark, 1965.

———. *War for the Colorado River,* vol. 2: *Above Lee's Ferry.* Glendale, Calif.: Arthur H. Clark, 1965.

Tocqueville, Alexis de. *Democracy in America.* The Henry Reeve text as revised by Frances Bowen and further edited by Phillips Bradley. New York: Vintage Books, 1945.

Tupper, Margo. *No Place to Play.* Philadelphia: Chilton Books, 1966.

Tyler, Daniel. *The Last Water Hole in the West: The Colorado–Big Thompson Project and the Northern Colorado Water Conservancy District.* Niwot: University Press of Colorado, 1992.

Ubbelohde, Carl, Maxine Benson, and Duane A. Smith. *A Colorado History.* 6th ed. Boulder, Colo.: Pruett Publishing, 1988.

Udall, Morris. *Education of a Congressman: The Newsletters of Morris K. Udall.* Indianapolis: Bobbs-Merrill Company, 1972.

Udall, Stewart L. *The Quiet Crisis.* New York: Holt, Rinehart and Winston, 1965.

Underwood, Kathleen. *Town Building on the Colorado Frontier.* Albuquerque: University of New Mexico Press, 1987.

Vandenbusche, Duane, and Duane A. Smith. *A Land Alone: Colorado's Western Slope*. Boulder, Colo.: Pruett Publishing, 1981.

Vogler, David J. *The Politics of Congress*. 2d ed. Boston: Allyn and Bacon, 1977.

Vranesh, George. *Colorado Citizens' Water Law Handbook*. Boulder: Colorado Endowment for the Humanities, 1989.

Wahl, Richard W. *Markets for Federal Water: Subsidies, Property Rights, and the Bureau of Reclamation*. Washington, D.C.: Resources for the Future, 1989.

Walton, John. *Western Times and Water Wars: State, Culture, and Rebellion in California*. Berkeley: University of California Press, 1992.

Walton, Roger Alan. *Colorado: A Practical Guide to Its Government and Politics*. Lakewood: Colorado Times Publishing, 1991.

Warne, William E. *The Bureau of Reclamation*. New York: Praeger, 1973.

Waters, Frank. *The Colorado*. New York: Rinehart & Company, 1946.

Watkins, T. H., and Charles S. Watson Jr. *The Land No One Knows: America and the Public Domain*. San Francisco: Sierra Club Books, 1975.

Weatherford, Gary D., ed. *Water and Agriculture in the Western U.S.: Conservation, Reallocation, and Markets*. Boulder, Colo.: Westview Press, 1982.

Weatherford, Gary D., and F. Lee Brown, eds. *New Courses for the Colorado River: Major Issues for the Next Century*. Albuquerque: University of New Mexico Press, 1986.

Weaver, Warren, Jr. *Both Your Houses: The Truth about Congress*. New York: Praeger Publishers, 1972.

Webb, Walter Prescott. *The Great Plains*. Lincoln: University of Nebraska Press, 1959.

Welch, Susan, and John G. Peters, eds. *Legislative Reform and Public Policy*. New York: Praeger Publishers, 1977.

Welsh, Frank. *How to Create a Water Crisis*. Boulder, Colo.: Johnson Books, 1985.

Wescoat, James L., Jr. *Integrated Water Development: Water Use and Conservation Practice in Western Colorado*. Chicago: Department of Geography, University of Chicago, 1984.

White, Richard. *It's Your Misfortune and None of My Own: A New History of the American West*. Norman: University of Oklahoma Press, 1991.

———. *The Organic Machine: The Remaking of the Columbia River*. New York: Hill and Wang, 1995.

Wild, Peter. *Pioneer Conservationists of Western America*. Missoula, Mont.: Mountain Press Publishing, 1979.

Wiley, Peter, and Robert Gottlieb. *Empires in the Sun: The Rise of the New American West*. Tucson: University of Arizona Press, 1982.

Wilkinson, Charles F. *Crossing the Next Meridian: Land, Water, and the Future of the West*. Washington, D.C.: Island Press, 1992.

———. *The Eagle Bird: Mapping a New West*. New York: Pantheon Books, 1992.

——. *Fire on the Plateau: Conflict and Endurance in the American Southwest*. Washington, D.C.: Island Press, 1999.

Worster, Donald. *Rivers of Empire: Water, Aridity & the Growth of the American West*. New York: Pantheon Books, 1985.

——. *Under Western Skies: Nature and History in the American West*. New York: Oxford University Press, 1992.

——. *An Unsettled Country: Changing Landscapes of the American West*. Albuquerque: University of New Mexico Press, 1994.

——, ed. *The Ends of the Earth: Perspectives on Modern Environmental History*. New York: Cambridge University Press, 1988.

Wright, Jim. *You and Your Congressman*. New York: Coward, McCann & Geoghegan, 1972.

Wright, John B. *Rocky Mountain Divide: Selling and Saving the West*. Austin: University of Texas Press, 1993.

Wyant, William. *Westward in Eden: The Public Lands and the Conservation Movement*. Berkeley: University of California Press, 1982.

Zaslowsky, Dyan, and T. H. Watkins. *These American Lands: Parks, Wilderness, and the Public Lands*. Washington, D.C.: Island Press, 1994.

Index

Douglas, Paul, 41–42
Dreyfuss, Dan, 88
Drury, Newton, 23
Durango (Colo.), 84, 154

Echo Park Dam, xvii, 29, 158, 159, 177n. 34; Congress and, 39–40, 45, 48, 50; conservation movement and, 33–36, 46–47, 58; opposition to, 36–39
economics: of Colorado River Storage Project, 37, 41–43; of Western Slope, 12–13
Eisenhower, Dwight D., xv, 27, 32–33, 175n. 17
elections: Fourth Congressional District and, 19–21, 125, 130–41, 172–73nn. 27, 28, 198n. 21, 202n. 51
Ely, Northcutt, 51
Endangered Species Act, 155
energy production: and Central Arizona Project, 118–19
Engle, Clair, 50, 70
environment: appropriate use of, 95–96, 99–101, 102, 103, 156–60; as campaign issue, 135–36, 139
Environmental Action, 135–36
environmental gap: and Democratic Party, 98–99
environmental impact statements, 155
environmental movement, 130, 157–59, 166n. 3; and congressional elections, 135–36, 139, 141. *See also* conservation movement
Exxon Corporation, 13, 147, 148

Farmington, 88, 154
Federal Bureau of Investigation, 23, 171–72n. 23
federal government: and Western

Slope, 12–13. *See also various agencies; bureaus; departments*
Fenno, Richard, 61–62
Field & Stream (magazine), 138, 201n. 46
Foley, Tom, 128
Ford, Gerald, 18, 22, 144
Fort Collins, 7, 125, 139
Fort Morgan, 126
Fourth Congressional District (Colorado), xiv, 20–21, 52, 172–73nn. 27, 28; campaigning in, 131–32, 134–35, 136–39, 202n. 51; environmental issues in, 135–36; political support in, 130–31, 139–40, 198n. 21; redistricting of, 124–25, 132–34, 141; voters in, 125–26
Front Range, 5, 15; and Colorado River Storage Project, 44–45; and Fourth Congressional District, 137–38, 139; water diversion to, 6–7, 86; and Western Slope, 7–8, 53
Fryingpan-Arkansas Project (Fry-Ark), xiv, 7, 45, 52, 115, 182n. 15; Aspinall and, 55, 56–58, 59–61, 66–68; Congress and, 58–59, 65–66
Fryingpan River, 55, 61
funding: for Bureau of Reclamation projects, 12, 25, 146

Garnsey, Morris, 42
Gavin, Tom, 139
Glen Canyon Dam, 33, 49, 76(fig.), 158, 159
Glenwood Springs, 8, 84
Goddard, Sam, 81, 188n. 30
Golden Gate Recreation Area, 138
Gold Rush, 4
Goslin, Ival, 161(fig.)
Gossard, Bill, 132
Gottlieb, Robert, 154

Ute Water Settlement Agreement,
155

Vanderhoof, Johnny, 143, 149
Vega Reservoir, 25
Verkler, Jerry, 64(fig.)
Vietnam War, 131
Vinger, Jack, 91

Walker, Walter, 18, 20
Washington Post, 96
water compacts, 8, 168n. 15. *See also*
   Colorado River Compact; Upper
   Colorado River Basin Compact
water development: in Colorado, 5,
   13–14, 53–54, 55–56
water diversion, 55; from Pacific
   Northwest, 74, 78–79, 84; from
   Western Slope, 6–7, 45, 53–56, 60,
   86
water law, 3–5
water rights: appropriative, 4–5; Front
   Range and, 6–7; Ute, 154–55
Watt, James, 143, 145–46, 149
Wayburn, Edgar, xvi, 128, 138, 143
Wayne Aspinall Conference Center,
   150
Wayne Aspinall Visiting Professorship,
   150
Wayne N. Aspinall Storage Unit, 150
WCPA. *See* Western Colorado Pro-
   tective Association
Weld County, 130

West Divide Project, 84, 85, 89
Western Colorado Protective Associa-
   tion (WCPA), 7
Western Mining Congress, 147
Western Outdoors Clubs, 49
Western Slope, xvi, xvii, 26, 126, 135,
   156–57, 163; and Colorado River
   Storage Project, 44–45; and federal
   goverment, 12–13; and Fourth
   Congressional District, 124, 133,
   134, 135, 139–40; and Front
   Range, 7–8, 53; oil shale and, 146–
   48; and water diversion projects,
   56, 60, 61, 68; water rights and, 5,
   6–7
Western State College, 150
Wild and Scenic Rivers Act, 151
Wilderness Bill/Act, 63–65, 151,
   184nn. 32, 33
Wilderness Society, 35, 40
Wilson, Charles, 57, 58
Wilson, Woodrow, 18, 33
Wirth, Tim, 142
Wyoming, 9, 11, 28, 29, 168n. 15
Wyoming v. Colorado, 11

Yampa River, 29, 33
Yosemite National Park, 34
Young, Don, 164
Young Democrats of Colorado, 99,
   101

Zahniser, Howard, 40

About the Author

STEPHEN C. STURGEON is Manuscript Curator in Special Collections and Archives at Utah State University as well as Adjunct Assistant Professor of History and an affiliated faculty member in the Natural Resource and Environmental Policy Program. He received his B.A. from Grinnell College, his M.L.I.S. from the University of California, Berkeley, and his M.A. and Ph.D. in history from the University of Colorado at Boulder. His research focuses primarily on the political and environmental history of the twentieth-century American West.